Frantz

'Few works have more creatively and comprehensively explored Fanon's perspective on gender relations, the family, and women's resistance to sexual violence. It provides an outstanding examination of the historical and political circumstances that shaped his least discussed book, *Studies in a Dying Colonialism*.'
—Peter Hudis, author of *Frantz Fanon:*
Philosopher of the Barricades

'Haddour is a foremost interpreter of Fanon – and here sheds important new light on this critical giant of the twentieth century by focusing on his radical, sadly neglected *Studies in a Dying Colonialism*, challenging the assumptions of many postcolonial readers.'
—Judith Still, Emeritus Professor of French
and Critical Theory, University of Nottingham

'A meticulously researched analysis looking beyond Fanon's most frequently-read works on Algerian society under French colonialism and during the War of Independence. Azzedine Haddour explores Fanon's analyses of gender, the family, medicine, and the use of torture, complementing Fanon's own writing with a wealth of historical information illuminating the devastating impact of French colonial policy on the Algerian people.'
—Jane Hiddleston, author of *Frantz Fanon:*
Literature and Invention

Frantz Fanon

Gender, Torture and the Biopolitics of Colonialism

Azzedine Haddour

PLUTO PRESS

First published 2025 by Pluto Press
New Wing, Somerset House, Strand, London WC2R 1LA
and Pluto Press, Inc.
1930 Village Center Circle, 3-834, Las Vegas, NV 89134

www.plutobooks.com

British Library Cataloguing in Publication Data
A catalogue record for this book is available from the British Library

ISBN   978 0 7453 4154 5   Paperback
ISBN   978 1 78680 831 8   PDF
ISBN   978 1 78680 832 5   EPUB

This book is printed on paper suitable for recycling and made from fully managed
and sustained forest sources. Logging, pulping and manufacturing processes are
expected to conform to the environmental standards of the country of origin.

Typeset by Stanford DTP Services, Northampton, England

Simultaneously printed in the United Kingdom and United States of America

EU GPSR Authorised Representative
LOGOS EUROPE, 9 rue Nicolas Poussin, 17000, LA ROCHELLE, France
Email: Contact@logoseurope.eu

In memory of Mum and Dad, who endured so much.
To Laura, Adam, and Sami, with all my love.

Contents

List of Photographs

List of Abbreviations

ALN	Armée de libération nationale, Algerian Liberation Army
AMG	Aide médicale gratuite
ASSRA	Adjointes sociales sanitaires rurales auxiliaires
CCE	Comité de coordination et d'exécution
CNRA	Conseil national de la Révolution algérienne, National Council of the Algerian Revolution
CRA	Croissant-Rouge algérien, Algerian Red Crescent
CSP	Comité de salut public
CTT	Centre de tri et de transit
DOP	Détachement opérationnel de protection
DPU	Dispositif de protection urbaine
ECPAD	Établissement de communication et de production audiovisuelle de la Défense
ELAK	Émissions des langues arabes et kabyles
EMSI	Équipes médico-sociales itinérantes
ENA	Étoile Nord-Africaine
FLN	Front de libération nationale
GADs	Groupes d'auto-défense
GCR	Groupement des contrôles radioélectriques
ICRC	International Committee of the Red Cross
IGAMEs	Inspecteurs généraux de l'administration en mission extraordinaire
IGRP	Inspection générale des regroupements de la population
ISA	Ideological State Apparatus
MSF	Mouvement de solidarité feminine, Women's Solidarity Movement
MTLD	Mouvement pour le triomphe des libertés démocratiques
OPA	Organisation politico-administrative, the FLN's civilian arm
OPA/ALN	Organisation politico-administrative/ Armée de libération nationale
OR	Officer of Information
PCF	Parti communiste français
POW	prisoner of war

PPA	Parti du peuple algérien
RALC	Radio de l'Algérie libre et combattante
RSA	Repressive State Apparatus
RTF	Radiodiffusion-Télévision Française
SAS	Section administrative spécialisée
SAU	Section administrative urbaine
SFIO	Section française de l'Internationale ouvrière
UDMA	Union démocratique du manifeste algérien

Acknowledgements

This book, through its long development, has benefited from the support and insights of many colleagues, to whom I am deeply grateful. Although it is impossible to name everyone, I offer my sincere thanks to all those who contributed to the ideas presented here. Special thanks go to Steve Brewer for his friendship, steadfast support, and exceptional collegiality. I am also grateful for the support of Vikki Bell, Russell Goulbourne, Max Silverman, Jean Khalfa, David Murphy, Judith Still, David Theo Goldberg, Charles Forsdick, Jane Hiddleston, Margaret Majumdar and Stephen M. Hart.

The anonymous readers, as well as the editors at Pluto Press, provided an encouraging report that led to several important improvements to the manuscript. Parts of Chapters 2 and 7 are based on work previously published in *Nottingham French Studies* (54:1, 2015, pp. 72–91) under the title 'Fanon, the French Liberal Left, and the Colonial Consensus', and in *Theory, Culture & Society* (27:7–8, 2010–12, pp. 66–90) under the title 'Torture Unveiled: Rereading Fanon and Bourdieu in the Context of May 1958'.

While the support of academic colleagues in the French Department and at SELCS, UCL, has been invaluable, this book would never have been completed without the immeasurable support of my family. I am deeply grateful for the Research Fellowship provided by the Leverhulme Trust, and especially for Anna Grundy's unwavering support during difficult times. Without this assistance, completing the book in time for the Fanon centenary would have been impossible.

Finally, I extend my thanks to the Archives nationales in Paris, the Service historique de la Défense, the Établissement de communication et de production audiovisuelle de la Défense, and the Archives nationales d'outre-mer for their help in providing access to materials that offered new perspectives on Fanon's work, as well as the opportunity to share this research with a wider audience.

Introduction

Frantz Fanon's posthumous legacy, particularly through his seminal work *The Wretched of the Earth*, transformed him into an iconic figure of anti-colonial resistance and third-worldism following his untimely death in 1961. His influence peaked briefly before waning by the early 1970s, only to undergo a resurgence in the 1980s with the republication of *Black Skin, White Masks*. While Fanon remained a relatively minor figure in France and Algeria, he gained central importance in Anglo-American critical circles, especially in cultural and postcolonial studies programmes. This revival coincided with civil unrest in Algeria and the failure of the socialist project he had envisioned in his critique of nationalism's pitfalls. The two decades following Algeria's decolonisation were marked by euphoric peace and calm. Although denunciation of French colonialism continued, the armistice terms effectively suppressed discussion and prosecution of war crimes. However, before the French government made some archives related to the Algerian war accessible in December 2021, and implemented further measures in August 2023, historians had already attempted to document some of the most horrific aspects of modern warfare in the Algerian conflict. While *Black Skin, White Masks* reflects Fanon's experience in Algeria during the Second World War, which heightened his awareness of race and racialised subjecthood, his subsequent work addresses the horrors of the Algerian war. This work was largely eclipsed due to the suppression of open discourse about the war's atrocities. Moreover, the renewed interest in his work from 1980s onwards shifted the discussion from decolonial politics to focus on the interplay of race, gender and sexual politics, moving the agenda away from its colonial context. It was as if colonialism had become irrelevant and obsolete; now that decolonisation had taken place, postcolonialism came to supplant it and involved rethinking Fanon in more global and universalising contexts, which disregarded the specific political sites from which he intervened. The universalising reading seems to occlude his other works and limit the scope of his main texts *Black Skin, White Masks* and *The Wretched of the Earth*.[1] Marxist and third-worldist perspectives on the latter, along with postcolonial critical interest in the former, further obfuscated the significance of Fanon's other works and their historical context.

My project in this book is to focus on one of Fanon's most significant yet often overlooked collections of essays. Published in 1959, following *Black Skin, White Masks* and prefiguring key themes in *The Wretched of the Earth*, the work initially bore the title *Réalité d'une nation* (*Reality of a Nation*). It underwent several titular transformations before settling on *L'An V de la Révolution algérienne* (*Year V of the Algerian Revolution*).[2] Originally published in 1959 by François Maspero, the work was later republished in 1972 under the title *Sociologie d'une révolution* (*Sociology of a Revolution*). The current French edition reverts to the original title while reproducing the 1972 version, which notably includes a previously unpublished introduction by Fanon from 1959. The English translation, *Studies in a Dying Colonialism*, by Haakon Chevalier, was published in 1965 by Grove Press. The original title of the French edition, *L'An V*, alluding to the French Revolutionary calendar, symbolised Fanon's belief in the dawn of a new historical era commencing on 1 November 1954.

Fanon's work was controversial due to its radical content. Seuil's 'Esprit' collection could not accommodate it, so it appeared in Maspero's 'Cahiers libres' series, a key platform for third-worldist perspectives. The preface's controversial statement about the 'death of colonialism' meaning the death of both colonised and coloniser likely prompted Maspero to omit it from the first edition.[3] Despite this omission, Fanon's work faced typical Algerian war-era censorship challenges, being seized three months after publication. It was one of 23 works seized between 1957 and 1962, with Maspero and Minuit being frequent targets, highlighting the contentious nature of publishing works critical of French colonial policies during this period.[4]

Studies in a Dying Colonialism, written by Fanon in a brief period of approximately one month,[5] examines the transformative impact of the Algerian Revolution on society from 1954 onwards. Fanon argued that a new nation had emerged in Algeria to replace the French colony, asserting the inevitability of formal recognition for this change. *Studies in a Dying Colonialism* comprises five studies examining key dimensions of the Algerian Revolution: (i) women's evolving roles, (ii) the FLN's (Front de liberation nationale) radio propaganda strategies, (iii) impacts on family structures, (iv) the intersection of medicine with colonisation, and (v) the position of the European minority. Two appendices by Geronimi and Bresson illustrate European involvement in the revolutionary process. In this present account, I engage with Fanon's studies as they appeared in his volume of essays, dedicating a chapter to each. Two additional chapters provide contextualisation: Chapter 1 offers a historical survey of the development of care institutions and their complicity with the colonial regime, while Chapter 6 addresses the issue of torture.

'From the sixties to the present day,' writes Alice Cherki:

> Studies in a Dying Colonialism is the least cited work among Fanon's various exegetes. Is it too dated? Are the options Fanon takes in this book so contradicted by the evolution of African countries, especially Algeria, causing a certain discomfort in returning to these statements? Can what is written about the place of minorities, and especially about the change in the status of women, their relationship to themselves, to family or society, be considered false?[6]

Before answering this question, let me first highlight the impact of *Studies in a Dying Colonialism* – often considered a minor and 'dated' text – on significant works like Gillo Pontecorvo's *La Bataille d'Alger*, Malek Alloula's *Le Harem colonial*, and Germaine Tillion's *Le Harem et les cousins*. Pontecorvo's classic film serves as a mise-en-scène of 'Algeria Unveiled', dramatising not only the historical Battle of Algiers but also the reality of a nation undergoing decolonisation. Just as colonialism affected every aspect of colonial society, decolonisation had an equally profound impact. The colonial influence was particularly evident in gender and sexual politics, as demonstrated by Alloula and Tillion. Endogamy intensified as a result of French colonial encroachment, which sought to conquer what was seen as the last bastion which stood against colonialism: the Algerian woman. Tillion, contrary to some interpretations, does not view Fanon's politics as retrograde. Instead, she argues that the veil is a manifestation of de-tribalisation and colonial urbanism. Alloula asserts that no women in history were subjected to the male gaze as intensely as Algerian women, with photography playing a crucial role in this process. Drawing from Fanon's work, he contends that unveiling Algerian women constituted a double violation akin to rape.

Pontecorvo acknowledges Fanon's influence on intellectuals of his generation, but emphasises the importance of contextualising Fanon's work within the lived experience of the Algerian war. *The Battle of Algiers* and Fanon's 'Algeria Unveiled' share significant thematic overlaps.[7] Both interpret the war against colonisation as a transformative historical and psychological process. Both Fanon's *Studies in a Dying Colonialism* and Pontecorvo's *The Battle of Algiers* emphasise the pivotal role of women in the Algerian Revolution and its transformative impact on society. They highlight women's active participation in armed struggle and their strategic use of fluid identities, alternating between Western attire and traditional veils to navigate colonial spaces. This dynamic illustrates the revolution's effects on gender roles and family structures. Both works portray the revolution as a regenerative process that reshaped social norms and cultural dynamics, revealing a shared understanding of its significance in redefining women's roles and identities. In Chapter 2, I explore a central theme in *Studies in a Dying Colonialism*: the evolving role of Algerian women in the revolution. Fanon argues that Algeria's decolonisation was inextricably linked to a revolution in gender and sexual politics, as demonstrated by women's participation in the struggle.

However, as Cherki and feminist critics note, Fanon's prediction of women's political and social equality in post-independence Algeria has been challenged by a more complex reality. While the liberation period initiated a genuine social and cultural revolution, particularly among women who actively participated in the struggle, the post-1962 era has seen significant impediments to this progress. This apparent regression should not be attributed to Fanon as one of his 'mistakes'. Cherki rightly argues that we must read *Studies in a Dying Colonialism* not as a factual description of a dated society, but as an enunciation of necessary changes for real liberation and national renewal.

In 'Algeria Unveiled', Fanon celebrated the emerging freedoms of Algerian women and advocated for their rights. He saw their changing roles as a crucial aspect of the revolutionary struggle against colonialism. As a participant, Fanon bore witness to the sufferings of Algerian women. An entire biopolitics developed, focusing on them to maintain colonialism.

Fanon made assertions about the historical complicity of medicine with colonialism without substantiating his claims. It is crucial to recognise that, as evidenced in Chapter 5, his interests in the role of medicine extend beyond these allegations. While denouncing this complicity by exposing some medical doctors' involvement in the abhorrent practice of torture, Fanon simultaneously attempted to reframe medicine practised by revolutionary Algerians as an instrument of anticolonial resistance, decolonisation and nation-building. The crux of his argument is that medicine, once a colonial agency, transformed into a vital aspect of decolonisation with the advent of the revolution. This central argument underpins Fanon's essays 'Algeria Unveiled' and 'This is the Voice of Free Algeria' as well, providing cohesion to his *Studies in a Dying Colonialism* and establishing the foundation for its liberationist discourse.

In Chapter 1, I address the gaps in Fanon's 'Medicine and Colonialism' by examining the historical complicity he alludes to but does not fully explore. It is important to contextualise his limitations: Fanon's intervention occurred at the height of the Algerian war, after his deportation, while operating as an FLN combatant in exile in Tunis. Without access to archives and historical data, his discussion was necessarily speculative and responsive to contemporary events, rather than grounded in comprehensive research. My work, benefiting from access to archives documenting the development of the colonial medical service, aims to fill these gaps. However, the full extent of the service's complicity remains elusive. The chapter offers a preliminary examination of how the service evolved in tandem with the establishment of the *Indigénat* regime.[8] Furthermore, this analysis not only addresses the historical complicity of medicine with the colonial regime but also demonstrates how medical discourse shaped what Fanon terms the 'Manichaean economy' of colonial society.

Medicine, hygiene and urban planning worked in concert to demarcate colonial space, confining the colonised within segregated areas. The chapter faces two challenges: it oscillates through historical periods without initially engaging Fanon's work (merely highlighting his omissions) and lacks a comprehensive analysis of Michel Foucault's concept of biopolitics. It is crucial to emphasise that this book is not primarily about Foucault and his theories. Instead, it examines the fundamental relationship between the administration of care and colonial governmentality, constituting a form of biopolitics. This system of care and governance optimised conditions for colonial settlements at the expense of the colonised population. Implicitly, this book challenges Foucault's assertion that institutions of confinement disappeared in the nineteenth century, suggesting that colonialism supplanted them. Racism, manifested in segregated spaces and institutions of care, was a key component of this system.

I use the term 'biopolitics' to refer to the strategic use of power to control and manage populations. Biopolitics, as an instrument of governmentality, promulgated contradictory laws that simultaneously created and mitigated crises: expropriating native populations while providing healthcare assistance. This system maintained control through a complex interplay of policies and seemingly benevolent interventions, keeping the indigenous population in a precarious state of bare existence.

Biopolitics weaponised healthcare to facilitate colonial settlement and maintain hegemony under the guise of care. Operating with inherent contradictions, it fostered optimal conditions for European settlers while deliberately withholding them from the indigenous population. This dichotomy was evident in spatial demarcation – the Manichaean economy of colonial society – and in its gender and sexuality politics, creating a stark contrast between colonisers and colonised. By prioritising settlers' interests, biopolitics enhanced their conditions while oppressing indigenous people through a health policy that engendered poverty, famine and disease. It exercised power over life and death, imposing a binary economy: prosperity for settlers and deprivation for natives. Fanon exposed this manipulative politics of life and health, highlighting its inextricable link to colonialism. Sartre, commenting on its violence, argued that it was experienced as a process determined by the expropriation of natives and their exclusion from colonising institutions. This process, maintained by brutal force, resulted in chronic malnutrition, galloping demographic growth, under-employment, famines, and diseases among the indigenous population – a 'controlled process' sustained by colonial biopolitics.

The book presents a chronological overview of the development of medical infrastructure in Algeria, spanning from the nineteenth to the mid-twentieth century. It begins with Jules Cambon's establishment of foundational medical care and assistance in the late 1800s, progressing to Célestin-Charles Jonnart's construction of indigenous infirmaries at the turn of the twentieth century. The narrative then advances to the 1930s, highlighting Maurice Viollette and Pierre-Louis Bordes' introduction of preventive medicine, and concludes with Jacques Soustelle and Robert Lacoste's establishment of the SAS (Sections administratives spécialisées) in the 1950s. These overarching historical patterns demonstrate the cyclical nature of violence perpetrated against the indigenous population, resulting in recurring ravages of poverty, famine and disease. Such devastation among the indigenous people necessitated the provision of assistance and care, primarily to mitigate potential impacts on the settler population. Notably, this regime of care and assistance targeted indigenous women, thereby seeking to medicalise the Algerian family. This medicalisation provides a lens through which to examine the intersection of colonial and gender politics, as explored in Fanon's works 'Algeria Unveiled', 'This is the Voice of Algeria' and 'The Algerian Family'.

Fanon provides a critique of biopolitics, arguing that the violence it engendered was fundamentally structural to colonialism's functioning. Medicine, in its complicity with colonialism, was one aspect of this system. His critique centres on colonialism's impacts on family structure, specifically referencing policies implemented by Soustelle and Lacoste that re-enacted nineteenth-century strategies of *terre brûlée* and rural population resettlement. *Studies in a Dying Colonialism* was written after Fanon's expulsion from Algeria, as the Battle of Algiers unfolded. Its narratives were firmly grounded in the context of this battle, the May 1958 putsch, and the political upheavals leading to the Fourth Republic's collapse. Remarkably, as I will have occasion to show in Chapter 7, the liberal left and French Communist Party maintained support for the French army, allowing it to assume extraordinary powers. This colonial consensus worked to uphold the raison d'état and justify colonial state interests at the expense of individual freedoms and fundamental rights. In his essay on the European minority, Fanon discusses the contradictions dividing the complicit liberal left in mainland France and the Dreyfusards in Algeria, who supported the Algerian Revolution. The Third Republic emerged on 4 September 1870, during the Franco-Prussian War, which culminated in France's humiliating defeat and the collapse of the Second French Empire. Amidst this turmoil, the Crémieux Decree was signed on 24 October 1870, granting French citizenship to approximately 35,000 native Algerian Jews while excluding Muslim Arabs and Berbers. This decree exacerbated French notions of racial superiority in Algeria and fuelled antisemitism among French colonists. The subsequent Dreyfus Affair epitomised these tensions, dividing France along ideological lines. The case was significant not only for its wrongful conviction to maintain the raison d'état but for scapegoating Alfred Dreyfus as a Jew who symbolised the perceived causes of France's imperial decline. Dreyfus came to represent revolutionary principles affirming individual sovereignty over the state, pitting Dreyfusards against anti-Dreyfusards in a profound national schism. Similarly, the Algerian war bequeathed France the Fifth Republic. However, unlike the Dreyfus Affair, a colonial consensus united left and right, enabling a putschist army to institute a regime akin to fascism, violating fundamental freedoms and individual rights. Fanon, in *Studies in a Dying Colonialism* and other writings, reminds us that this violence was not an aberration but had a long history fundamental to colonialism and its biopolitics.

1

Colonisation Medicine and Colonial Biopolitics

COLONISATION AND MEDICINE

During the entire period of France's conquest of Algeria, the French army and its health service took prophylactic measures to forestall endemic diseases and bore the burden of providing care to the settlers. The colonising army encountered severe health challenges in a country whose climate was murderous: frequent epidemics decimated soldiers and settlers alike.[1] The army was responsible for hygiene and public health, a particularly demanding task in a country, where epidemics and contagious diseases posed a more serious danger for French troops and settlers than enemy bullets.[2] Care provision and hospitals evolved with the historical vicissitudes of the military and civil administrations which developed side by side. In 1853, with the creation of the colonial medical service, and later with the transfer of medical care to the civilian administration, hygiene protocols were put in place by epidemiologists and enforced by departmental or municipal hygiene councils; the administration of hygiene was only one of the many functions carried out by the Department of the Interior, which also dealt with matters relating to departmental and communal administration, notably the prison service, public education and social work.

The growth of colonial settlements meant that military doctors were no longer sufficient to provide medical care to the small but ever-increasing European population. Contagious diseases were rampant; during epidemics in particular, military doctors could not adequately care for this population scattered throughout the Algerian countryside.[3] The success of France's colonial mission depended on these settlements, which in turn relied on the medical provision made available to European settlers. On 12 April 1845, the minister of war made the decision to establish a special service tasked with providing free healthcare to settlers.[4] Subsequently, the colonial medical service was organised by an order of the Ministry of War on 21

January 1853. 'Colonial doctors' (*médecins de colonisation*) were henceforth deployed to treat the needy free of charge, making regular visits to the *douars* and *mechtas*,[5] administering vaccinations, and promoting public health.[6] It is important to note that this service was established not to benefit indigenous populations, but rather to facilitate their colonisation.

Nevertheless, four native hospitals were built to address the aftermath of famine, typhus, cholera, earthquakes and locust infestations that devastated Algeria between 1866 and 1868.[7] In 1874, Cardinal Lavigerie, Archbishop of Algiers, founded Sainte-Elisabeth hospital (also known as Saint-Cyprien des Attafs) with the help of General Wolff, who sought to use France's 'civilising mission' to win the hearts and minds of the natives in the propaganda war.[8] A year later, Governor-General Chanzy decided to build Saint-Augustin hospital in the mountainous Aurès region of Arris. In 1894, Governor-General Cambon inaugurated the third hospital, Sainte-Eugénie, in Michelet. This decision came a year after the 1893 famine that ravaged native populations in the Chélif plain. In 1895, Cambon approved the plan to build the Lavigerie hospital in Biskra. He was motivated by the belief that charitable work would alleviate the suffering of the indigenous population decimated by famine, bring them closer to France, and curb their religious fanaticism.[9]

These 'native' or 'auxiliary' hospitals were nonetheless rejected or seldom frequented by native patients. Saint-Augustin hospital ceased operations in June 1915 due to its failure to attract the sick among the Chaouïa tribes.[10] The signage at the front of Sainte-Elisabeth hospital, bearing the inscription بيت الله ('House of God' in Arabic), written incorrectly from left to right as in French, was symbolic of this failure. The Orientalising inscription, meant to appeal to the native population, clearly gestured to their rejection of Western medicine. Under the administration of Governor-General Jonnart, several native infirmaries – such as Hôpital de Rabelais, Hôpital indigène d'Ammi-Moussa, Hôpital auxiliaire d'Oran – were constructed to resemble mosques. Their Moorish style, contemptuously dubbed 'infirmaries à la Jonnart', was merely a ploy used to attract the natives and make them feel at home. French settlers derided the Jonnart style for its assimilationist tendency, while natives rejected the infirmaries for the same reason. This style was nothing but an exterior, a façade without an inner function – a vacuous cultural artefact – designating effectively empty infirmaries. These 'native infirmaries' were constructed with a stylish exterior but lacked the basic internal equipment essential to their use.[11] Fanon was the first to highlight this failure in *Studies in Dying Colonialism*; YvonneTurin provides further elaboration in a detailed and archival study, *Affrontements culturels dans l'Algérie coloniale: Ecoles, médecines, religion, 1830–1880.*[12] Before delving into Fanon's discussion of 'Medicine and Colonialism', it is important to examine the politics of health established by the colonial administration in Algeria. From the outset, Cambon set the stage for the complicity of medicine and colonialism that Fanon would later critique, as the colonial health system became a means of exerting control and perpetuating the inequalities of the colonial order.

If we interpret the Foucauldian terms 'noso- and biopolitics' to broadly mean the politics of containing and treating diseases while maximising life, it is fair to say that Cambon was a noso- and biopolitician par excellence. This politics operated with the dual aim of simultaneously containing poverty-induced diseases among the indigenous population and optimising the living conditions and prosperity of European settlers. Focused on two critical issues for the settlers' survival – healthcare assistance and security – Cambon developed essential infrastructure. He built hospitals, established the Pasteur Institute in Algiers, and implemented measures to combat contagious diseases.[13] Healthcare provisions and assistance offered to the natives constituted an integral part of colonial biopolitics, which primarily sought to ensure security and create the necessary conditions for colonial prosperity and expansion. In fact, while this assistance mitigated the impact of poverty and famine on the European population, it did not address the root causes of these issues among the natives.

The Sénatus-consulte of 1863, enacted during the Second French Empire, introduced two key provisions that had a devastating impact on the political economy of indigenous populations: land indexation and parcelisation. Despite the far-reaching consequences of colonial policies, which often led to the displacement and dispossession of indigenous communities and negatively impacted their social, cultural, and economic wellbeing – resulting in appalling poverty, famines, and diseases – Cambon was keen to emphasise their purportedly positive aspects. He claimed they 'consisted in recognising individual property where it existed and [in] establishing it where it did not'. While war was a factor, expropriation – brought about by the Sénatus-consulte and the Warnier Law of 1873 – was the main instigator of famine. The Warnier Law became, in the hands of speculators, 'an instrument of expropriation and ruin'.[14] However, Cambon commends this law for being based on 'rational thought', as it opened up indigenous property that would otherwise have 'remain[ed] forever closed to [colonial] activity'. As he opines:

The National Assembly passed the law of 1873, under the inspiration of the excellent Doctor Warnier, a law whose aim was to open up to colonisation, to European activity and capital, this indigenous property which, by its very nature and its state of undivided ownership, was absolutely closed to our action. In 1882, the Chambers also sought to constitute the Muslim family in a way more similar to ours, by creating civil status.[15]

In Cambon's view, colonial and social issues were inextricably linked. Colonisation and expropriation had one intended outcome: destroying existing social structures and reconfiguring the family unit. At the intersection of his nosopolitics lies this connection that Cambon establishes between the traditional laws regarding the inalienability of land property and those structuring the Muslim family and homestead. Two interrelated consequences resulted from the implementation of the Warnier Law: socioeconomic and medical. This law brought about the alienability of what was previously inalienable, and the divisibility of land went hand in hand with the fragmentation of the family structure, giving rise to poverty and disease. The expropriation of Algerian land was a key feature of Cambon's 'nosopolitics' – a term I am using to underscore that the politics of health was not one that provided remedies, but rather one that conversely occasioned diseases. While acknowledging that unscrupulous speculators used the provisions of the Warnier Law to expropriate and ruin entire families, Cambon nonetheless underplays its devastating effects on the indigenous people. Simply put, the impact of the Warnier Law on the socioeconomic and familial structures of Algerian society was a central component of Cambon's noso- and biopolitical agenda, which prioritised the health and security of the European settler population over the wellbeing of the native population.

Attributing the nineteenth-century famines not merely to inclement weather, but also to Malthusian pressures, Cambon writes:

> In the two and a half years that I have been in Algeria, not an hour has passed when I have not heard of famine, drought, locusts, fires. It seems that all the calamities have been accumulating in the colony for several years. It is the law of this country, so rich and so poor at the same time, it is the law in all Mediterranean countries, that periods of great rain succeed those of great droughts and bring abundance and fertility to a soil which, without them, is rebellious to all production.[16]

The apparent paradox of Mediterranean countries being both rich and poor was not merely a result of climate, but primarily a consequence of colonial policies. The plight of famine was not a tribute paid by the natives to a capricious soil that refused to yield, but rather a result of the Sénatus-consulte and Warnier Law. These laws served as tools of colonial biopolitics which, by expropriating land and preventing natives from working it, gave rise to famine. The workings of this biopolitics were ambivalent and contradictory: colonialism provided assistance to the natives against diseases and famines which it had created in the first place. In Cambon's account of the early 1860s, disastrous events struck Algeria: the insurrection of the Oulad-Sidi-Cheikh ravaged the south of the province of Oran; cholera, soon followed by a terrible famine, caused the death of large segments of the indigenous population throughout Algeria. An enquiry conducted by Count Le Hon resulted in a programme of liberal reforms, but nothing came of it as it was consigned to oblivion with the outbreak of Franco-Prussian War in 1870.[17] What motivated Cambon, in his capacity as governor-general (1891–97), to put in place healthcare provisions for the natives three decades after the Sénatus-consulte (1863) instigated their expropriation and two decades after Dr Auguste Warnier completed this task? The contradictions inherent in colonial biopolitics were reflected in Cambon's initiatives, which paradoxically sought to institute healthcare provisions while simultaneously expropriating the natives. *Expropriation* and *assistance* went hand in hand; clearly, colonial biopolitics strategised to kill or keep the natives in a vegetative state, living between life and death.

According to Cambon, it was legitimate and necessary to spread education among the natives and ensure that they received the benefits of medical care and assistance, since they were made to pay taxes.[18] However, while the 'Arab tax' constituted the largest part of the resources for assistance, these resources were devoted exclusively to hospitals placed in the centres of colonisation, which the natives could not attend.[19] It is important to clarify that these taxes did not conform to the rules and laws mandating taxation; they consisted of plundering and pillaging the indigenous people. It is erroneous to think of the latter as taxpayers; they were expropriated and dispossessed subjects, victims of the ruthless *razzias* carried out by the French army. Ferdinand-Auguste Lapasset describes the *razzia* as a sort of 'hawk strike on populations hidden or fleeing': an operation commonly used against tribes, culminating with their subjugation. Usually, the raids took place early in the morning, as the *razeurs* (*goum*,[20] cavalry, infantry) launched their attacks 'killing men, seizing women, children, unarmed men, herds, booty, etc.

... burning items they cannot take'.[21] *Razzias* differ from the pillaging and *mise-en-sac* that typically accompany military conquest. As Olivier Le Cour Grandmaison elaborates, these operations had specific aims and intended consequences: clear tribal land by uprooting and displacing inhabitants; make land available for colonial settlements; dislocate and destroy traditional economic structures; cause economic hardship, famine, and diseases, leading to the destruction of native populations.[22]

The devastating famine of 1866–68 decimated Algeria's population. Contagious diseases also gripped the native people, posing a serious threat to colonial settlements. In response, mobile units were organised to provide medical care to remote tribes, especially in the Aurès region. The native population avoided French hospitals due to cultural insensitivity and their association with military atrocities. Hospital regulations disregarded indigenous religious, dietary, and cultural practices,[23] while colonial doctors in military uniforms resembled soldiers who had committed violent acts against the native population – pillaging food stores, stealing livestock, burning villages, and perpetrating sexual violence against women. Though Cambon took the initiative to build special hospitals in remote and densely populated regions, he seemed oblivious to the ramifications of the natives' impoverishment. This impoverishment, caused by so-called taxes collected through *razzias*, led to famine and its sequelae, which manifested as plagues and contagious diseases. This initiative to bring assistance and medical care to the natives was, in fact, one of the public measures used by the colonial administration to impose confinement on the roving, destitute indigenous populations carrying the scourges of famine and other communicable diseases, which posed a serious threat to French colonisation. The French colonial authorities recognised the need to provide healthcare to native Algerians, but their efforts were hampered by a lack of cultural sensitivity and the underlying exploitation and violence of the colonial system itself. Ultimately, therefore, the provision of medical care was far more a means of control and containment than a humanitarian gesture.

The Franco-Prussian War (1870–71) and the El-Mokrani insurrection (1871–72) accelerated the process of colonisation and settlement in Algeria. At the behest of M. d'Haussonville, the French government allocated funds to resettle displaced immigrants from Alsace and Lorraine in Algeria. Following the 1871 insurrection, Governor-General de Gueydon imposed a severe collective penalty: a tax on the insurgents to punish the natives, resulting in the sequestration of tribal land. Of the 400,000 hectares confiscated, approximately 350,000 were allocated for colonisation.[24] This sequestration and expropriation deprived the natives of their livelihoods and brought about significant hardship. While these 'brutal dispossessions' were morally dubious, Cambon felt compelled to accept the inevitable recourse to expropriation, which once again opened up native property for colonial activity. As he elaborates:

> So you have before you people with property rights based on inviolable legislation. Therefore, just as the existence of that population was an obstacle to colonisation by force, so the existence of that legislation and property is an obstacle, not only to colonisation by force, but also to private initiative.[25]

Two factors impeded colonisation: an indigenous society with a large and rapidly growing population and the indivisibility of their property. These populations could neither be exterminated nor ignored; consequently, colonial laws were introduced as a 'weapon of war',[26] to wreak untold havoc on them by violating their property rights and destroying the sustainability of their existence. This weapon of war was, nonetheless, double-edged: it curbed the natives' political resistance by impoverishing them, but simultaneously created unfavourable living conditions for the settlers. As a result, hygiene became paramount, with medicine intervening in colonial biopolitics. The colonial administration was very mindful of the need to attenuate the impact of these conditions on the settlers and their survival.

It is worth reiterating that, contrary to Cambon's assertion, famine was not a natural calamity but an instance of colonial biopolitics. Its mechanisms were geared towards altering the demographic landscape that favoured the native populations. In this regard, sequestration and expropriation were key strategies employed to address this demographic imbalance and promote colonial settlements. These tactics effectively defined France's colonial politics, which aimed to benefit European settlers at the expense of the indigenous population. Cambon's establishment of Provident, Relief, and Mutual Loan Societies, along with the construction of auxiliary hospitals, provided financial assistance and medical care. These measures were intended to mitigate the pernicious ramifications of expropriation on the native economy and to attenuate endemic diseases – namely cholera, typhus and other plagues exacerbated by famine. Furthermore, Cambon proposed keeping the natives working the land, not for themselves but for the settlers on starvation wages. He argued for a form of assimilation that amounted to little more than exploitation. His policies exemplified the contradictory nature of colonial biopolitics, which simultaneously sought to control and 'improve' the native population while maintaining their subordinate status. Cambon identifies two opposing tendencies among Algeria's French inhabitants: those favouring assimilation and those seeking autonomy. He rejects both on similar grounds. Autonomy was not viable for a minority of 250,000 European settlers 'in the presence of a large indigenous population', while assimilation was inconceivable as it would negate the settlers' political and economic dominance as a minority. Assimilation was thus unworkable; its logic confronted Malthusian pressures created by the indigenous population of 4 million.[27] He also dismisses the notion that these indigenous people could be granted the same rights as the French. He describes this population as having 'its own customs, traditions, habits of mind, religion, intellectual culture and civilisation' that resisted European education, cultural values, and ways of being. 'In Algeria,' he affirms, 'France finds itself in the presence of diverse population elements, distinct from one another, anxious to differentiate themselves, that will continue to live without mixing either their ideas or their intimate feelings.'[28] Cambon cautioned against imposing institutions upon the colony that would conflict with its established cultural practices and traditions.

Rejecting both assimilation and autonomy, Cambon asserts that colonialism created Algeria's institutions, 'exercising a local authority, but linked to and closely subordinated to the metropolis'.[29] He proposes to maintain the *Indigénat* with an administration 'invested with special powers', enabling the governor-general to balance opposing interests and 'pursue with perseverance the colonising work of France', while protecting 'the prosperity of … French settlers on the Mediterranean coast'.[30] In Cambon's view, Algeria was culturally too different from France to be assimilated, but its geographical proximity to France and strategic position in the Mediterranean were nonetheless crucial to France's imperial ambitions. The dynamic of these 'special powers' ultimately shaped colonial biopolitics.

Biopolitics not only created the necessary conditions for settlers to work but also devised methods to extract labour from native populations. Cambon believed it would be misguided to ignore these 'constantly increasing' and 'considerably large and active' populations, as the success of colonisation depended on their labour. He argued it was 'in France's interest and duty to make use of them to develop her power in the world'.[31] Cambon sought to employ the indigenous workforce 'intelligently and rationally' by cultivating conditions conducive to native labour productivity. His concern for the expropriated natives extended only as far as they could be subjugated to French colonialism and thus contribute to 'the general prosperity of the country and that of the settlers'.[32] The financial and medical assistance offered to the native inhabitants did not stem from the principles of altruism and beneficence but from ruthless colonial calculus. 'Care' and 'assistance' must be inscribed within the context of policies advocating new colonial settlements after France's humiliating defeat in 1871. Cambon's policies were part of a biopolitical system that established healthcare to create optimal working conditions in the colony and increase its European population. Cambon viewed Algeria simultaneously as a 'colony of settlement' and a 'colony of exploitation', asserting that the Sahara – the gateway to Africa – made it also a 'colony of influence or better still of political and commercial domination'.[33] The promotion of colonial settlement aimed to compensate for France's defeat and restore its imperial status. For Cambon, exploiting the Sahara represented a crucial step in France's colonial project to extend its imperial rule over an entire continent and achieve world domination.[34]

NOSOPOLITICS: MEDICALISING GENDER AND FAMILY

During the mission assigned by Cambon to provide medical assistance to the natives, Drs Lucien Raynaud and Henri Soulié travelled through the Aurès region and were appalled by the lamentable state of the population and the lack of medical aid. While Soulié applauded Cambon for paving the way for his successors (Célestin-Charles Jonnart, Charles Lutaud, Théodore Steeg, Maurice Viollette, and Pierre-Louis Bordes), who further developed medical assistance for the natives,[35] he also revealed the true motives behind Cambon's charitable work and beneficence: (1) to bridge the gap between French civilisation and that of the indigenous Muslims, who represented the majority of the Algerian population; (2) to 'penetrate into the native family and reach the woman who had been inaccessible until then'. Cambon understood the significance of the interplay between gender and colonial politics. He underscored the importance of women in native families while criticising, in Orientalising terms, the inferior state in which they were kept. He condemned the secluded existence of native women, forced 'not to leave the house, to show [themselves] only to [their] husbands, families, and a few friends'.[36]

The development of 'auxiliary hospitals' and 'native infirmaries' was a manifestation of nosopolitics of the social body, as care and assistance became blunt instruments of colonial propaganda. Nosopolitics – as practised by Jules Cambon, Dorothée Chellier, Henri Soulié, and others – instantiated what could be termed the 'medical police', primarily concerned with demographic growth and work: natality, morbidity, mortality, life expectancy, family, sexuality, education, work and professional development.[37]

Following Cambon's directives and recognising the failure of assimilation policies, Chellier asserted that women doctors could facilitate the introduction of French ideas into 'a milieu so obstinately, so deliberately distant from [the French]'. She also noted that Cambon employed doctors 'not only to bring enlightened care to the natives and curb the influence of the *toubibs* ... but also to hasten the work of assimilation'. Chellier identified one of the key reasons for the failure of assimilation: French colonisation had not succeeded in conquering the domestic sphere, or as she put it, 'penetrat[ing] the gynaeceum'. Chellier believed that strategically deploying women doctors could bridge the gap between the French and the native population, both in terms of providing modern medical care and facilitating broader cultural assimilation.[38] Her mission, undertaken at Cambon's behest, had a dual purpose, medical and strategic: to study practices surrounding childbirth, abortion, and prevalent uterine diseases in Algeria; and to gain access to and influence Algerian women while unveiling the secluded native culture. Inspired by Cambon, Chellier aimed to penetrate the domestic sphere of Algerian society, which had remained largely inaccessible to French colonial influence. Chellier strategically positioned women doctors as agents of both medical care and cultural change, envisioning a more effective means of introducing French ideas into the insular indigenous society, thereby advancing Cambon's broader objective of leveraging medicine to expedite the assimilation process.

Chellier observed that Chaouïa women, unlike their Arab counterparts who concealed their faces with veils, were more accessible to the male gaze. However, they refused examination by male physicians, instead placing their trust exclusively in female doctors. Chellier suggested that 'it would be in our interest, while respecting Arab customs, to act on women through women'.[39] Chellier was adamant that assimilation could be achieved only by 'operating on the mind of the woman' and 'infiltrating' the family.[40] She attributed the failure of assimilation to its primary focus on adult men while overlooking the crucial role women could play in the process. Chellier advocated for a nosopolitics involving the establishment of a new, diverse medical corps that was not exclusively male. This corps would work with Algerian women in educating children by: (1) gaining the trust of mothers through regular visits and interactions; (2) encouraging mothers to follow medical guidance and recommendations; (3) adopting and promoting new cultural norms that would facilitate assimilation. She identified French women doctors as prime movers in an assimilationist project that would 'hasten progress in Muslim countries'.[41] Chellier hence brought a feminist perspective to medical care and added a feminine touch to France's colonial endeavour and assimilationist policies.

According to Chellier, the indigenous population was largely unaware of the fundamental benefits offered by Western medical science. She posited that native resistance to French cultural practices and customs stemmed primarily from religious adherence. In her view, the indigenous people's fidelity to their traditional beliefs created an insurmountable barrier to the full adoption of French lifestyles, including colonial medical advancements. Writing two decades before the promulgation of the *laïcité* law (1905), Chellier posed a thought-provoking question: 'Would it not be possible to avoid any idea of religious proselytising and to respect their faith while teaching them to relieve their illnesses?'[42] This query reflected her belief that science and French colonialism could conquer the population and penetrate its cloistered culture, but only by becoming resolutely secular.[43] Chellier was adamant that the key to success lay in teaching the colonised population 'how to save themselves from illness without demanding conversion in exchange for medication'. She believed that, by respecting the religion they practised, European settlers would be 'almost certain to see them rally to our civilising ideas'.[44] For Chellier, humanism and colonialism went hand in hand. She saw the potential to bring the benefits of science and medicine to the colonised population, but only if done in a respectful way. This delicate balance between respecting local cultures and advancing the colonial agenda was a central tenet of Chellier's nosopolitics.

Nonetheless, religion and gender remained significant obstacles to the colonial agenda. Chellier cautioned against an assimilation which would 'bring the natives into our civilisation and at the same time keep them segregated from the settlers, and leave [the indigenous] women uneducated'.[45] She recognised that indigenous women were more resistant to assimilation than men. As a result, she advocated for the deployment of medicine as an instrument of coloniality, specifically targeting the female component of indigenous society. In her view, only female doctors could facilitate their assimilation by 'bring[ing] relief to their sufferings and gradually initiat[ing] them into all the benefits of [French] civilisation'.[46] Castigating the *toubib* (doctor) and *qabla* (matron) as obstacles to Western medical practice, cultural instruction and development, Chellier advocated replacing them with French doctors and matrons. She viewed French matrons and white sisters as symbols mediating childbirth's transformation from a physical experience into an abstract and politicised agency of colonial propaganda. She presented women doctors, especially those who knew the Arabic language, as 'family friends' to native women and as prime movers in the implementation of the colonial agenda. These doctors would be tasked with discovering the intimate life of the indigenous people, unveiling their secluded culture, and penetrating the 'gynaeceum'.[47] Chellier's nosopolitics and efforts to medicalise Algerian women and regulate familial units ultimately faltered, as indigenous women and the family unit, which the latter maintained, proved resilient against French colonial intrusion. The interplay of gender norms and religious beliefs presented insurmountable obstacles to French colonialism.

Raynaud, Soulié and Chellier's missions provided medical and obstetric care to the impoverished indigenous and numerically increasing population.[48] These efforts were part of a broader biopolitical strategy to contain and manage communicable diseases and native women's reproductive capacities. However, native populations resisted these initiatives. According to Soulié, the hospitals established by these missions remained largely empty, as women refused to visit them. In the countryside, the natives, especially women, were reluctant to be hospitalised. Soulié noted the small number of hospitalisations, with only one admission every two or three days in a population of more than 20,000 inhabitants. The infirmaries in the southern territories were often deserted.[49] In the city of Constantine, a 20-bed ward built to meet the needs of 30,000 native women was almost always empty. Native women were unwilling to leave their homes and families to enter these European-run hospitals.

The interwar period (1918–39) saw several organisations playing crucial roles in administering medical care and promoting public health. Organisations like the Union of the Women of France (UFF), the Red Cross, and its affiliates – the Association of French Ladies and the Military Casualty Relief Society (SSBM) – established dispensaries and consultation centres staffed by white sisters. These groups, along with other charitable foundations, contributed to preventive medicine initiatives.[50] The focus on women by these organisations raises questions about their motivations: disease containment, demographic surveillance, or regulation of indigenous sexuality. Inscribed within the framework of nosopolitics – which medicalised the family, particularly women, as part of a broader colonial strategy that employed healthcare as a means of control and influence over indigenous populations – their activities were crucial for understanding Soulié's proposal to replace auxiliary hospitals with first aid stations (precursors to the SAS) in order to improve rural healthcare.

The decree of 1 March 1926, and the circular of 30 October of the same year, issued by Governor-General Viollette, regulated the recruitment of visiting nurses. By 1930, there were 80 visiting nurses working at the auxiliary hospitals and consultation centres, tasked with managing women's services, providing midwifery and obstetric care, delivering vaccinations, detecting diseases, and reporting suspected cases to doctors. During rounds in *mechtas* and *douars*, which Fanon references in 'Medicine and Colonialism', visiting nurses instilled basic hygiene principles and ways to prevent contagion. As agents of colonial propaganda and medical surveillance, they monitored diseases and native population growth, perceived as threats to colonisation.

Unlike Chellier, Soulié was not concerned with the failure of assimilation. Instead, his primary preoccupation was colonial hygiene. He excoriated officials from mainland France for treating the natives by European standards, arguing that these French officials erroneously believed that what was good and applicable in France must also apply in Algeria, ignoring the significant gap between the two civilisations. Soulié highlighted the visiting nurses' failure to attract the natives to their consultation centres in the countryside. He attributed this failure to two factors: the nurses' ignorance of the culture was compounded by the natives' 'stubborn prejudices'. 'In certain communes,' writes Soulié, 'the distribution of condensed milk, flour, fabric, soap and small bottles of cologne attracts a certain number of mothers, but in a large number of centres, nurses and doctors find themselves in the presence of emptiness.'[51] Soulié criticised French officials and visiting nurses for treating natives like settlers, a fundamental mistake in his view. He insisted on maintaining the cultural divide, which justified excluding natives from hospital care benefits. This subtext underscored his belief in preserving the distinction between colonisers and colonised.

Soulié advocated for reducing the number of hospitals and replacing them with first aid stations, arguing that natives rarely utilised hospitals and only sought medical consultations when free drugs were offered.[52] These stations were, in his view, more cost-effective than 'auxiliary' hospitals equipped to treat large numbers of patients, and were able to 'isolate the contagious, and to destroy the vermin, source of propagation of the most serious epidemic diseases of Algeria'. For Soulié, first aid stations represented a new organisational development that aligned with natives' cultural habits and addressed their medical needs through treatment and prophylaxis. He promoted this assistance method based on three key points: it was the preferred method among native populations; it was the method recommended by the colonial administration; and it was the most cost-effective.[53] The primary aim of these stations was to treat patients at home. In Soulié's words: 'They impose a minimum of disturbance to patients; they are thus closer to home assistance [...] the most desired.'[54] Clearly, Soulié was concerned more with the spiralling cost of care and the pressing issue of tackling the spread of epidemics at source than by the exclusion of the indigenous populations from hospital care. His proposal to replace hospitals with first aid stations must be interpreted in this light as a sort of cordon sanitaire imposed by colonial hygiene. A close examination of Soulié's proposal to replace hospitals with first aid stations exposes its underlying implications. While purporting to bring healthcare to natives' homes, it effectively denied them the comprehensive care that hospitals could offer. Instead, it kept them confined to their often miserable conditions in the countryside without adequate medical provision.

While Soulié might diverge from Chellier's assimilationist views, he shared her belief in medicine as a colonial instrument. He advocated for urgent improvements to consultation centres for women and children to 'attract ... this very interesting part of the indigenous society: the Arab woman'. Soulié cited the success of the Miliana consultation centre, where a female, Arabic-speaking doctor attracted large numbers of indigenous women.[55] He aimed to replicate the El-Affroun initiative across numerous localities to achieve three primary objectives: deliver healthcare to sick people; reduce the financial burden of care on public funding; interpose French authority on native culture and extend French influence into the previously inaccessible 'Muslim gynaeceum'.[56] In an effort to infiltrate Algerian households, first aid stations and consultation centres, primarily targeting women, were strategically deployed as part of a propagandistic schema that sought to co-opt – or more accurately, interpellate – women through medical discourse and care provision. Paradoxically, these initiatives replicated colonial segregation policies by imposing quarantine on the indigenous population, thereby reinforcing the harem culture that Soulié, Chellier and Cambon simultaneously Orientalised and demonised.

HYGIENE, URBANISM AND COLONIAL MANICHAEANISM

The administration of hospitals and care provision in colonial Algeria was governed by a series of decrees and orders.[57] The decrees of 16 May and 21

June 1849, along with Louis Napoléon's decree of 23 March 1852, restructured hospital administrative commissions. The decree of 23 December 1874 organised medical services in Algeria, transferring the colonial medical service from the Ministry of War to the Ministry of the Interior.[58] Subsequently, the decree of 11 September 1920 placed it under the direct authority of the governor-general.[59] Notably, these care provisions were not intended for the indigenous population; rather, 'treatment' effectively maintained their physical confinement and segregation. Native care fell under the *Indigénat* regime, characterised by arbitrary and exclusive regulations, further reinforcing colonial control. The *bureaux arabes*,[60] functioning as agencies of surveillance and colonial propaganda, were tasked with providing care to the indigenous population. In analysing Fanon's 'Medicine and Colonialism', it is crucial to recognise the pivotal role of hospitals in mediating Algeria's colonisation history. As a primary organ administering care and hygiene, and an emblem of colonial architecture and urbanism, the hospital significantly influenced the development of colonial structures and policies. It played a key role in shaping the colony's political evolution from military to civilian rule while simultaneously mediating the tension and complicity between these two forms of governance.

The status of doctors and pharmacists in France was established by the presidential decree of 28 August 1851, and later redefined by the law of 30 November 1892.[61] This legislation was extended to Algeria through the decree of 7 August 1896, effectively denying indigenous empiric doctors the right to practise traditional medicine among their co-religionists.[62] Initially, as evidenced by his instruction to local authorities on 1 September 1897, Governor-General Cambon advocated leniency towards Algerian 'medics' who 'have never been the object of any complaint and knew how to impose themselves on the populations concerned'.[63] However, this policy was reversed in 1923 when Governor-General Steeg, perceiving these practitioners as potential instigators of anti-French sentiment, decided to take action against them. Steeg favoured French medicine as a more reliable tool for colonial governmentality, believing that 'qualified' doctors would facilitate local administration while serving as agents of colonisation and propaganda.[64] As Fanon suggests in 'Medicine and Colonialism' (which I will elaborate on in Chapter 5), colonial antagonism manifested as a conflict between traditional healing and Western medicine.

The law of 15 July 1893 mandated care for elderly and poor sick people in mainland France. Prior to this law, Picard remarks, the charity office assisted those in need; free medical care was not a right.[65] However, this law did not apply to Algeria, where assistance was provided by the European charity office.[66] Given this office's limited resources and the absence of a designated charity for the indigenous poor, the latter had to resort to private charity or begging, which was an infraction of the law. Although the Commission for the Reform of Hospital Assistance made proposals that were adopted by the Financial Delegations and approved by the Board of Governors in June 1902, the provisions stipulated by the law of 15 July 1893 were not enforced in Algeria. The 'ethnic diversity' of the population complicated the situation so much that the governor-general made the following pronouncement on 28 September 1909: 'The law of 14 July 1905, relating to compulsory assistance to the elderly, the infirm and the incurable deprived of resources, reserves the benefit of its provisions only to persons of French nationality.'[67] On 12 December 1912, the minister of the interior was reminded that the law of 1905 remained ineffective in Algeria, as it was not applicable to the impoverished Algerians.[68] Cost was a crucial factor limiting healthcare provisions for Algerians. As we shall see, treatment kept them in a permanent state of physical confinement and segregation.

Municipal healthcare provided hospital consultations and home visits for patients who were unable to travel to hospitals. Home visits helped municipalities to reduce high and potentially crippling hospitalisation costs. The civil administration highlighted the severity of the problem in providing care to an indigent society. On 5 March 1907, the governor-general issued a circular to the prefects, stating that home care was the only way to reduce municipalities' heavy financial burden of treating the impoverished in hospitals.[69] In a circular dated 4 May 1908, the governor-general, expressing concern about the spiralling costs of hospital care, declared: 'When the patient can be effectively cared for at home, hospitalisation must be ruthlessly refused.'[70] In his report to the Financial Delegations in 1927, Dr Charles Aboulker informed the Assembly that providing care at home would cost less than covering the enormous expenses incurred by hospitalisation.[71] The colonial administration could not bear the financial burden for the reorganisation of care if the law of 1905 were implemented in Algeria. In the early 1920s, 84 per cent of the population was destitute. Of 6 million inhabitants, the budgetary burden fell on fewer than half a million European taxpayers. Almost the entire population required free care services yet contributed nothing financially.[72]

To mitigate high care costs,[73] the colonial administration adopted a policy antithetical to medical assistance, embracing the mantra 'prevention is better than cure', or more precisely, prevention as aid. In practice, this translated to prevention for the indigenous population and medical aid for European settlers. While hospitals were constructed for Europeans, home visits were imposed upon natives, effectively containing them within a cordon sanitaire. Hygiene and prophylaxis gained prominence in the colonial medical service, with Drs Lucien Raynaud and Paul Picard asserting that this preventive medicine contributed to public health and 'racial preservation' ('*préservation de la race*').[74] This term carried dual implications: preventing European–native intermixing and protecting European settler demographics from decline due to infectious diseases prevalent among indigenous populations. Thus, 'preservation' functioned simultaneously as a medical intervention and a political practice imposed by a racialised regime of care.

Social assistance and medical care were implemented as preventive measures against diseases by optimising individuals' hygienic conditions. Picard contends that poverty, devastating entire families, posed the most severe social threat, necessitating worker protection against illness and unemployment for its eradication.[75] Picard elucidates the deleterious effects of poverty on productive and reproductive processes, highlighting several significant consequences. First, the poor, unable to resume an active life, became a burden on society. Their living conditions made them prone to communicable diseases like tuberculosis, typhus, or syphilis, turning them into vectors of contagion endangering not only the indigenous populations but the European ones as well. Contagion did not discriminate between these two populations; it was in the Europeans' interest to help fight against poverty and prevent communicable diseases.[76] Second, in a society with a scarce workforce, social hygiene and medicine gained paramount importance: the sick colonised contributed neither to production nor to care costs. Poor health and hygiene impeded colonial infrastructure and productivity, while also exacerbating the already declining birth rates among European settlers. Picard assigns medicine a crucial role in France's colonial project in Algeria, combating poverty, morbidity, and mortality.[77] He argues that pursuing public health simultaneously ensured European settlers' prosperity and demographic growth.[78] With European immigration halting in the 1920s and settlers outnumbered ten to one, the native population, perceived as disease carriers, represented both a financial burden and an existential threat to settlers. Picard thus questions how to prevent the spread of disease given natives' unhygienic living conditions near European settlers.

Taking a cue from Foucault and Fanon, it is possible to demonstrate that France's colonial enterprise in Algeria was underpinned by a 'social economy' and by the development of 'medico-administrative' knowledge, which invested medicine with a 'surplus of power'.[79] The 'modern' doctor, the hygienist, and the epidemiologist were co-opted in this regard as colonial agents, working together with the philanthropist to eradicate one of the main causes of morbidity and social diseases: poverty. Paradoxically, this poverty was engendered by the very colonial enterprise they served. Colonial doctors assumed a dual function as both public and private practitioners. As government and military officials, they administered care and ensured public hygiene. This dual function made them effective agents of colonial propaganda. They fulfilled a crucial function by 'bring[ing] the benefits of civilisation to the most remote corners of [the] colony' and by monitoring its 'very backward population, living in deplorable hygienic conditions', by preventing outbreaks of dangerous epidemics.

Picard contends that the physician, functioning as both hygienist and epidemiologist, was instrumental to the colonial enterprise, a view corroborated by Governor-General Jonnart's assertion that a compassionate doctor could potentially supplant a military battalion in maintaining public order and solidifying France's moral authority. This sentiment was echoed in the Chamber of Deputies session of 21 December 1903, where Marcel Sembat and Charles Jonnart emphasised the urgency of providing medical assistance for indigenous populations. Sembat argued that France should be perceived not only as an educator but also as a healer, while Jonnart declared medicine to be the 'true conqueror' in Algeria. Malinas and Tostivint further elaborated on this perspective, asserting that multiplying medical assistance services was the surest way to gain the trust and affection of Muslim populations.[80]

This rhetoric of maximising healthcare contrasted sharply with political reality. As we have seen, on 28 September 1909, the governor-general restricted free healthcare assistance (mandated by the 14 July 1905 law) to French nationals only. It is worth reiterating that financial constraints significantly limited healthcare provisions for Algerians, resulting in a system that effectively maintained their physical confinement and segregation. Both Jonnart and Cambon, as biopolitical strategists, worked to consolidate French colonialism through the establishment of medical care. The *bureaux arabes* served as a conduit for introducing military doctors into these populations, effectively creating a mechanism for surveillance and control under the guise of healthcare provision.

In the early twentieth century, health offices and departmental services were established to combat severe epidemics.[81] Governor-General Maurice Viollette's decree of 9 July 1927, created a sub-directorate of social work and hygiene, which was further developed by Governor-General Pierre Bordes and ratified in the law of 17 July 1928.[82] This legislation established the Central Service of Hygiene and Preventive Medicine, responsible for public health and social hygiene, focusing on contagious and social diseases.[83] Notably, mobile units were created in each department to extend hygiene services to rural areas, conducting disease prevention, sanitation, and health education campaigns.[84] Adopting the mantra 'prevention better than cure', the Territorial Protection Service emphasised proactive measures to improve public health in colonial Algeria, marking a shift towards preventive healthcare strategies. The Office national d'hygiène sociale, inaugurated on 4 December 1924, launched an extensive propaganda campaign in France and its colonies to promote public health measures, combat social diseases, and ensure 'racial preservation'.[85] On 14 May 1928, the Algerian Office for Preventive Medicine and Hygiene was founded, with similar objectives: to disseminate public health information through propaganda, emphasising hygiene and prophylaxis for combating social diseases and 'racial preservation'; to facilitate communication between public authorities and private organisations; and to advance medical technologies for improving hygiene and public health across the colony. This office also aimed to establish centres for combating social diseases and to support both public and private organisations in realising these objectives.[86] It created dispensaries and organised a propaganda service to educate the public. Undoubtedly, doctors, nurses, and visiting social and health workers were the best propagandists in this service.

Colonial hygiene not only ensured the biological wellbeing of settlers but also created particular conditions of existence that differentiated them from natives, ostensibly to prevent contagion. Sanitary measures upheld an institution of colonial domination that managed the native population. Inscribed within the protocols of the Office national d'hygiène sociale were Soulié's epidemiology and programme of hygiene. As noted earlier, Soulié endorsed first aid stations and homecare provisions as strategies to monitor the interface between public and private spaces, control native domestic spheres, and limit the movement of natives from rural areas to urban hospitals. Mobile units were deployed to contain the spread of contagious diseases and their carriers, pejoratively referred to as 'vermin' and 'native' populations – terms that intermingled in the settlers' racist lexicon. Effectively, colonial epidemiology and hygiene established a cordon sanitaire, rooted in racist logic, that segregated indigenous villages, districts, and territories from European cities. The economy of care in colonial Algeria was inherently Manichaean, with hygiene serving as a vital instrument of colonial governmentality. As Fanon illustrates in *The Wretched of the Earth*, Algeria was partitioned into distinct zones, each inhabited by different peoples and governed by different laws.[87] The rural–urban divide was demarcated along ethnic lines, with natives confined to prevent the spread of communicable diseases. Ultimately, this Manichaean economy determined the mapping of colonial space. It was compartmentalised and segregated, with its functioning conforming to racialised hygiene principles, reinforcing the colonial power structure through spatial and medical surveillance mechanisms.

Colonial hygiene played a crucial role in regulating interracial relationships, policing the demarcation between public and private spaces and determining the Manichaean economy of colonial life. The *bureaux arabes*, the *Indigénat*, and the colonial territories functioned as medico-administrative institutions, instrumental in maintaining the segregation of indigenous populations and reinforcing settler hegemony. Confinement and racial segregation were primary measures employed to ensure hygiene standards. Drawing on Foucault's theorising, colonial society can be viewed as a multifaceted entity: a physical ensemble, a social construct, an economic system, and a sexualised body. This complex societal structure was regulated by hygiene measures designed to safeguard both its productive and reproductive processes. These measures served not only as health protocols but also as mechanisms of power and control, reinforcing the colonial hierarchy and justifying the separation of coloniser and colonised.

To comprehend the mechanisms of the colonial apparatus, its dominance and inherent instability, it is crucial to examine demography as a determining factor, particularly given the numerical superiority of the native population over European settlers. Control of reproduction played a vital role in maintaining colonial equilibrium, with interracial sexuality violating both the racialised colonial order and endogamous norms, thereby symbolically undermining the political economy of colonial society.[88]

This economy, predicated on a Manichaean logic, structured colonial society to keep natives and Europeans apart in clearly segregated and demarcated spaces. Racism and misogyny functioned as defence mechanisms, maintaining a cordon sanitaire to ensure colonial hygiene and prevent prostitution, sexual disorder, and miscegenation – all perceived as threats to the demographic growth of white settlers. In colonial Algeria, segregated communities were sustained by endogamy and racism, which collectively established prevailing norms. Colonial Manichaeanism further partitioned space along racialised lines, creating an environment inhabited by two species and governed by a multitude of barriers – religious, social, and sexual. These barriers perpetuated a state of permanent coloniality for the natives, reinforcing the power dynamics of the colonial system.

Hygiene played a pivotal role in maintaining colonial control, serving dual purposes: safeguarding the colonial project's viability and preserving white racial supremacy, both physically and politically. Operating at the intersection of public and private spheres, hygiene policed sexuality, contained social diseases threatening the social body, and articulated its powers through the urbanisation of colonial life. Cities were sanitised by removing elements that posed threats to public health and internal security. As Fanon argues, colonial society was compartmentalised: European cities were segregated from quarters inhabited by natives. This colonial Manichaeanism was governed by the rules of colonial hygiene and urbanism. European cities were constructed in accordance with principles of order, rationality, modernity, and hygiene. In contrast, quarters inhabited by the pullulating native populations were characterised by poverty, disorder, pollution, and deprivation. Colonial presence was inscribed in urbanism – in buildings and monuments emblematising France's imperial power and civilisational work. Cities were conceived as social bodies that required protection from contagion; colonial hygiene intervened to implement measures regulating these bodies and confining disease-carrying vectors. Propaganda supported these efforts, with agents including military officers, doctors, matrons, visiting nurses, and school teachers working in unison to inform and contain the masses, and reform native customs. 'Racial preservation' and colonial dominance depended heavily on this propaganda.

Colonial urban planning and medicine were deeply intertwined, with doctors and urbanists working in tandem to regulate the colonial city and distinguish it from native quarters. The sanitisation of space was governed by a logic of supplementarity, as described by Jacques Derrida, which effectively relegated native inhabitants to the urban periphery. This strategy created a secure space for settlers to live and work, protected from communicable diseases prevalent among native populations. Urbanism and hygiene were maintained by principles akin to those outlined in Derrida's discussion of pharmacy, which excluded elements deemed dangerous to urban harmony. Hygiene and public health measures were instituted primarily to safeguard white European urban areas, revealing a racist conception of space that sought to 'whiten' these areas by expelling and ghettoising the native population. Even hospitals, ostensibly places of care, were governed by these exclusionary, racialised principles of urbanisation under the guise of prophylaxis.[89] This ethnic and racial purification served as a defence mechanism to protect the perceived order and health of the colonial social body. In stark contrast to the meticulously planned colonial city, native quarters were characterised as not conforming to Western hygiene standards – overcrowded, and inadequate for the 'circulation of people' and 'goods' – thus hindering the functioning of a modern economy.[90] After the conquest of Algiers, large parts of the old city were demolished to make way for the European city, with its wide streets and open, airy spaces. This design was not merely aesthetic but functional, aimed at preventing the concentration of masses, who were viewed as potential hotbeds of contagious diseases.

Exemplifying urban design principles, hospitals were constructed in conformity with principles of segregation, separation, confinement, surveillance, and discipline exercised over indigenous populations. Indigenous medical facilities were often relegated to the status of ancillary dispensaries, exemplified by the native hospitals à la Jonnart, reflecting the broader compartmentalisation of settler and native spaces. In territoires de plein exercice, hospitals built for Europeans followed healthcare standards akin to those in mainland France. In contrast, colonial territories were equipped with 'auxiliary' hospitals for native populations, manifesting an apartheid-like system in healthcare administration. Urban hygienists and epidemiologists recommended establishing distinct hospitals for Europeans in colonial cities, justifying racial segregation on health grounds. They perceived the 'propagation of diseases' associated with indigenous populations as a threat to colonial hegemony. Segregated hospitals in Algeria were first introduced in 1874, with the construction of Sainte-Elisabeth Hospital, also called Saint-Cyprien des Attafs. Subsequently, in 1903, Jonnart established 'special' infirmaries specifically for the indigenous population. These facilities were notably substandard, lacking basic amenities such as beds and blankets, forcing patients to sleep on the floor.[91]

Picard and his colleagues, in the two volumes of Hygiène et pathologie, highlight the dire conditions of native populations in colonial Algeria: mortality rates in the Casbah were double those in the rest of Algiers, and indigenous inhabitants were six times more likely to contract tuberculosis than their European counterparts. Algeria endured devastating famines in 1866, 1867, 1868, 1893, 1932 and 1945, decimating its indigenous populations. These recurring famines were compounded by infectious diseases such as cholera, syphilis and typhus. In combating contagious diseases, colonial hygiene – guided by the logic of supplementarity – structured and organised space along ethnic and racial lines. Hygienists viewed indigenous populations as potential vectors of communicable diseases; consequently, they advocated for their containment and segregation from European settlers.[92] The European city stood as an emblem of power and progress, while the Casbah, with its narrow lanes and dilapidated, overcrowded houses, symbolised the perceived inferiority of the natives. This dichotomy reaffirmed the perceived superiority of the European city as an epitome of progress and civilisation, while simultaneously demonising the Casbah. The latter was characterised by its purported 'worrying promiscuity' and 'degeneration', with descriptions emphasising its 'offensive odours' and the 'raucous voices of rowdy veiled women'.[93]

Segregation contradicted France's rhetoric of political assimilation, a promise consistently made to indigenous peoples but never fulfilled. At the 1905 Congrès colonial français, proposals emerged for complete separation of indigenous and European settlements, including demarcated urban quarters.[94] Plans for separate European habitats were suggested, ostensibly to protect settlers from perceived poor hygiene in native areas. Hygienists such as the Sergent brothers viewed natives as vectors of contamination and recommended social distancing measures of 1 kilometre between European and native habitats.[95] They advised the administration about the potential hygiene impacts on the European settler population, whose demography was already in rapid decline. This segregationist approach reflected an anti-assimilationist sentiment, articulated by Georges Hardy, in his advocacy for association rather than assimilation. By the turn of the century, this shift represented a significant change in colonial policy. However, contrary to Hardy's suggestion in *Nos grands problèmes coloniaux*,[96] this policy change served to maintain racial hierarchies and colonial power structures, rather than to respect native traditions and preserve indigenous cultures. The Sergent brothers' approach articulated broader trends in colonial management emphasising racial separation and the maintenance of European privilege. Their prescribed measures of containment, zoning, and segregation, primarily framed as public health initiatives, pertained to a 'pharmaceutical operation' aimed at expelling elements deemed threatening to European security and hygiene. These segregationist measures formed part of a comprehensive strategy to insulate European enclaves from perceived indigenous threats.

In the early 1920s, amid stalled colonial expansion, the socialist Lucien Deslinières advocated for a policy of '*colonisation d'état*' (state colonisation) to uphold France's global standing, believing it depended on rapid population growth to balance power with other major nations.[97] In *La France nord-africaine*, he contended that the state needed to implement a settlement and development policy in North Africa; a policy which aligned conceptually with the ideas of Cambon, key architect of colonial medicine and hygiene. Nevertheless, Deslinières called for fortifying colonial settlements with 'all exterior walls in a continuous enclosure, with a walkway, bastions, and loopholes'. To deter indigenous encroachment in unstable areas, he recommended additional defences, including 'gates, a central redoubt, barbed wire, some machine guns, and a wireless telegraph post'.[98] As part of this fortification and colonial hygiene, he supported segregation, asserting: 'The essential differences that exist and will exist for a long time between the way of life of the natives' and French settlers precluded cohabitation. He claimed '[the natives] feel more comfortable among themselves' and '[they] would poorly adapt to [European] civilised demands'. He insisted that '[Europeans] would not tolerate their laxity in matters of hygiene, good order, and cleanliness', which 'would lead to continuous conflicts'.[99]

Likewise, Dr Lucien Raynaud advocated for legislation to monitor vagabonds and itinerant workers as potential disease carriers. He proposed regulating population concentrations by forcibly removing harmful elements threatening public health and imposing segregation. While acknowledging that such measures infringed upon individual liberty, Raynaud deemed them necessary.[100] Hygienists employed containment, zoning and urban planning as effective strategies against contagion, with European quarters designed to keep natives at a distance. Urbanism and hygiene worked in tandem to 'whiten' the colonial city, inscribing Western architectural concepts and cultural norms onto its space while expelling native elements considered threats to the city's health and moral order. Biopolitics wielded medicine, hygiene, and urbanism as its arsenal to manage indigenous populations and consolidate colonial hegemony. Urban planning in the colony articulated colonial power and dominance, manifested in architectural edifices – buildings and monuments – as expressions of French imperial presence.

L'Urbanisme aux colonies et dans les pays tropicaux, two volumes compiled by Jean Royer in 1932, contain proceedings from the 1931 international congress on colonial urban planning, highlighting the segregationist policies that shaped colonial space. This event occurred one year after the centenary of Algeria's colonisation, during which Marshal Lyautey inaugurated Radio Poste Colonial. In his 'Preface' to *L'Urbanisme aux colonies et dans les pays tropicaux*, Lyautey implicitly criticised mainland France's assimilationist politics as 'negative formalism',[101] envisioning an urbanism focused on creating and safeguarding European cities rather than preserving indigenous heritage. As he explained: 'Urban planning, understood in its broadest sense, belongs to the same family as Indigenous Policy. It brings ease of life, comfort, charm, and beauty.'[102] In the 'Introduction' to these volumes, Edmond du Vivier de Streel, Director of Congresses for the Colonial Exhibition (1931), called for an urban planning strategy to encourage rapid population growth and extensive development of colonial urban centres.[103] His vision encompassed liveable and healthy settlements in open spaces, featuring wide thoroughfares, multi-storey buildings, and green areas. Central to this plan was the careful selection of sites, the prompt establishment of civic amenities and the incorporation of elements designed to cater to the needs of European settlers. This framework sought to balance urban expansion with public health considerations, reflecting broader colonial objectives of increasing European presence overseas. Crucially, both Lyautey and du Vivier advocated for segregation. Du Vivier justified this as a necessity, citing indigenous populations' fear of contact with Europeans and concerns for the health of whites. He emphasised Lyautey's principle, established as law, to never mix indigenous and European populations in urban settings.[104] This policy, consistent with Hardy's views, was fundamentally segregationist in nature.

Urbanism, as a discipline, brought together architects, planners, geographers, sociologists and epidemiologists. It emerged as a powerful biopolitical instrument operating at social, political and economic intersections to optimise productivity. Race and ethnicity were crucial in mapping colonial cities. As Fanon argued, clear boundaries delineated spaces inhabited by colonised natives and white European settlers. This demarcation was governed by an economy of supplementarity – opposing coloniser/colonised, high/low, inside/outside, same/other, European/native – and by pharmaceutical measures maintaining hygiene and colonial order. Colonial power was established through monumental superstructures, visibly articulating the coloniser's dominance as the architect – etymologically meaning 'chief creator'. The difference engendered by this Manichaean economy was inscribed at the symbolic level, within language, and the space inhabited by coloniser and colonised. The colonial city provided the necessary medical and social hygiene for the white settlers, while the native quarters, the old city and the Casbah became sites of confinement for those who lacked hygiene and threatened the internal security of the colonial city. The colonised were considered a 'dangerous class', and their presence was not tolerated in the city. Clearly delineated boundaries maintained the Manichaeanism of colonial order, and these boundaries were coloured by colonial racism.

The 'villages nègres',[105] agglomerations of 'gourbis' that morphed into 'bidon-villes' from the 1920s onwards, served as sites of containment. Fanon pithily describes them in this phraseology:

> The town belonging to the colonized people, or at least the native town, the Negro village, the medina, the reservation, is a place of ill fame, peopled by men of evil repute. They are born there, it matters little where or how; they die there, it matters not where, nor how. It is a world without spaciousness; men live there on top of each other, and their huts are built one on top of the other. The native town is a hungry town, starved of bread, of meat, of shoes, of coal, of light. The native town is a crouching village, a town on its knees, a town wallowing in the mire. It is a town of niggers and dirty Arabs.[106]

In L'Algérie sous l'égide de la France, Said Faci observed that in 1936 Algeria was compartmentalised, consisting of two distinct societies living side by side: settlers inhabited well-appointed houses forming the colonial city, while natives, whose gourbis constituted what were improperly called 'villages nègres', were relegated to its margins.[107] Like Faci, Fanon demonstrated how racism came to colour space. In The Wretched of the Earth, he echoes Faci, dubbing these gourbis 'ville de bicots'.[108] Space was coloured, excluding natives from the colonial city and reinforcing their inferiority. Racism functioned to sanitise space and was an integral component of colonial biopolitics, operating at the intersection of biology, sociology and politics. Hygiene and urbanism intervened in the administration of colonial populations to ensure, sustain and optimise the regime of coloniality. This biopolitics was predicated on segregation and exclusion, establishing a cordon sanitaire that excluded a class of people considered dangerous. While nineteenth-century Europe, according to Foucault, announced the failure of the institution of confinement, Fanon's account suggests that colonialism reinstated it as a feature of biopolitics.

In conclusion, the extended discussion of the role played by medicine and hygiene in the conquest and colonisation of Algeria provides valuable insights and context for Fanon's essay 'Medicine and Colonialism', explaining why Algerians refused to adopt Western medical technologies. The complicity of the medical establishment with France's colonising efforts was one of the main reasons for this rejection. Building on this historical context, the discussion in this chapter not only provides an account of the historical complicity that Fanon overlooks in his essay but also offers a fresh perspective to reinterpret the Manichaean economy he formulates in *The Wretched of the Earth*. This new perspective considers the role of epidemiology, hygiene, and urban planning in mapping colonial space, and takes into account the laws and policies implemented to dispossess, uproot and displace native populations while facilitating colonial settlements. Furthermore, the historical overview outlines the contradictory workings of colonial biopolitics. On the one hand, it created and optimised the necessary conditions for settlement, work and life for Europeans. On the other, it denied these conditions to natives. Most significantly, gender and sexuality were at the core of colonial biopolitics. The emphasis that the institution of care and assistance placed on the conquest of Algerian women is particularly noteworthy. Gender and sexuality became not only a site of colonial conflict and ideological contestation but a battleground where the Algerian war was fought. Given gender's centrality in colonial politics, it is crucial to engage with Fanon's concept of 'the historical dynamism of the veil', the instrumentalisation of gender in the Algerian war, and the weaponisation of sexuality as a torture tool. The economy of care gave rise to the Manichaeanism which divided colonial society; care was not just a medico-administrative service, but an almost exclusively military operation, crucially important in the conquest and in maintaining colonial domination. Care was administered by the *bureaux arabes* set up by Governor-General Thomas Robert Bugeaud in the early 1840s as his columns adopted one of the most devastating tactics of warfare: the *razzia*. Significantly, Cambon used care to palliate the pernicious effects of colonial politics which promoted European settlements, expropriated, uprooted and displaced the native population, broke down family unity and brought about the pulverisation of Algerian society. At the pinnacle of the Algerian war, Soustelle and Lacoste pursued a similar strategy to Cambon. In his *Studies in a Dying Colonialism*, Fanon formulates a critique of this economy by throwing into sharp focus the complicity of medicine and colonialism. In this critique, he also directs his attention to the weaponisation of care and welfare – that is, the role played by the SAS in administering care, managing the population and promoting colonial propaganda – as the French army undertook a massive programme of *deconstructing* and *reconstructing* Algerian society.

2

Torture Unveiled:
Rereading Fanon and Bourdieu
in the Context of May 1958

In recent critical studies, according to Nigel Gibson, 'the most sustained and profound critique of Fanon over the past decade has been launched by feminist and postcolonialist theorists focusing on "Algeria Unveiled"'.[1] This critique largely explores Fanon's concept of the 'historical dynamism of the veil', examining women's roles in the Algerian war and their strategic use of veiling and unveiling to subvert French colonialism. Critics are divided in their interpretation of 'Algeria Unveiled'. Alluding to the vicissitudes of history Fanon delineates, Tillion writes: 'Algeria, where during the Seven Year War the veil played various strategic roles, is still going through a process of self-examination.' In both urban and rural areas of Algeria, the veil gained ground and assumed a symbolic role in the struggle for Algeria's independence which is, in her words, 'the work of modernist, not retrograde elements'.[2] Christine Achour praises Fanon's astute analysis of the veil as a mechanism of resistance,[3] citing the testimony of *moudjahida* Safi Bazi on Fanon's importance in highlighting women's changing attitudes, in mediating the profound mutations in their traditional family structure, and in raising awareness about the necessity of change.[4] Tracy Denean Sharpley-Whiting maintains that Fanon's work demonstrates a pro-feminist consciousness.[5] However, other critics diverge from this view. Marie-Aimée Helie-Lucas questions the myth constructed by Fanon that Algerian women would be liberated with decolonisation. She argues that women's revolutionary role was largely symbolic, burdening them with safeguarding Algerian culture and identity. Helie-Lucas cautions against Fanon's praise of the veil's revolutionary virtue, highlighting the difficulty of addressing its oppressive nature without betraying national and revolutionary ideals.[6] Furthermore, Helie-Lucas criticises the retrograde and repressive anti-woman legislation implemented in post-independence Algeria, particularly the Family Code, which deprived women of constitutional rights and legalised their inferiority. Contrary to Fanon's vision in 'Algeria Unveiled', the radical changes in Algerian society during the war were largely thwarted post-independence, with women forced to return to traditional roles rather than experiencing liberation.

It is important to note that this failure is not Fanon's; it is the outcome of a narrow nationalism. In *The Wretched of the Earth*, Fanon cautions against 'the danger of perpetuating the feudal tradition which holds sacred the superiority of the masculine element over the feminine'. Decolonisation meant that '[w]omen will have the same place as men, not in the clauses of the constitution but in the life of every day: in the factory, at school, and in the parliament'.[7] A number of critics confuse his pronouncements on the impact of the Algerian war, which revolutionised Algerian society and gender relations, with the reactionary policies implemented in post-independent Algeria. Fanon's 'Algeria Unveiled' must not be read simply as an FLN manifesto that failed to adhere to its pledges. Fanon fought for the institution of freedom and democracy and could not possibly condone the repression of women: his writings could not make any concessions to the establishment of a 'mutilated Algeria' in which half of its population, namely its feminine component, is denied existence.[8]

Such a stance goes against the grain of feminist criticism that rebukes Fanon for eulogising the retrograde tradition of the veil, for perpetuating gender inequality and for espousing Orientalist views. The significance of Fanon's discussion of the instrumentalisation of the veil lies in comprehending the 'transformations of the relationships between the two sexes, between parents and their children and between women and men'.[9] Pierre Bourdieu grasps these transformations in his discussion of colonial traditionalism. To fathom the political and ethical concerns raised by Fanon, I propose to read his 'Algeria Unveiled' alongside Bourdieu's *The Algerians* (*Sociologie de l'Algérie*), against the physical and symbolic violence to which Algerian women were subjected.[10] Both texts explicitly refer to the mass demonstrations during which women were coerced by the French army to unveil to the chanting of 'Long live de Gaulle'. Fanon intervened not only to counter the myth of assimilation that de Gaulle was promoting in Algeria but also to protest against the physical and symbolic rape of Algerian women. My argument is that Fanon's 'Algeria Unveiled' raises an alarm against torture and rape, degrading methods deployed as part of psychological warfare to break anticolonial resistance.

FEMINIST CRITIQUE OF 'ALGERIA UNVEILED'

Some feminists denounce a brand of retrograde nationalism in Fanon's work which completely subsumes gender agency, while others chide his misogynistic views. For instance, Anne McClintock identifies in Fanon's 'Algeria Unveiled' an inherent phallocentrism which reproduces the phantasm of 'colonial conquest as an erotics of ravishment'.[11] She excoriates Fanon for masculinising the Algerian female militant, by 'turning her into a phallic substitute, detached from the male body but remaining, still, the man's "woman-arsenal"'.[12]

McClintock contends that in embarking on a critique of the libidinous economy of French colonialism, Fanon unwittingly performs an act of striptease: 'the Algerian woman is seen as the living flesh of the national body, unveiled and laid bare for the colonials' lascivious grip, revealing "piece by piece, the flesh of Algeria laid bare"'.[13] Moreover, McClintock rebukes Fanon for his instrumentalist appropriation of the female gender, which eroticises and sexualises the colonial conflict by projecting a view of the Algerian woman '[c]arrying the men's pistols, guns, and grenades beneath her skirts, [as] "[she] penetrates a little further into the flesh of the Revolution"'. In this characterisation, the Algerian woman is perceived as a victim of 'a masculinized rapist'.[14] This chapter will argue that this charge is at odds with the ethical imperative which urged Fanon to intervene against the symbolic rape of Algerian women.

Like McClintock, Ato Sekyi-Otu provides a feminist interpretation of Fanon's 'Algeria Unveiled'. While the former overlooks the significance of the interplay between public and private, the latter makes it one of the central parts of his argument. Ato Sekyi-Otu takes issue with Fanon for underplaying the racist and Orientalising stereotypes which project a negative view of the Algerian woman – of 'her alleged confinement, her lack of importance, her humility, her silent existence bordering on quasi-absence'.[15] He bemoans Fanon's 'eagerness to satirize Orientalism', which misled him to 'regurgitate nationalist evasions and denials of woman's internal subjugation'.[16] In Sekyi-Otu's view, Fanon colludes with a repressive nationalism: his text mediates the wilful exclusion of women in Algerian society or, simply put, the 'systematic censorship of the experience of half of its human constituency'.[17] 'How to register, even vindicate,' he asks, 'the anti-imperialist "love of one's own," knowing that this homestead of the particular is in many respects a house of bondage, the refuge of ancestral and recrudescent institutions of repression and exclusion, particularly of women?'[18]

Fanon does not condone the sequestration of women, as Sekyi-Otu intimates; in fact, in *Studies in a Dying Colonialism* and *The Wretched of the
Earth*, he calls for a genuine decolonisation, a radical mutation of an inert
tradition, and a revolution in gender relations. He establishes a correlation
between gender and colonialism, or more precisely, between family life and
the life of an occupied nation, contending that the subjugation of women is
metaphorical for Algeria's colonial domestication. Sekyi-Otu concurs with
Fanon's view that the colonial relation is re-enacted in the domestic sphere.
However, he is adamant that 'structures of women's subjugation precede and
prefigure colonial domination; and that the colonial context reproduces and
reorganises the institutions of patriarchal lordship and bondage'.[19]

In terms echoing Albert Memmi, he constructs a portrait of the colonised
male as an 'emasculated' figure in the public sphere who vents his frustration
at home. The family is the site where the colonial relation is replicated: in the
refuge of family life, where he nurses his 'battered and bruised masculinity',
the colonised man reasserts his authority by subjugating and sequestering
the woman.[20] By arguing that these structures of domination pre-existed
the colonial state, Sekyi-Otu unwittingly writes an apologia for colonialism, placing the blame squarely on tradition, which harbours a regressive
nationalism and works to re-establish male supremacy. The central plank
of Sekyi-Otu's argument is not so much that Algerian women should be
decolonised but rather that they should be 'decloistered'. The women who
removed the veil in the Algerian struggle for independence must now wage
another battle to liberate themselves from a cloistered existence.

Sekyi-Otu fails to adequately analyse how the colonial conflict played out
at the intersection of public and private spheres. Colonisation succeeded in
occupying territory but could not conquer the domestic space of the colonised.[21] Religious and sexual barriers impeded the French colonial conquest.
The veil was not just a signifier of an inert and rigid tradition that kept
women in a state of sequestration and a 'perpetual infantilism'; nor did it
simply represent an 'ambulant harem'. Rather, it constituted an insurmountable barrier, a frontier, separating the inside from the outside, the public
sphere from which the colonised were excluded and the private one where
they enacted and re-enacted their cultural belonging. This ambivalent signifier represented, to borrow Memmi's expression, 'a portable ghetto'; or better
still, a 'cultural corset', which prevented an intrusive colonialism from interfering in the private affairs of the natives.[22] Sekyi-Otu also fails to grasp the
sexualisation of colonial discourse. In a battle where the Algerian woman's
body became a site of contestation, the veil was raised as the standard of

Algerianity against a rampant colonialism. It is worth stressing that the first wave of French feminists was implicated in the colonial endeavour and that their campaign was not to liberate the Algerian woman but to maintain colonial hegemony over Algeria. As Fanon perceptively observes: 'Converting [her], winning her over to the foreign values, wrenching her free from her status, was at the same time achieving a real power over the man and attaining a practical, effective means of destructuring Algerian culture.'[23]

In sum, Sekyi-Otu's critique is inattentive to the historical and political specificities of 'Algeria Unveiled'. An examination of Bourdieu's work throws into sharp relief the lacuna in Sekyi-Otu's reading, which overlooks the significance of gender as a site of anticolonial struggle and also neglects the impact of colonialism on the mummification of tradition and the diremption of public and private. Like Sekyi-Otu, McClintock is oblivious to the implication of colonial feminism in the pacification of Algeria. As we shall see, far from occupying the posture of a 'masculinised rapist', Fanon raises serious ethical and political concerns regarding rape and torture perpetrated by the French army.

Unlike McClintock and Sekyi-Otu, David Macey provides a well-documented contextualisation for Fanon's text. Macey's focus is nonetheless narrow, situating it in the context of the Battle of Algiers. Invoking the role played by women in the Battle of Algiers, he disputes the accuracy of Fanon's claim that at first 'the combat was waged exclusively by the men'.[24] Macey challenges Fanon's assertion that after 1955, the FLN political leadership mobilised the entire nation by involving married women, 'trusted' widows and divorcees, and that later they had 'to make another leap, to remove all restrictions, to accept indiscriminately the support of all Algerian women' including unmarried girls.[25]

Although strategic operations led by Saadi Yacef were kept secret, Macey writes, 'Fanon's account of how dress codes were used to outwit the French army is not entirely inaccurate.'[26] Two pointers to help better situate Fanon's 'Algeria Unveiled': first, during the Battle of Algiers, he was not an FLN member and was certainly not involved in strategic decisions. He wrote the essay in 1959, after joining the FLN following his exile in Tunisia. Second, and more importantly, his discussion in 'Algeria Unveiled' centres not so much on the Battle of Algiers but on the events of May 1958.

Although noting regional differences in Algerian men's attire ('the *fez* in urban centres, turbans and *djellabas* in the countryside'), Fanon maintains that the veil is a rigid signifier that cannot accommodate change – 'a uniform which tolerates no modification, no variant'.[27] Dismissing Fanon's assertion, Macey points out that 'the *haïk*, or the square of the white cloth that veils a woman from head to foot, is indeed subject to modifications. A *haïk* can be made of plain cotton, of silk or of a man-made fabric.'[28] It must be noted that the veil in Fanon's discussion is not simply a referent to a physical object but also constitutive of an 'outlook' – a phenomenology in which the female component of Algerian society appears to the coloniser as an undifferentiated Other. The veil as a uniform, both literally and symbolically, unifies the coloniser's perception of Algerian women, projecting a stereotypical view of them. Indeed, there are different ways to wear the veil, or, in Macey's phraseology: 'it can be held around the body and drawn across the face in different ways. It can be held beneath the chin, and a smaller veil can be fastened below the eyes. There can be variations in the stitching, and there are regional variations.'[29] Moreover, there are also variations in colour: the black veil is called *m'laya* in the east of Algeria. In certain rural areas women do not wear it, and in some regions where the Touareg live it is men who wear the veil. As Pontecorvo's film *The Battle of Algiers* shows, cross-dressing was not practised just by women, men also put on the veil as camouflage. Macey reads Fanon's assertion literally: the veil is not just a referent to a physical object, nor is it merely a symbol of a rigid tradition. To focus on the materiality of the object is to miss the nuance of Fanon's discussion of this ambivalent signifier which acquired a revolutionary signification in Algeria's anticolonial struggle.

To the feminist critique, however, Macey adds a perspective exploring latent Orientalism in 'Algeria Unveiled'. He objects to Fanon's description of the *moudjahida* who takes off her veil and walks 'naked' into the European city. He argues that such a description, although couched in terms drawn from Merleau-Ponty, has more than a phenomenological interest for Fanon.[30] Macey situates this interest within a scopophilic Orientalism, akin to the libidinous economy of Jean Geisor's late nineteenth- and early twentieth-century ethnographic and erotic photographs of Algerians, many of which were widely circulated as postcards. Such a reading contradicts Fanon's critique of the colonial fantasy of unveiling the Algerian woman as metaphorical for rape. The epithet 'naked' is loaded with sexual connotation, but in colloquial Algerian Arabic, the same epithet denotes the condition of being 'unveiled'. Fanon's intention is not to portray the Algerian woman in summer clothes, as Macey intimates, but to discuss her being-in-the-world-of-the-European: unveiling is tantamount to being naked, feeling vulnerable and exposed to the European gaze. Neil MacMaster attributes her reluctance to unveil to 'religio-cultural factors and the psychological shock of exposure that was subjectively experienced as a form of gross nudity.'[31] Fanon conveys not only this psychological shock but also the association of nudity with promiscuity and dishonour in Algerian society.[32]

It is possible to identify in Macey's singular reading of the unveiled-woman-outside a conflation of three distinct portraits offered by Fanon: (1) the acculturated woman who travelled in the city with a 'bare face and free body'; (2) the *fidaïa* who unveiled and assumed an identity other than her own, and who did not feel comfortable in the skin of a Westerner wearing European clothes; (3) the veiled woman who was forcibly unveiled. Two distinct discourses are at play in Fanon's discussion of the corporeal patterns of the unveiled woman: one pertains to phenomenology; the other is strictly political.

To start with the political: Fanon explicitly refers to the Battle of Algiers and the role played by the *fidaïa* who 'manipulated, transformed [the veil] into a technique of camouflage, into a means of struggle.'[33] Is Fanon's project to wax lyrical, as Helie-Lucas intimates, on the revolutionary virtue of the veil for allowing the *fidaïa* to outwit the French army and travel incognito? There was nothing lyrical about the conclusion of the Battle of Algiers, which was fought and lost; it culminated with General Jacques Massu dismantling the FLN organisation in the Algiers.

Politically, the Battle of Algiers is of little interest to Fanon. He seems to be engaging with a completely different political context – namely the putsch of May 1958 which brought de Gaulle back to power and, more specifically, the Franco-Muslim fraternisation ceremonies during which women were forcibly unveiled by the French army. Contrary to Macey's claim, Fanon does not confuse the date of the 13 May putsch with that of these ceremonies, which he clearly identifies as having taken place on 16 May.

Let us now turn to establish how politics is inextricably bound up with phenomenology. Gibson is right to draw a parallel between the being-looked-at in 'Algeria Unveiled' and that presented in *Black Skin, White Masks*: like the unveiled Algerian woman, the Negro at the end of the white man's look feels vulnerable and exposed. To convey the 'ontological nudity' of the Negro, Fanon uses a corporeal language describing the being-of-the-Negro 'as a zone of non-being, an extraordinarily sterile and arid region, and utterly naked declivity.'[34] Unlike the Negro, who had no ontological resistance and whose corporeal schema shattered as he encountered the white man's gaze, the Algerian woman could return the look because the veil afforded her protection.[35] Simply put: the veil empowered her to look at the European without being looked at. Removing the veil in the public

Photo 1. A demonstration organised in Constantine in support of the Franco-Muslim fraternisation. On Monday, 26 May 1958, Constantine hosted a staged 'fraternisation' demonstration, where Chérif Sid Cara, passed through a crowd of over 300,000 people expressing loyalty to French colonialism. (© ECPAD)

sphere altered the patterns of her corporeality – that is, her view of her own body in its interaction with the outside world. In the Battle of Algiers, the *fidaïa* who willingly removed the veil to infiltrate European quarters had to relearn the patterns of her corporeal schema. She had to rethink the dialectical relationship between her body and the world in a revolutionary fashion, and overcome her timidity and awkwardness, the feeling of being exposed.[36] Contrary to the *fidaïa* who was empowered by casting away her *haïk*, the woman coerced into unveiling publicly in the Franco-Muslim fraternisation ceremonies was violated. Critics believe they detect in Fanon a regressive movement, falling back on traditional practices that valorised the veil and the sequestration of women, a tendency to regurgitate nationalist slogans which were retrograde and anti-feminist. These critics, however, ignore the historical specificities of Fanon's intervention against these infamous ceremonies, which were part of the psychological warfare adopted strategically by the French army to destroy the corporeal schema of the Algerian woman and crush her resistance. It is at the intersection of the phenomenological and the political that his discussion of the veil must be situated. As we shall see later, breaking the patterns of her corporeal schema was experienced as a form of torture; unveiling was tantamount to rape.

MAY '58: UNVEILING ALGERIA

Unveiling the Algerian woman evokes the history of the French conquest, the violence, pillage and rape which accompanied France's colonisation of Algeria, or, to put it in Fanon's words, 'the sadism of the conqueror' and his 'eroticism'.[37] Gibson is quick to establish an easy equivalence between the repressive practices of the colonisers and those of the nationalist leaders who 'discover[ed] unexpected power in the revalorization of "tradition"';[38] or simply a correspondence between the colonisers' will to unveil the Algerian woman and the nationalist leaders' desire to impose on her the garb of tradition.

It is important to note that the work of culture must not be confused with the resistance of the nationalist leaders. As Pierre Nora contends, throughout the history of colonisation, women played a crucial role in safeguarding Algerian culture; this role was not dictated to them by nationalist leaders. It is unclear to whom Gibson refers when evoking the expression 'nationalist leaders'. Anticolonial resistance from 1900 onwards until the Algerian war was not an organised movement: it was represented by diverse political and cultural interests which did not necessarily subscribe to the agenda of the religious reformists (*ulemas*). Nonetheless, Gibson astutely presents the colonial conflict as a Manichaean struggle over an 'elementally gendered nation'[39] – colonisation as a violation of both Algerian nationhood and womanhood. As women entered the arena of politics and 'became historical protagonists',[40] they not only challenged 'men's monopoly over what constituted nationalist militancy'[41] but also exploded 'the tight, hermetic, and hierarchical structure of the family'. Gibson rightly describes women's entry into the public sphere and the arena of politics as 'a disruptive making of history'.[42] Let me now turn to explore this 'disruptive making of history', which is central to both Bourdieu and Fanon in their discussion of the symbolic function of the veil that worked to demarcate the public from the private, and the coloniser from the colonised.

Colonialism produced a disjunction between private identity and public citizenship, between family life and the life of the nation, between past and present. The colonised were no longer subjects of history, enjoying publicly the rights which citizenship conferred upon them. As Memmi explains, their exclusion from public life forced them to re-enact their identity and sense of cultural belonging privately, either by retreating into the domestic sphere or seeking refuge in religion.[43] This exclusion, according to Fanon, forced them to fall back on archaic cultural practices from a congealed past. Bourdieu concurs with the view that colonialism marginalised the Algerians and forced them to live a cloistered existence. He considers tradition as a set of cultural conventions, constituting a framework of reference within which self-knowledge and self-identification are realised. He coins the expression 'traditional traditionalism' to describe how society became caught within its own signifying frame of cultural reference. Colonialism established a self-reinforcing cultural framework and a closed system of ingrained values. Society henceforth focused on its norms as the primary lens for interpretation, hindering new ideas and adaptation. This frame served as both source and justification for traditions, trapping society in a cycle of reinforcing values and leading to cultural stagnation and resistance to change. 'Traditional traditionalism', he writes, 'meant following a tradition that was considered, not as the best possible [...], but as the only possible tradition.' The colonial situation, he explains, gave rise to a 'new traditionalism', also dubbed 'colonial traditionalism'. It emerged to institute a cultural closure that kept the colonised society and its institutions alive by 'artificial means'.[44] It stood as a rampart against colonialism, providing a refuge for the colonised society from the encroachment of the colonising culture.

At the centre of Bourdieu's discussion of the veil and the Algerian war are two negations. Colonial traditionalism acted as a negation of colonialism: it fulfilled a symbolic function and was a language of refusal. The veil constituted its materiality, representing one of the 'impregnable ramparts' against colonial intrusion. This first negation instantiated what Nora calls a 'blocus historique', that is, the halting of the historical processes of Algerian society, which took the conscious decision to turn inward by imposing on itself the restrictions of an inert tradition. Such closure effected a diremption between colonised and coloniser, between inside and outside, between private and public, between past and present. This disjunction gave rise to a peculiar view of the past situated at the immutable origin of time but not in history – a congealed representation of the past, out of joint with the present and not inscribed within a diachronic perspective. Colonialism expropriated the colonised and perpetuated their exclusion from public life and the processes which motivated history. Private life provided them with a refuge, tradition with a shield as they hid behind the law of anachrony, which fulfilled a dual function: it demarcated the cultural space they inhabited but also led to its dehistoricisation. The veil, as the garb of an inert tradition, represents both the demarcation and dehistoriciation of Algerian culture and tradition. The second negation, engendered by the Algerian war, gave a voice to the Algerian people and empowered them to renounce colonial traditionalism without renouncing their cultural heritage. This negation was not the refusal of their own cultural tradition per se but worked in the same direction as colonial traditionalism by challenging French colonial impositions. Bourdieu argues that the Algerian war was undoubtedly the most important event that occurred in Algeria since its colonisation. Like Fanon, he examines the sociological changes it occasioned, the cultural shocks it has provoked, the political and military consequences it brought about. Commenting on the ramfications of the war in the sociological field, he writes: 'It's as if this society, which, more or less consciously, had chosen to stop and close in on itself, opposing any intrusion of novelty with a thousand invisible and impregnable ramparts, had suddenly opened up and started moving again. How are we to interpret this kind of sudden, global mutation, to which a thousand details bear witness?'[45]

The war represented the first radical challenge to the colonial system, one that was not merely symbolic, as in the past, but had real political implications. Before the war, Bourdieu writes:

> We have seen that a number of cultural traits, such as the attachment to certain details of clothing (the veil, for example, or the chechia), to certain types of conduct, beliefs and values, can appear as a way of expressing, symbolically, that is, through behaviors implicitly invested with the function of *signs*, the refusal to adhere to Western civilization identified with the colonial order, the will to remain oneself, to assert a radical and irreducible difference, to deny the negation of the self, to defend a threatened and beleaguered personality.[46]

'Colonial traditionalism', opines Bourdieu, 'had essentially a symbolic function: it played the role, objectively, of a language of refusal.'[47] From a sociological viewpoint, another language developed, as a result of the war, giving the Algerian people a voice and initiating a deconstructive movement with two interrelated aspects: first, the relationship of domination could no longer be exercised in its 'essential purity'; second, from that moment onwards, this language intervened in this relationship. Not only was France's colonial authority subverted, but colonial traditionalism was also rendered obsolete and 'all magical negations and symbolic refusals [lost] much of their function and significance'.[48] The war empowered Algerians to proclaim adherence to the values of Western civilisation without falling into contradiction, and without renouncing their own cultural heritage.

Let us focus on the materiality of this essentially symbolic function. The veiled woman with a 'hidden face', inhabiting a 'separate world', with violence gleaming in her eyes which 'look like two black holes in a silent mask',[49] hypostatises the historical condition of Algerian society, which Bourdieu delineates in his discussion of colonial traditionalism. In terms that echo Fanon's and Memmi's characterisation of colonial culture as mummified and colonised society as secluded, he describes its retreat into tradition as follows:

> It is as if this society had chosen to remain tightly closed upon itself, as if it had taken great pains to set up a thousand invisible, impregnable barriers against the intrusion of new methods and ideas. Feeling that they were constantly exposed to the critical eye of the Europeans, anxious not to give them any pretext or reason for their unfavorable judgments, the Algerians, by their behavior, their clothing and their whole way of life, created a language of refusal. Such a refusal, to be sure, could only be expressed in a symbolic fashion.[50]

The garb of tradition, the veil, was not just the signifier of gerontocracy and patriarchy; it was also adopted as an effective weapon to counter French colonialism. 'It was, to be sure,' Joan Scott writes, 'a refusal of French appropriation of the country, a way of insisting on an independent identity for Algerians.'[51] According to Jacques Berque, it pertained to a semiology of 'co-presence', but one that expressed 'a certain failure between the sexes' and 'the mutual obsession of two races'. The garb of tradition proved to be 'bewildering' and 'overwhelming'; it draped 'a muffled figure with a triangular face, transfixing [the European] with a terrible gaze' – a glance that reveals 'a sense of presence or of emptiness, a denial which is affirmation'.[52] Citing Fromentin and Gautier, Berque underscores that the historical and colonial situation was revealed by the interplay of the gaze and the donning of the veil. Bourdieu concurs with Scott's assessment that the veil was invested with an essentially symbolic value: it was the signifier par excellence of colonial traditionalism, which created a situation of non-reciprocity between coloniser and coloniser, defended privacy, and protected against foreign intrusion. Bourdieu also captures this interplay as he ascertains that vestimentary habits constitute a language of refusal. However, alluding to the unveiling ceremonies during the fraternisation demonstrations in May 1958, Bourdieu contends that the Algerian war brought radical changes to these habits. As he explains:

> The most obvious transformations have occurred in the traditions endowed with an essentially symbolic significance, such as the customs pertaining to dress. A second function has been added, for example, to the traditional function of the wearing of the veil. Like the *chechia* (distinctive cap worn by the men), the veil has the role of a symbol that expresses both an alliance and exclusion; it is primarily a defense of the inner self and a protection against any intrusion from without. But in addition to this, by the wearing of the veil, the Algerian woman is also creating a situation of non-reciprocity; like a cheating gambler, she can see without being observed; and it is through her that the whole of this dominated society is symbolically refusing to establish any reciprocal relations, is looking on without letting itself be observed. The veil is the most obvious symbol of this closing in upon oneself, and the Europeans have always obscurely felt it to be such. In this way it becomes evident why all attempts at assimilation have taken the discarding of the veil to be their primary objective. The demonstrations of May 13, 1958, in the course of which several Algerian women removed their veils or 'burnt them symbolically' (as the newspapers reported), amid the applause of the crowd of Europeans present, was tantamount to a ceremonial magic rite by which the whole of Algerian society was offering itself, naked and willing, to the embrace of the European society.[53]

Bourdieu's trope of the veiled woman as a 'cheating gambler' that 'see[s] without being observed', symbolically representing a society closed in upon itself, chimes with Fanon's description of the Algerian woman who, by donning the veil, creates a situation of non-reciprocity.[54] For Bourdieu, the discarding of the veil represented a radical transformation: the Algerian society began to open up to the modernising influences of French culture. This change in vestimentary habit was all the more remarkable since traditionally the veil, as a cultural signifier, shielded indigenous society from the intrusion of French colonialism.

Bourdieu characterises the Algerian war as a 'revolution within a revolution', representing effective political resistance against colonialism. The war gave rise to new cultural forms and practices, challenging and opposing the dominant culture, as well as representing an alternative to the ossified and necrotised tradition which had hitherto shielded colonised society. In short, it provided a new lease of life to a dying tradition; it set in motion a historical process, activating what used to be a relatively inert culture. The war presented Algerians with an alternative, indicating the end of traditional and colonial traditionalism as agencies of symbolic resistance against colonialism. Bourdieu observes that the war put to rest many ghosts from the colonial past: it announced the demise of 'a number of traditions, institutions and beliefs, which they had tried to keep alive by artificial means'.[55] He is adamant that the veil, as the signifier par excellence of colonial tradition, became redundant.

Photo 2. The unveiling ceremony and the 'burning of veil' which took place on 17 May 1958. In front of the General Government building in Algiers, a dozen Algerian women performed a symbolic *auto-da-fé*, burning the veils that had concealed their faces, before the gathered crowd. A delegation was then received by General Massu. (© ECPAD)

The above quotation, taken from *The Algerians* (the English translation of the 1961 revised edition of *Sociologie d'Algérie*), reproduces material previously published in two articles: 'Guerre et mutation sociale en Algérie' and 'Révolution dans la révolution'.[56] Remarkably, the points of overlap and amendments made in the revised and translated edition of *Sociologie d'Algérie*, *The Algerians*, diverge from the articles in their interpretation of the unveiling ceremonies, as the following passage from 'Guerre et mutation sociale en Algérie' demonstrates:

The most manifest and also the most spectacular renunciations are perhaps those which concern traditions invested with an essentially symbolic value, such as the wearing of the veil or the chechia. To the traditional function of the veil had been added, as a superimposition, a new function, in reference to the colonial context. Without pushing the analysis very far, we can see in effect that the veil is above all a defence of privacy and a protection against intrusion. And, confusedly, Europeans have always perceived it as such. By wearing the veil, the Algerian woman creates a situation of non-reciprocity; like a dishonest player, she sees without being seen, without giving herself to be seen. And it is the whole dominated society which, through the veil, refuses reciprocity, which sees, which looks, which penetrates, without letting itself be seen, looked at, penetrated. It is common to hear from the mouths of Europeans indignant proclamations against this kind of disloyalty, this refusal to play the game, which means that Algerians have access to the privacy of Europeans while they deny them any access to their own privacy. The veil can therefore be considered the symbol of self-closure. However, in recent years, we observe, among young women and girls, a very marked tendency to abandon the veil, with a slowdown and a regression at the time of 13 May [1958] – the wearing of the veil then resumed its sense of symbolic negation and the abandonment could be grasped, objectively, as a sign of allegiance – and, currently, a very clear resumption of the movement, observable even in the countryside.[57]

A number of textual echoes in 'Guerre et mutation sociale en Algérie', 'Révolution dans la révolution' and *The Algerians* suggest that Bourdieu read *Studies in a Dying Colonialism*. Like Fanon, Bourdieu argues that the war revolutionised Algerian society: the custom of wearing the veil was abandoned, Western technologies like the radio and medicine were put at the service of the revolution, and the war curbed paternal authority, changing fathers' relationships with their sons and daughters. Like Fanon, Bourdieu also evokes the events of 18 May 1958. Before exploring the ways in which Fanon's views diverge from Bourdieu's, it is important to recover the political specificities of these events. Generals Salan and Massu exploited these circumstances to summon General de Gaulle back to power, producing major repercussions on French politics.

The demonstration of 13 May – organised in protest against the execution of three French soldiers held by the FLN – could have turned into a *ratonnade* – a mob frenzy hunting for Arabs. It could have culminated, like the crisis of 8 May 1945, in the massacre of scores of Algerian people.[58] This was fortunately averted with the promotion of the 'fraternisation' ceremonies, which seemed to have brought together French and Algerian people, irrespective of class, ethnic difference or dress codes. Many photographs documenting the news reports in *L'Echo d'Alger* show turbanned Algerians joining hands with Europeans. The demonstrations, organised by the colonial authorities, involved not only Algerian men but also extended to include women.[59] The upsurge of brotherly feelings putatively brought Europeans and Muslims together into one single embrace. Bourdieu expressed these sentiments in his depiction of Algerian women in the Forum unveiling – 'offering' themselves, 'naked and willing', to the fraternal embrace of the French.

However, behind the 'show of solidarity', deep political divisions existed: the French army and the *harkis* on one side, and the FLN on the other; those who believed in Franco-Muslim fraternisation and those, like Alain de Sérigny, the editor of *L'Echo d'Alger*, who wanted to maintain France's colonial dominance. According to Yves Courrière, nobody actually believed in fraternisation; for most European settlers, integration meant the annexation of Algeria to mainland France – the *status quo ante*.[60] Commentators like Courrière maintain that the putsch of 13 May was a purely Franco-French operation: an affair involving mainland French and European settlers in Algeria. The Muslims viewed the turmoil of this political moment in which they were caught up with fear and trepidation. The end of the Battle of Algiers brought a moment of reprieve for Algerian women who, draped in their white veil, hastily rejoined the mysterious and enclosed world of the Casbah after the havoc Massu and his paratroops had wreaked on them.

As a symbolic gesture for Franco-Muslim fraternisation, the Massus adopted two Algerian children, a boy and a girl. Malika, the 15-year-old girl, was paraded in front of a large crowd to express her allegiance to French Algeria.[61] To be sure, it is difficult to separate the events of 18 May from the broader context of the Battle of Algiers, also dubbed the 'battle of the veil'.

While Massu waged the Battle of Algiers, his wife engaged in another battle targeting Algerian women. Her Mouvement de la solidarité féminine paved the way for several women's associations aimed at helping Algerian women break free from oppressive traditions and follow the path of emancipation taken by French women.[62]

These associations became instruments of colonial propaganda. As Mac-Master shows, women were targeted by army propagandists in a media campaign against the veil. In July 1957, Radio-Alger broadcast the programme 'Magazine de la femme', calling on Algerian women to remove the veil.[63] On 8 April 1958, weeks before the May events, women were urged to petition Radio Casbah for a modern French Algeria, freed from the constraints of traditional garb, such as the veil or *cachabia*, which suffocate Muslim women, 'hinder them from working and learning, and, above all, deprive them of freedom, imprisoning them within four walls'.[64] On 6 May,

Photo 3. Massu and an Algerian girl addressing the crowd in Blida, 28 May 1958. (© ECPAD)

General Allard, Commander of the Algiers Army Corps, forwarded the
Radio Casbah letter to the Army General commanding the 10th Military
Region and the Joint Forces. Allard emphasised that the year-long efforts
through medical teams, women's circles, and propaganda had yielded unexpected results. He insisted that it was time for an official gesture towards

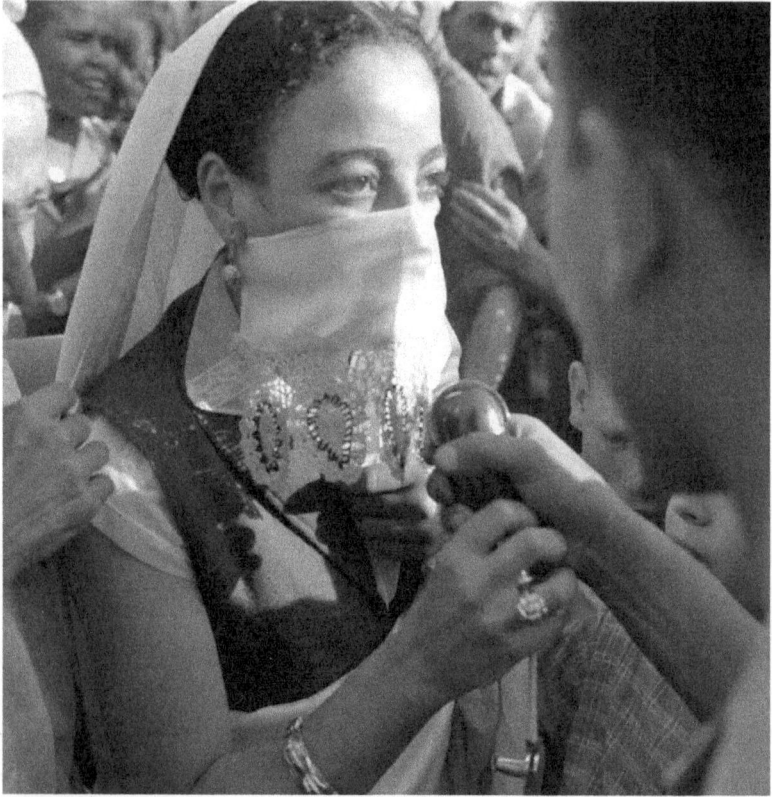

Photo 4. This photograph was taken on the afternoon of 18 May 1958, when nearly
100,000 residents gathered in the square facing the General Government building
in Algiers. The crowd cheered Algerian women from Algiers and its suburbs.
A woman (pictured above) addressed the assembled people. While Jacques
Soustelle paid tribute to them, General Raoul Salan, Commander-in-Chief of the
Armed Forces and head of both civil and military powers in Algeria, praised their
dedication. Chérif Sid-Cara, Secretary of State, concluded with a speech supporting
French Algeria. In attendance were General Edmond Jouhaud (Commander of
the 5th Air Region), General Jacques Massu (Commander of the 10th Parachute
Division and President of the Comité de salut public (CSP – Public Salvation
Committee), Léon Delbecque (Vice-President of the CSP), and General Jacques
Allard (Commander of the Algiers Army Corps). (© ECPAD)

Muslim women's emancipation, to prevent the rebellion from exploiting the evolving mindset achieved through considerable effort.[65] On 12 May, Salon's cabinet forwarded the petition to Massu through Colonel Goussault, head of the Fifth Bureau, marked 'Wearing of the Veil' and 'For All Useful Purposes.'[66] Massu, receiving it on 13 May, unsurprisingly endorsed unveiling as a central aspect of the fraternisation demonstration. He argued that the anonymous Radio Casbah letter revealed Muslim women's desire for rapid change, confirming surveys that showed young women seeking greater freedom. Massu stressed that removing the veil was both crucial and eagerly awaited by many. He also expressed concern that the FLN might exploit this desire for emancipation. Citing social, psychological and national reasons, he called for a ban on the veil, emphasising the need to issue the 'unveiling' order immediately, with clarity and resolve.[67]

The campaign undertaken by the colonial administration to unveil Algerian women engendered what Marnia Lazreg dubs 'military feminism'. This campaign was carried out by the Équipes médico-sociales itinérantes (EMSI), together with the Adjointes sociales sanitaires rurales auxiliaires (ASSRA) and the Attachées féminines des affaires algériennes (AFAA). It provided lessons to women on topics such as housekeeping, child rearing and personal hygiene.[68] Couched in medical language, this brand of feminism pathologises the veil and those who wear it. 'In villages and towns,' Lazreg writes, 'the ASSRA were given step-by-step instructions on how to make women remove their veils. Fighting veils was on a par with getting rid of "flies", "ticks" and "lice".'[69] Social groups and radio talks were organised with the sole intention of advising women to rid themselves of the veil.[70] The EMSI's campaign against the veil culminated in unveiling ceremonies, which the military ordered to be organised 'with applause and expressions of sympathy'.[71]

Colonel Goussault spearheaded the campaign undertaken by the SAU/CSP (Sections administratives urbaines/Comité de salut public) to mobilise women for the Franco-Algerian fraternisation demonstrations. Wives of political ex-servicemen helped design the tricolour with three *haïks* dyed in red, white and blue; this emblem of Frenchness was displayed on the balcony of the General Government building.[72] Feminist organisations and social clubs organised the ceremonies that took place on 18 May. MacMaster recounts the case of an Algerian woman chosen to address the crowd from the balcony through a microphone: 'We are aware of how far our traditional dress, our reclusive existence, are factors that separate us from our French sisters of a different religion to ours. We wish to engage fully in the route to modernity and to profit from the exciting epoch which Algeria is currently traversing to accelerate our progress.' Then she addressed the crowd in Arabic, asking them to remove the veil, which constituted a 'barrier between two communities'.[73] As we shall see, the same mise-en-scène occurred in Constantine, and the same text – scripted by the army – was read by Monique Améziane.

The Franco-Muslim fraternisation took place not only in Algiers but also in Tizi-Ouzou, Constantine and Bône, where women ceremoniously removed their veils. As MacMaster affirms:

> the most elaborate ceremonials of unveiling, which make the biggest impact through the media, took place in a series of massive demonstrations organized by the army in the major towns from 18 May onwards. In particular the leaders of the military coup (Soustelle, Salan, Massu, Allard) and other generals and dignitaries, transported by helicopter, engaged in a lightning tour of Orléansville, Mostaganem, Blida, Boufarik, Oran, Philippeville, Bône, Sétif, Constantine, Tizi-Ouzou and Biskra between the 18 and 28 May. On each occasion an almost identical and theatrical *mise en scène* took place: groups of veiled women marched in mass parades through the streets alongside medalled Algerian ex-servicemen associations and *harkis* to the traditional locations of official ceremonial (central squares, town halls, war memorials). On arrival the young female delegates, dressed either in a modern European style or with *haïks*, shared the rostrum or balconies with the generals and dignitaries and presented them with bouquets, before making speeches in favour of emancipation and casting their veils to the crowds.[74]

Clearly, the demonstrations were not 'spontaneous'; coercion and manipulation of the crowd were commonplace, as evidenced by the telex sent by the Fifth Bureau to the commanders of the three army forces and by the so-called 'Operation Lorry'.[75] Muslim demonstrators were rounded up from the neighbouring villages and forcibly brought to 'express' their solidarity with banners given to them by the French army. As Helie-Lucas explains, at the behest of French officials, army trucks transported women from rural areas to city centres where they were forced to unveil publicly.[76] This was the case with the French Algerian Monique Améziane, who had never donned the veil but was made to put it on in order to perform the act of removing it publicly in Constantine. Her step-brother Mouloud Améziane was detained and tortured; the French army threatened to execute him if she did not participate in the symbolic act of unveiling.[77]

Monique Améziane was coerced to take part in a charade where she was presented as an example of a young Muslim woman faithful to France, calling on other women to renounce their outworn traditions.[78] In the pay of the colonial administration, Cheikh Lakhdari Abdellali, Imam of Sidi-El-Ketani mosque, came out in support of Jacques Soustelle's call for women to symbolically remove their veil.[79] He affirmed that the tradition of donning the veil was not Islamic and that Frenchness and Islam were not incompatible.[80] He was keen to advise women to follow Améziane's example. On 27 May, photographs of Améziane – wearing a dress with a tricolor rosette, standing next to a soldier who held a microphone for her – were printed in *La Dépêche de Constantine* with a caption that read: 'A Young Algerian woman, Miss Améziane, daughter of *bachagha*, has just spontaneously removed her veil and invites all the other Arab women to follow in her footsteps.'[81]

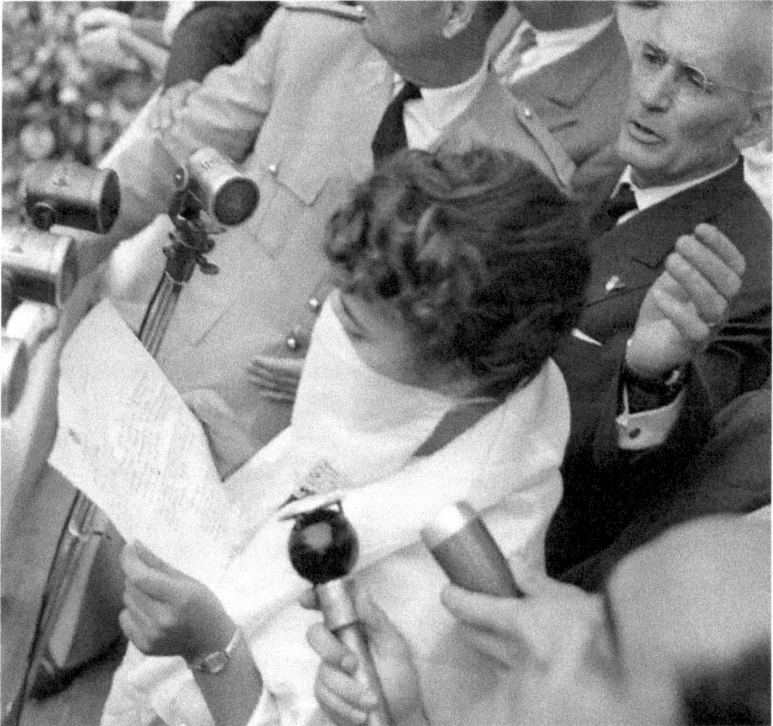

Photo 5. On Monday, 26 May 1958, during a demonstration in Constantine supporting Franco-Muslim fraternisation, Monique addresses the crowd. (© ECPAD)

However, this unveiling covers up more than it reveals. These ceremonies were part of psychological warfare strategically exploited by the French army to obliterate one of the cornerstones of Algerian society, destabilise the revolutionary movement and break the FLN's resistance. Military strategists targeted Algerian women; the catchphrase of 'military feminism' was that only with the FLN's defeat would women be fully liberated and integrated into French society.[82] As Lazreg astutely points out, women's emancipation was not an end in itself but was used as a stratagem in psychological warfare to both quell the FLN's resistance and maintain France's colonial hegemony. The partisans of military feminism were adamant that 'Algeria was truly and genuinely French. Differences of customs as exemplified by the veil were simply a vestige of a past that the FLN was allegedly fighting to maintain. They could be removed symbolically by the public unveiling of a few women.'[83] Lazreg contends that the hollow rhetoric of this brand of feminism threatened the FLN leadership. Alastair Horne also makes the same point, arguing that:

> [t]he official line of the FLN, as well as that of French sceptics, is that the whole demonstration was phoney, rigged by the psychological warfare experts of the French Cinquième Bureau; that the women who had so joyfully cast away their *haïks* were simply tarts rounded up for the occasion.[84]

Written in a style countering the propaganda of the colonial administration, 'Algeria Unveiled' expresses the threat posed by military feminism to the FLN leadership. Fanon clearly toes the official line on the issue of the ceremonies of unveiling. He argues that neither de Gaulle nor the ultras would liberate Algerian women, who were rounded up and forced to unveil while chanting 'Long live French Algeria' and 'Long live de Gaulle'. Instead, Fanon asserts that only through revolutionary praxis and the culture which they helped preserve throughout colonisation would these women achieve freedom. At the height of the 13 May crisis, he writes, the colonial administration 'reenacted its old campaign of Westernising the Algerian woman'. The women chosen to perform these public unveiling ceremonies were not representative of the Algerian people. Fanon describes them as '[s]ervants under the threat of being fired, poor women dragged from their homes, prostitutes, [who] were brought to the public square and *symbolically* unveiled to the cries of "*Vive l'Algérie française!*"'[85]

It is worth reiterating that Fanon's text, written in 1959, conflates two historical moments in the Algerian war: the Battle of Algiers and the events of May 1958. As we have seen, these two moments were interconnected. While the Battle of Algiers ended, the battle of the veil continued, opening a new front in the Algerian war where gender became a site of political struggle. Arguably, Fanon wrote 'Algeria Unveiled' to address the strategic and psychological effects of this battle waged by the French army.

Fanon, both implicitly and explicitly, psychoanalyses the effects of public unveiling. He explains that the veil not only covered the body of the Algerian woman but also determined her corporeal schema: her self-perception, her view of her body, her sexuality and her place in society were all intricately bound to the physical structure of the veil. Without it, the Algerian woman felt exposed, having the 'impression of being improperly dressed, even of being naked.'[86] The unveiling ceremonies of 18 May 1958 were intended to humiliate and degrade Algerian women. Similar to the cases of interrogation documented by Jean-Luc Einaudi, the intended effect of unveiling the Algerian woman was to destroy her corporeal schema.

UNVEILED, TORTURED AND RAPED

Like Bourdieu, Fanon contends that the Algerian Revolution gave tradition a new lease of life. For instance, the veil – once a symbol of inert colonial traditionalism – was adopted as a stratagem against the advances of French colonialism and transformed into a revolutionary weapon. However, Fanon presents a different view from Bourdieu: he argues that the 'burning of the veil' did not symbolise that 'the whole of Algerian society was offering itself naked and willing to the embrace of the European society'. Commenting on the efforts undertaken by the agents of the colonial administration to convert the Algerian woman, Fanon writes:

After each success, the authorities were strengthened in their conviction that the Algerian woman would support Western penetration into the native society. Every rejected veil disclosed to the eyes of the colonialists horizons until then forbidden, and revealed to them, piece by piece, the flesh of Algeria laid bare. The occupier's aggressiveness, and hence his hopes, multiplied ten-fold each time a new face was uncovered. Every new Algerian woman unveiled announced to the occupier an Algerian society whose systems of defense were in the process of dislocation, open and breached. Every veil that fell, every body that became liberated from the traditional embrace of the *haïk*, every face that offered itself to the bold and impatient glance of the occupier, was a negative expression of the fact that Algeria was beginning to deny herself and was accepting the rape of the colonizer. Algerian society, with every abandoned veil, seemed to express its willingness to attend the master's school and to decide to change its habits under the occupier's direction and patronage.[87]

This rape, in Fanon's terms, was a 'double deflowering';[88] or, as Malek Alloula describes it, 'a double violation'. It represented the unveiling of what was forever forbidden to the coloniser, and this unveiling violated the *horma* (honour) which constituted a symbolic obstacle to the fulfilment of colonial desire.[89] The history of the French conquest of Algeria – characterised by *razzia*, pillage, and the rape of both women and land – gave rise to a highly sexualised discourse in which violence crystallised in the body of the veiled Algerian woman.[90] Politically, unveiling her meant breaking the core of resistance in indigenous society, opening the inner sanctum of its tradition to European colonisation.

The rape of women paralleled the rape of land, leading to widespread immiseration and destitution throughout Algeria's colonial history. The veil afforded the destitute, dressed in rags, a cover of decency. 'At the mass unveiling of 18 May in the Forum', MacMaster notes, 'women shouted, "Give us clothes so that we can dress like our European sisters!"'[91] In response, collections of second-hand clothes were made to help Algerian women divest themselves of their outworn traditions. Fanon remarks that charitable organisations, social workers and feminist associations embarked upon the project of liberating the sequestered Algerian woman from the clutches of an unyielding patriarchy. However, this was with a view to implementing colonial propaganda. Charitable work went hand in hand with their mission to convert the Algerian woman: 'The indigent and famished women were the first to be besieged. Every kilo of semolina distributed was accompanied by a dose of indignation against the veil and the cloister. The indignation was followed up by practical advice.'[92]

For Fanon, the conversion of native Algerian women was not an innocent humanitarian gesture, but a manifestation of a colonialist attitude tinged with sexualised exoticism. It articulated an Orientalising discourse whose ultimate interests were not the liberation of women but the enactment of France's colonial policies. Unveiling the Algerian woman meant not only breaking the resistance of native Algerian society but also making her available to the coloniser's sexual advances. In the European's dreams, Fanon remarks, the act of unveiling was almost always accompanied by sadistic brutality and rape, invariably performed in an orgiastic context evocative of the harem, where more than just one individual woman was subjected to this ritual. 'The European always dreams of a group of women,' he adds, 'of a field of women, suggestive of the gynaeceum, the harem – exotic themes and deeply rooted in the unconscious'.[93] As we will see in Chapter 6, Fanon subtly establishes a connection between colonial exoticism and the orgiastic, sadistic brutality of the torture methods taking place. 'The old fear of dishonor', he writes, 'was swept away by a new fear, fresh and cold – that of death in battle or of torture of the girl.'[94]

Crucially, critics have overlooked the extent to which the ceremony of removing the veil was intertwined with the practice of unspeakable torture, as Jean-Luc Einaudi documents in La Ferme Améziane.[95] In the case of Monique's brother, sadistic brutality merged with the exoticism associated with the Turkish bath where his questioning took place. The public unveiling of his sister was an extension of the questioning Mouloud experienced in private; her torture, executed in public, was a show of public power that the French exercised over the veiled woman. The ceremonies of unveiling, as in Monique's case, were endured as a 'symbolic public rape' and were resented equally by Algerian men and women. 'Many young women, even those brought up in liberal families,' Helie-Lucas argues, 'chose to don the veil as a demonstration of their belonging to the oppressed Algerian people – in their lives and in their symbolic existence.'[96]

In La Torture et l'armée, Raphaëlle Branche establishes a correlation between torture and rape, arguing that they symbolically reproduced the power of a conquering force.[97] She contends that rape mediated the power relation between coloniser and colonised, serving as both an act of colonial conquest and a sign of profound humiliation for the colonised. Although not an official policy, rape was nonetheless a strategy the army adopted to maintain French presence in Algeria.[98] Lazreg also affirms that rape was practised as a form of questioning and that entire villages were turned into free brothels for French soldiers. Lazreg provides documentary evidence of torture and rape as strategies in psychological warfare, contradicting the avowed aims of military feminism to liberate Algerian women.

In May 1959, a year after the Franco-Muslim fraternisation ceremonies, the army, at Massu's behest, subjected women to the same questioning as men; rape and sexual violence were deployed as torture techniques.[99] In a letter to Zohra Drif, a prominent figure in the Battle of Algiers, Cixous alludes to rape while eulogising the Casbah for its femininity, asserting that 'it resisted rape'.[100] Assia Djebar also references '[t]orture with electricity' in the opening paragraphs of *Women of Algiers in their Apartments*: 'The motor begins to run dangerously, the "gene" – generator – is wired, place of torture ...'[101] In the 'Postface', Djebar reveals that some women involved in the Battle of Algiers – the 'carriers of the bombs' – 'came back later with their sex electrocuted, flayed through torture'.[102] One protagonist laments that '[Algerian women] suffered the pain of their legs torn apart by the rapist soldiers'.[103] Djebar observes that rape – or what she calls the 'tradition of war' – was experienced as trauma by women in particular and Algerians in general.[104] Female genitalia became a new site of interrogation, an opening through which violence was exercised.[105] Branche cites the case of Djamila Boupacha, arrested for planting a bomb in an Algiers café, who endured the *gégène*, cigarette burns, drowning, and ultimately rape.[106] Published in the same year as Boupacha's arrest, Fanon's 'Algeria Unveiled' explicitly addresses the torture and rape of Algerian women: 'With an Algerian woman,' Fanon notes, 'there is no progressive conquest, no mutual revelation. Straight off, with the maximum of violence, there is possession, rape, near-murder.'[107]

Upon the methods of questioning adopted by the French army, Scott elaborates:

> So potent an instrument did the veil become that French soldiers patrolling the countryside violated women first by forcibly removing their veils and then by raping them. Those suspected of being nationalists were treated even more harshly. Aahia Arif Hamdad told of her arrest along with her husband. As one soldier tore off her veil, another commented on its inauthenticity: 'enough is enough; the game is over.' She was then beaten and subjected to electric shock as she stood nude.[108]

Scott argues that it was the Algerian war, not 11 September 2001, that brought about the politicisation of the veil.[109] One must add to Scott's observation: Fanon's 'Algeria Unveiled' seems to have written the prologue to events that would unfold fifty years later in Iraq's infamous Abu Ghraib.

The veil establishes a situation of non-reciprocity; the veiled woman, whom Bourdieu calls a 'gambling cheater', sees without being seen. In the torture scenario, Scott contends, this situation is reversed: 'her interrogators get to look at her without limit'.[110] The same perverse scenario is at work in Geisor's colonial postcards, which sought to unveil the mystery of the Algeria woman as a figure of exoticism. This perverse scopophilia contradicts Fanon's ethical concerns. Fanon disagrees with Bourdieu's view that the ceremonies during which Algerian women removed their veils symbolised the Algerian society 'offering itself, naked and willing, to the embrace of the European society'. Fanon is adamant that 'She does not yield herself, does not give herself, she does not offer herself'.[111] 'Algeria Unveiled' should not be read as re-enacting the phantasm of 'colonial conquest as an erotics of ravishment', as McClintock argues. Rather, it should be interpreted as a protest against the public rape of Algerian women and an indictment of torture and psychological warfare. These tactics, by forcibly unveiling women, sought to break their corporeal patterns. The political and historical specificities of Fanon's intervention point to a lacuna in Sekyi-Out's discussion of the interface of public and private: it was not a retrograde tradition that led to the cloistering of Algerian women; colonial politics determined both the marginalisation of men and the tradition of women's sequestration. In *Republic of Cousins*, echoing Fanon, Tillion provides a cogent study of colonialism's nefarious impact on this tradition. As Scott aptly points out, the veil was not just 'emblazoned with the stigma of ethnicity' or merely a symbol of religious and cultural affiliation; it was adopted as a stratagem of subversion and political resistance.[112] The veil was not essentially the emblem of women's servitude; it was also 'an impenetrable membrane, the final barrier to political subjugation'.[113] 'In Fanon's "Algeria Unveiled"', Diana Fuss sagaciously remarks, 'the wearer of the veil *becomes* a veil, the inscrutable face of a nation struggling to maintain its cultural inviolability'. What was put in question in the fraternisation ceremonies, as well in the torture chambers, was the cultural symbolism in which the veiled Algerian woman came to represent the 'guarantor' of an endangered national identity and of its 'continued visibility'.[114]

3

The Battle of the Veil and of the Waves: Colonial and Anticolonial Radio Transmission

The invention of radio revolutionised communication, serving as a precursor to radar, television, the internet, and mobile communication. The golden age of wireless, spanning from the mid-1920s to the late 1950s, brought diverse forms of entertainment and information into homes. As T.A.M Craven notes, 'radio microwave transmission had the characteristics of invisible light',[1] ushering in the age of modernity and playing a crucial role in conquering time and space, thus advancing globalisation. While radio cemented the 'nation' as a political and sociological construct, it paradoxically obliterated cultural and national borders by transcending or making them porous. This new technology eliminated constraints of time and space, bringing peoples, cultures and nations closer together. However, it also reconfigured warfare, heralding the battle of the waves during the Second World War and the period leading to decolonisation of Third World countries in the 1950s. Before engaging with Fanon's 'This Is the Voice of Free Algeria', it is worth noting that de Gaulle, dubbed 'Général micro', deployed the wireless as an effective tool in his military operations, helping transform the BBC into an instrument of war.[2] The wireless also played a crucial role in radicalising the 18-year-old Fanon: the BBC's 'Ici Londres' and de Gaulle's call to arms influenced him to join the Free French Forces in North Africa, an influence that proved lasting. In 'This Is the Voice of Algeria', Fanon emulates 'Général micro' and 'La Voix de la France libre' broadcasting from London. Invoking the popular BBC programme 'Les Français parlent aux Français', Fanon underscores the historical contradictions engendered by France's colonial war in Algeria. Like de Gaulle, Fanon weaponised the radio. To fully appreciate Fanon's intervention, it is important to situate it within a broader historical context, considering the Hertzian developments of the 1930s and 1940s and the propaganda and counter-propaganda that dominated the airwaves at the time.[3]

In 1930, a French Ministry of Foreign Affairs inquiry revealed France was lagging behind in radio technology and failing to deploy it strategically as a propaganda instrument. In response, the radio statio Le Poste colonial was launched on 6 May 1931, with its inaugural broadcast featuring Marshal Lyautey's speech at the Paris Colonial Exhibition. Although aiming to transcend time and space constraints by informing, teaching, reassuring and entertaining settlers in distant colonial outposts,[4] Le Poste colonial struggled to keep pace with rapidly evolving political developments. By 1935, Rome, Berlin and Moscow were engaged in a battle for airwave dominance. Mussolini's radio station broadcast in multiple languages, including Greek, Albanian, Bulgarian, Romanian and Arabic; Goebbels disseminated Nazi rhetoric in approximately thirty languages; and the USSR dominated with 1560 kW, broadcasting in sixty-five languages.[5] Amidst this cacophony of fascist and communist propaganda, the voice of Le Poste colonial, intended to reassure distant colonial settlers, became increasingly inaudible.

Georges Mandel, Minister of Posts, highlighted the need to overhaul France's broadcasting strategy in a letter to Albert Lebrun.[6] Consequently, on 23 March 1938, Le Poste colonial was relaunched as Paris ondes courtes, renamed Paris-mondial a week later. This revamped radio station aimed to counter fascist and communist propaganda targeting France and its empire. The development of radio broadcasting in the 1930s occurred against a politically fraught background. The centenary of Algeria's colonisation was marred by political tensions, culminating in the 1945 uprising and the massacres of nationalists in Guelma, Kharata and Sétif. As Rebecca Scales demonstrates, transnational radio stations exacerbated these tensions and fostered the development of an auditory culture in colonial Algeria.[7]

In her study of fascist and anticolonial propaganda broadcast by Radio Bari and Radio Seville, Scales demonstrates how these transnational stations threatened French colonial hegemony. She argues that 'French authorities came to view radios and phonographs as dangerous and subversive technologies because the sounds they produced so consistently evaded the disciplinary mechanisms of the colonial state.'[8] The dissemination of incendiary propaganda in Arabic via stations like Radio Bari necessitated changes in Radio-Alger's programming strategy,[9] reflecting a broader agenda in Blum's Popular Front government to counter the rise of fascism, pan-Islamic propaganda, and nascent nationalism threatening France both domestically and abroad.[10] Against this backdrop, Scales offers a nuanced interpretation of Fanon's authoritative piece 'This Is the Voice of Algeria', reassessing his perspective on radio's weaponisation during the Algerian war.[11]

Scales excoriates Fanon for overlooking the fact that the airwaves were a site of competing discourses in the 1930s and 1940s: the wireless was an instrument of propaganda and counter-propaganda deployed by fascist and Nazi states, by communist USSR, by the Popular Front against the rise of fascism, by colonial France to thwart anticolonial resistance and maintain its hegemony in its colonies, by transnational radio stations to mobilise the colonised against French colonialism in Indochina, in the Middle East and in North Africa. She assembles an impressive, apposite corpus of archival material dismissing Fanon's assertion that, before the 1954 revolution, Algerians did not listen to the wireless and that the ownership of a radio set was considered as 'a sign of Europeanization in progress, of vulnerability'.[12] Far from being implements of coloniality, she contends, the radio and the phonograph empowered Algerians to stymie the disciplinary control of the colonial state. In her attempt to debunk Fanon's assertion, Scales clearly ignores three key issues which are central to his piece: the gendering of the radiophonic message; the psychological warfare carried out by the Fifth Bureau; and the role played by the nationalist radio stations in the Algerian struggle for independence.

AUDITORY CULTURE, ITS COLONIAL AND GENDERED POLITICS

The modus operandi of radio is vulgarisation and 'propaganda', in the sense of 'broadcasting' and 'disseminating' speech. The Latin phrase *verba volant* aptly describes this dissemination: 'spoken words that fly away' are difficult to monitor and control. These words are intangible and equivocal, as they inhabit a slippery medium that straddles the public and private spheres. From the early 1930s, radio traversed both spheres, shuttling colonial and anticolonial propaganda. Scales observes that during Radio-Alger's 1929 inauguration, Constantine lawyer and Centenary Commissioner Gustave Mercier envisioned the station as a crucial instrument of colonial propaganda. Mercier believed it would advance the spiritual conquest of Arab hearts and minds by transgressing the public–private divide, reaching the previously impenetrable spaces of Algerian domestic life and furthering the 'civilising mission'.[13] Indeed, the wireless medium transcended the masculine public sphere, penetrating the 'cloistered life' of Muslim women and disseminating the colonial message.[14] However, the transmission of this message was ultimately thwarted by undercurrents of nascent nationalism.[15] Drawing upon Bachaga Smati's report 'Le disque de langue arabe',[16] Scales expands on the ambivalence of the radio as an elusive medium, maintaining that Algerian society had an auditory culture. However, she overlooks the fact that this ambivalence stemmed from the fundamental separation between public and private spheres. Furthermore, she overlooks a crucial aspect of Smati's argument: the capacity of radiophonic messages to traverse gendered spaces.

Scales's analysis thereby neglects the significant role of radio broadcasts in challenging and potentially reconfiguring traditional spatial boundaries defined by gender norms. To explore the gaps and blind spots in Scales's reading it is important to refer to Smati's report and to explore the politics which bifurcated Algeria's colonial space.

In the early 1920s, Smati observes, the phonograph significantly impacted indigenous Muslim cultural life, pervading public spaces and domestic spheres with Oriental music. Considering the nationalistic potencies of such music, played in *cafés maures*, *gargottes*, souks and shops, Smati also particularises the sexual politics that bifurcated the space along gender and ethnic lines. As he explains, the 'infatuation' with this new trend in music had discernible causes: 'the cloistered life of women, the convenience of the record as a means of entertainment at home'.[17] It was with ease that the phonograph was adopted because it did not confuse the lines of demarcation, and, unlike the wireless, it did not operate on the ambivalent medium of radio frequency.

Despite the advances in radio technology, the phonograph was more predominant than the wireless in the 1930s and 1940s. Initially, the phonograph, just like the radio in the 1940s and 1950s, was demonised by a conservative society for promoting 'immodest love songs'.[18] Nonetheless, the phonograph captured the indigenous imagination, overcoming traditional constraints. After the First World War, it became ubiquitous: it insinuated itself into all aspects of culture. The phonograph did not just blare Oriental music. From 1926 onwards it acquired an ideological function: it reproduced and disseminated nationalistic discourses, interpenetrated with pan-Islamism and Arabism.[19] In her critique of Fanon, Scales aptly demonstrates that the phonograph proved to be more subversive than the radio as the former disseminated anticolonial propaganda in Arabic language in public places. However, a closer reading shows that her account is not at variance with Fanon's: the auditory culture enjoyed by the Algerians was notably male-centred and consumed predominantly in the public and seldom in the domestic sphere. The recipients of this culture, subverting colonial state control, were primarily recruits of nascent Algerian nationalism in the late 1920s and 1930s.

The roots of Algerian nationalism can be traced to French colonial policies instituted in the late nineteenth and early twentieth centuries, which effectively excluded native Algerians from the public sphere. The Sénatus-consulte of 1865 introduced a provision for naturalisation of native Algerians, albeit with a significant caveat: individuals were required to relinquish their Muslim status to attain political citizenship. This stipulation created a complex interplay between religious identity and civic participation, effectively institutionalising a system that led to the segregation and bifurcation of colonial space. In the aftermath of the First World War, the Jonnart Law of 1919 attempted to revive the assimilationist policy that the 1865 Sénatus-consulte had failed to implement.[20] However, these reforms stood in stark contrast to the 1905 *laïcité* legislation by maintaining religion as a crucial factor in determining political access. Contrary to the principle of separating religion and state, French law continued to require indigenous Algerians to renounce their personal status to acquire citizenship rights. Rather than fostering integration, the Jonnart Law exacerbated the marginalisation and exclusion of the native population from the public and political spheres. This legislation contributed to what can be described as the 'cloistering' of Algerian culture, further deepening the divide between coloniser and colonised.[21]

The Jonnart Law, with its extremely limited applicability to only a small fraction of the Algerian population, exacerbated colonial relations in the 1920s and 1930s, foreshadowing the antagonism that peaked with the failure of the Blum–Viollette Bill in 1936[22] and the crisis of 1945. Transnational radio broadcasts, particularly fascist and Nazi propaganda, exploited this colonial antagonism. Radio Bari, broadcasting Mussolini's propaganda, stoked anticolonial nationalism by calling for *jihad* against French colonialism.[23] The colonial mission started to falter at a time when France was celebrating the centenary of its occupation of Algeria. Contemporary writers like Lecoq and Pomier acknowledged the settlers' precarious position and the religious divisions hindering assimilation, which they paradoxically argued against.[24] Pomier argued that harmony could only be achieved by confining religion to the private sphere, stating, '**Algeria will live, that is to say, it will be one, when all religions are confined to their own domain – that of the heart and the family.**'[25] While official reports like 'Postes, télégraphes et téléphone en Algérie' lauded radiophony's potential to consolidate France's colonial enterprise,[26] this rhetoric masked underlying tensions. In his 1937 report to the Haut Comité Méditerranéen, 'La Radio diffusion et les populations indigènes d'Algérie', Delahaye alluded to this malaise and emphasised the wireless as a tool to reinvigorate France's colonising mission and counter growing Algerian nationalism and transnational propaganda. Two crucial points can be gleaned from this report: first, Delahaye called for the instrumentalisation of the radio as a tool of colonial propaganda, to help implement the assimilationist policies which the Jonnart Law and the Blum–Viollette Bill failed to promulgate; second, he warned against transnational radio stations broadcasting in Arabic which became a source of anxiety for the colonial administration.

The report identified a particularly susceptible audience for indoctrination: illiterate men who listened to radio broadcasts in *cafés maures*. According to Delahaye, this audience was prone to political manipulation owing to its reliance on translators, who could imbue interpretations with nationalistic sentiments and ideological biases. Furthermore, the report cautioned against listening to the radio as a group activity, especially in urban environments, where it intersected with other activities such as religious preaching, political discourses, phonograph recordings, Oriental music performances, and Arabic theatre and film productions, all of which could potentially reinforce these sentiments and biases. The introduction of Arabic programming on radio stations like Le Poste colonial, Paris-mondial, and Radio-Alger was not intended primarily to promote indigenous culture. Instead, this initiative served two strategic purposes: countering fascist propaganda and penetrating the indigenous cloistered culture. It was not without irony that the *sans-filistes* thanked Mussolini and Radio Bari for promoting the Arabic language, which hitherto had been exiled from its own cultural landscape by French colonialism.[27] However, the use of colloquial Arabic in these programmes divided opinion: the anti-assimilationists adhering to the cultural project of the *oulemas* found these programmes vulgar and inappropriate and feared that their reach to a wide audience could jeopardise their nationalist agenda. The *élus* took the opposite position.[28] *La Voix indigène*, epitomising such position, rejected the use of literary Arabic and considered the radio as a very useful tool which could facilitate the assimilation of the natives.

To reiterate, the Algerians' auditory culture was male-centred and experienced in the public sphere. To counter an incipient nationalism, the radio was deployed as a stratagem of coloniality, having 'the triple advantage of reaching even illiterate populations and of penetrating the most jealously guarded homes and of having an almost unlimited range in space'.[29] In *Le Monolinguisme de l'autre*,[30] echoing Memmi's view that the colonised never experienced nationality and citizenship, except privately,[31] Jacques Derrida describes the perverse effects of colonisation in terms of the 'ossification' and 'necrotisation' of the colonised culture. The colonised sought refuge in this cocooned culture, which became a source of anxiety for the coloniser, prompting the use of radio as a tool to penetrate and hegemonise it.

Ambivalence is at the centre of radiophonic transmission: on the one hand, it broadcast anticolonial propaganda and disseminated Algerian nationalism; on the other, it was used as a stratagem to promote coloniality. Scales argues that radio was a slippery medium, evading colonial state control and facilitating fascist and anticolonial propaganda. Conversely, it was weaponised to advance France's 'spiritual conquest of Arab hearts and minds', a civilising mission that faltered in the 1920s and came to a halt in the 1930s and 1940s. Operating at the intersection of public and private spheres, radio targeted the final bastion of resistance: Algerian culture, emblematised by the Algerian woman.

Scales overlooks that the radiophonic medium was gendered. Contrary to her interpretation, Fanon does not argue that Algerians lacked an auditory culture pre-1954. Rather, he contended that the wireless disrupted traditional modes of sociability. Economic, sociological and cultural factors limited radio ownership among Algerians, and the device blurred gendered spatial divisions, threatening traditions of respectability and modesty. As Fanon explains, it was not possible to listen to radiophonic programmes because of some of their lewd and lascivious talk.[32] En Nadjah newspaper criticised the lewd programmes of Radio-Alger for offering a 'lesson in licentiousness [leçon de libertinage]' to its 'decent' listeners,[33] thereby highlighting its perceived threat to traditional values. Some listeners reportedly turned off their receivers to protect their children's morals from the 'love of pleasure'. Nonetheless, Fanon's analysis, corroborated by contemporary reports and newspaper articles, reveals that the colonial administration used radio to infiltrate Algerian homes and disrupt traditional modes of sociability.

In the appendix to 'Algeria Unveiled', Fanon provides an account which concurs with Delahaye's report and Pomier's and Lecoq's assessment of the political situation in the early 1930s: France colonised Algerian soil but not Algerian culture. The domestic space was the last bastion that stood against French colonialism and the colonial administration made a concerted effort in the 1930s to assimilate Algerian women. As Fanon elaborates:

The decisive battle was launched before 1954, more precisely during the early 1930s. The officials of the French administration in Algeria, committed to destroying the people's originality, and under instructions to bring about the disintegration, at whatever cost, of forms of existence likely to evoke a national reality directly or indirectly, were to concentrate their efforts on the wearing of the veil, which was looked upon at this juncture as a symbol of the status of the Algerian woman. Such a position is not the consequence of a chance intuition. It is on the basis of the analyses of sociologists and ethnologists that the specialists in so-called native affairs and the heads of the Arab Bureaus coordinated their work. At an initial stage, there was a pure and simple adoption of the well-known formula, 'Let's win over the women and the rest will follow.'

Furthermore:

This enabled the colonial administration to define a precise political doctrine: 'If we want to destroy the structure of Algerian society, its capacity for resistance, we must first of all conquer the women; we must go and find them behind the veil where they hide themselves and in the houses where the men keep them out of sight.' It is the situation of woman that was accordingly taken as the theme of action. The dominant administration solemnly undertook to defend this woman, pictured as humiliated, sequestered, cloistered ...[34]

In 'This Is the Voice of Algeria', Fanon expands on this theme, arguing that colonial administration used radio to infiltrate Algerian homes, particularly targeting women. Alluding to colonial feminism, which initiated social and charitable works in the 1920s and 1930s, Fanon contends that the movement developed 'technique[s] of infiltration' into the domestic space that aimed at co-opting Algerian women into the assimilationist project.[35]

The 'social' and 'charitable' works of colonial feminists such as Hubertine Auclert and Marie Bugéja in the 1930s, later championed by Massu and Salan in the 1950s, constituted a critical element of nosopolitics. Fanon argues that this represented colonialism's final onslaught, seeking to insinuate itself into the core of Algerian culture to mutilate and erase it. From 1930 onwards, he opines, French colonialism contested and disfigured Algerian people, culture and history, recognising that territorial occupation required cultural hegemony.[36]

Scales intimates that Fanon's 'bifurcated' views may have overlooked the radio's strategic development as a propaganda tool in the 1930s and 1940s. However, his main preoccupation was not the competing discourses which dominated the airwaves in the 1930s and 1940s but the events leading to the 1958 putsch, particularly Massu's paratroopers' use of radio for psychological warfare during fraternisation demonstrations. Fanon feared these demonstrations were attempts to integrate Algerian women and undermine the Algerian Revolution. While Scales presents extensive archival material, she notably omits crucial context: the mid-1950s 'battle of the waves' and political efforts to silence the 'Voice of Free Algeria'. This oversight represents a significant gap in her analysis regarding radio's role in Algeria's decolonisation. In what follows, I will recover this context, before exploring the connection between the battle of the waves and the battle of the veil.

BROADCASTING ON THE RUN, SILENCING THE VOICE OF FREE ALGERIA

In the 1940s and 1950s, owning a radio set meant belonging to an emerging consumer society that was keen to display its consumer goods, such as the car, the refrigerator and the telephone, as signifiers of class status. The radio was not only a symbol of cultural membership but was also a medium that brought the colonial margins back to the metropolis, connecting remote rural locations and cities with mainland France; it was the only link with civilisation. The radio provided cultural capital and reassurance for the settlers; it reminded them of their historical mission and reinforced their cultural dominance. They adopted radio technology without any hesitation; its development, observes Fanon, 'proceeded at a rate comparable to that of the most developed Western regions'.[37] Just like medicine, this technology constituted one of the most important instruments of biopolitics which ensured the necessary condition for colonial life. As Fanon elaborates:

For a European to own a radio ... gives him the feeling that colonial society is a living and palpitating reality, with its festivities, its traditions eager to establish themselves, its progress, its taking root. But especially in the hinterland, in the so-called colonization centers, it is the only link with the cities, with Algiers, with the metropolis, with the world of the civilized. It is one of the means of escaping the inert, passive, and sterilising pressure of the 'native' environment. It is, according to the settler's expression, 'the only way to still feel like a civilized man.'

On the farms, the radio reminds the settler of the reality of colonial power and, by its very existence, dispenses safety, serenity. Radio-Alger is a confirmation of the settler's right and strengthens his certainty in the historic continuity of the conquest, hence of his farm. The Paris music, extracts from the metropolitan press, the French government crises, constitute a coherent background from which colonial society draws its density and its justification. Radio-Alger sustains the occupant's culture, marks it off from the non-culture, from the nature of the occupied. Radio-Alger, the voice of France in Algeria, constitutes the sole center of reference at the level of news. RadioAlger, for the settler, is a daily invitation not to 'go native,' not to forget the rightfulness of his culture. The settlers in the remote outposts, the pioneering adventurers, are well aware of this when they say that 'without wine and the radio, we should already have become Arabized.'[38]

As Roland Barthes affirms in *Mythologies*, wine was the symbol par excellence of French colonialism; the radio was another symbol. Radio-Alger, as an 'instrument of colonial society and its values', served to maintain cultural distinctions between the European settler minority and the larger colonised native population, and to protect European settlers from racial intermixing and from their 'Arabization'.[39] In Algeria before 1945, settlers appropriated the radio as an instrument of political and cultural domination. 'Among European farmers', writes Fanon, 'the radio was broadly regarded as a link with the civilized world, as an effective instrument of resistance to the corrosive influence of an inert native society, of a society without a future, backward and devoid of value'.[40] Conversely, Algerians largely rejected the radio for promoting Western content that clashed with their family tradition and cultural values.[41] In urban areas, prior to the Algerian war, well-to-do families refrained from purchasing a radio set; their reticence – which Fanon describes as 'a dull absence of interest in that piece of French presence' – was based on an inchoate attitude without an explicit political rationale. In remote rural areas, it was inconceivable for Algerians to own a radio. Economic constraints and colonial traditionalism were key factors.

Print and audio media played a significant role in the 1954 revolution, bringing about radical mutations in the consciousness of the colonised, changing their perception vis-à-vis tradition as well as calling into question a hegemonic French colonialism. In 'This Is the Voice of Algeria', Fanon argues that the war gave rise to new attitudes in the struggle for independence. As has been noted, in the 1930s and 1940s, the auditory culture that contributed to Algerian radicalisation was primarily disseminated through phonographs rather than radios and consumed in the public space rather than in private. Before 1945, radio ownership in Algeria was starkly divided along colonial lines, with 95 per cent of sets owned by Europeans and only a privileged few Algerians possessing them.[42] This distribution reflected the Manichaean economy Fanon describes in *The Wretched of the Earth*, where clear socioeconomic divisions separated coloniser from colonised, haves from have-nots, and the well-fed from the starving.[43] Malika Mokeddem's *Les Hommes qui marchent* vividly illustrates this disparity, depicting Algerians foregoing bread to save for a radio set, underscoring the extreme sacrifices made to access this technology within the oppressive colonial economic structure.[44]

Fanon identifies two main sources of disseminating messages and information, and two distinct sorts of news consumers. The first source was the written press, which served a very small segment of the native population. In the urban centres, Algerians could buy either colonialist newspapers (like *L'Echo d'Alger*) or French democratic newspapers (such as *L'Express*, *France-Observateur*, *L'Humanité*, and *Le Monde*). Purchasing 'democratic' newspapers was deemed a dangerous 'nationalist act', equivalent to publicly declaring 'allegiance to the Revolution'.[45] Consequently, the urban elite stopped purchasing the written press and turned instead to the radio for information, as it provided anonymity and reduced the risk of being identified as revolutionary sympathisers. After 1956, radio became the most accessible and popular medium, catering to the entire population, particularly rural and illiterate masses previously excluded from the written press.

Since these masses could neither read nor write, Fanon affirms, the radio reported to them, via broadcasts 'from Cairo, from Syria, from nearly all the Arab countries, the great pages written' by Algerian freedom fighters. 'La Voix de l'Algérie', inaugurated on 12 December 1956, brought about a radical change; the portable battery-operated receiver was purchased not just by individual families but by groups of houses, by entire *douars* and *mechtas*.[46] Traditional resistance to the radio all of a sudden disappeared with an emergent cultural and social formation in cities as well as in *douars*; new ways of thinking and being, henceforth, brought together 'groups of families in which fathers, mothers, daughters, elbow to elbow, would scrutinise the radio dial waiting for the Voice of Algeria'.[47] This change of attitude was tantamount to a religious conversion; listening to the radio in groups constituted a ceremonial rite.

Fanon is adamant that 'the technical instrument of the radio receiver lost its identity as an enemy object' and was no longer considered 'a part of the occupier's arsenal of cultural oppression'.[48] Algerians decided to 'embrace' radio technology, by 'tun[ing in] on the new signaling systems brought into being by the Revolution. The Voice of Fighting Algeria was to be of capital importance in consolidating and unifying the people.' The radio mobilised them and strengthened their unity; purchasing a radio receiver meant effectively joining 'the struggle of an assembled people'. This development was not lost on the French authorities: a number of steps were taken to control radio media outlets and deny Algerians access. Spare batteries were withdrawn from the market; the sale of radios, without a permit issued by the police, was prohibited. More importantly, nationalist radios were scrambled, instigating what Fanon calls 'sound-wave warfare'. Before exploring the ramifications of this sort of warfare, carried out by the 'highly trained French services' at the Groupement des contrôles radioélectriques (GCR), it is important first to provide the historical and political context.

Since July 1953, Radio Cairo had conducted a sustained anticolonial campaign against French interests in North Africa.[49] As early as 11 February 1954, General Guillaume called upon the Radiodiffusion-Télévision Française (RTF) to consider countermeasures in order to scramble 'La Voix des Arabes' by transmitting on the frequencies used by the Egyptian radio station. This was not jamming per se, but an 'occupation of frequencies outside of any pre-established international plan'.[50] The Brazzaville, Allouis and Issoudum transmitters were deployed, in this regard, to occupy these frequencies. On 17 September 1956, Resident Minister and Governor-General of Algeria, Lacoste, cautioned the President of the Council about Radio Tunis's and Radio Rabat's vociferously anticolonial broadcasts, which were transmitted around 21:00 and were highly audible to an increasing Muslim audience in Algeria. He called for the jamming of their transmitters which represented a 'dangerous' interference in France's colonial affairs.[51] On 28 September 1956, the President of the Council was again urged 'to make these stations inaudible given the intolerable situation created by Radio Maroc and especially Radio Tunis, which are very popular in Algeria'.[52] The government decided to scramble them on 13 October that same year.[53]

Referring to Lacoste's request to jam these two 'subversive' and highly 'dangerous' radio stations, Maurice Bourgès-Maunoury emphasises that urgent action was needed to scramble not only the already neutralised La Voix des Arabes and Radio Damas, but also the daily programme of 'Algérie soeur', the weekly 'La Voix de l'Algérie', and 'Le Grand Maghrèb'. 'The scrambling technique', he specifies, 'could be, if necessary, replaced by that of "intrusion" which consists in carrying the contradiction during the broadcast and on the same frequency'.[54] This was one of the main scrambling techniques used to silence Radio de l'Algérie libre et combattante (RALC), which Fanon's 'This

Is the Voice of Free Algeria' discusses. As we will see, jamming constituted an unauthorised appropriation of radio frequencies beyond international agreements and violated Copenhagen Convention protocols through frequency misuse and harmful interference. Moreover, it represented a form of 'intrusion' or 'effraction': a violation of space. On 3 August 1957, Radio Cairo launched its daily broadcast in French, 'La Voix de l'Algérie libre'. In an information sheet for the Secretary General of the Government, Director of GCR, Veyron La Croix, reported on 'subversive' Arab radio propaganda. He noted the resumption of broadcasts by 'La Voix de l'Algérie libre' and RALC after technical issues.[55] Attempts to scramble these programmes paradoxically highlighted growing interest in such content across Algeria and other Arab countries. La Croix identified eight anticolonial broadcasters, including La Voix des Arabes, Radio Damascus, Radio Tunis, Radio Tétouan, Radio Tanger and Radio Rabat, recommending their scrambling to counter their influence.[56] These radios used ten short and four medium waves and broadcast at different times, and in different languages. As mainland transmitters were ineffective, the GCR's scrambling of 'subversive' radios relied heavily on the Brazzaville transmitter.

Anticolonial radio stations introduced a number of modifications between 15 September and 10 October 1957. An increase or drop in frequency was used as a strategy to avoid jamming. Radio Tunis adjusted its programme to transmit on 629kc/s instead of 962kc/s; the RALC suspended its programme entirely from 26 September to 1 October 1957 but resumed transmission thereafter.[57] From 2–4 November, its daily programmes were presented not in three tranches but in four, with a change in frequencies for each section.[58] It broadcast in French, Arabic and Kabyle. Significantly, in addition to its own transmitters, the FLN had at its disposal the microphones of other radiophonic platforms, such as Radio Tétouan and its programme 'La Voix de l'Algérie'; Radio Cairo and 'La Voix de l'Algérie libre'; Radio Rabat and 'La Voix de l'Algérie combattante'; Radio Tunis and 'La Voix de l'Algérie arabe soeur'. The proliferation of these programmes made scrambling virtually unworkable, as the FLN operated on different channels, broadcasting at different times and on different radiophonic platforms, from different countries. Fanon captures the sonance of these radiophonic voices and the problems which they posed for the GCR trying to scramble them.

After 1957, the French troops in operation formed the habit of confiscating all the radios in the course of a raid. At the same time listening in on a certain number of broadcasts was prohibited. Today things have progressed. The Voice of Fighting Algeria has multiplied. From Tunis, from Damascus, from Cairo, from Rabat, programs are broadcast to the people. The programs are organized by Algerians. The French services no longer try to jam these powerful and numerous broadcasts. The Algerian has the opportunity every day of listening to five or six different broadcasts in Arabic or in French, by means of which he can follow the victorious development of the Revolution step by step.[59]

The jamming of broadcasts from Egypt, Tunisia and Morocco proved ineffective.[60] From 3 August 1957, Radio Cairo began broadcasting on a new frequency;[61] its programme 'La Voix de l'Algérie libre' aired in French every evening at about 19:00 for ten minutes, with fairly good reception in mainland France.[62] 'Since the inauguration of its new bi-weekly programme titled "The Voice of Algeria" on 13 June 1957', writes La Croix, 'Radio Tétaoun ha[d] become, after RALC, the most violently anti-French Arab-Muslim radio station.'[63] 'La Voix de l'Algérie' denounced torture and the violation of fundamental rights and freedoms as Nazi methods adopted by French authorities in Algeria, and called on Muslims and Arabs to rally against French colonialism. Significantly, 'La Voix de l'Algérie' had a wide audience as it was broadcast in colloquial Arabic. Radio Tunis aired 'La Voix de l'Algérie Arabe soeur' thrice weekly, while Radio Tangier and Radio Rabat provided two additional outlets for anticolonial discourses. Radio Tangier was clearly audible in Algeria's western regions. In his report, La Croix noted that Radio Tétaoun and Radio Tangier were particularly popular due to their clear reception, quality music variety programmes, and the virulence of their news commentary. La Croix suggested that jamming these stations might discourage listeners from tuning in.

The GCR pursued the jamming of broadcasts on medium wave, namely targeting Radio Tunis, Radio Rabat and Radio Tétouan. Serious concerns were raised with regard to Radio Tanger, also called Radio Africa Maghreb; its incendiary transmissions belied the fact that its management and capital were French.[64] The GCR encountered difficulties in jamming 'La Voix des Arabes' and Radio Damascus.[65] Resources were diverted from the RTF and General Salan deployed military personnel to assist in the operation.[66] On 24 December 1957, Pierre Maisonneuve requested the deployment of twelve specialist technicians from RTF to serve under the colours. Resources were needed urgently at the Eucalyptus centre to help scramble 'subversive' radio transmissions.[67] In addition to the 48 million francs which were pledged,

RTF's regional director in Algiers estimated that 114 million francs were required to cover the cost of jamming.[68]

The GCR's claim that it completely stifled the RACL's voice of dissent should not obscure the fact that other radio stations, like Radio Cairo, Radio Tunis, Radio Damascus, Radio Baghdad, Radio Tanger or Radio Rabat, continued to broadcast and led the charge against France's colonial 'hatred' and 'blind racism',[69] condemning de Gaulle's manoeuvres in the slaughter of the Algerian people, discounting his new constitution as a blunt instrument of colonialism, and affirming that the Algerian people would never grant him a mandate in the upcoming referendum. If the GCR momentarily managed to silence the RALC, Radio Tanger took on the anticolonial mantle by providing a platform for the FLN to announce their communiqués and for the RALC to continue its anticolonial broadcasts.[70] Significantly, the FLN had access to a transmitter in Libya, which further complicated the task of jamming the 'Voice of Free Algeria'.[71] La Croix warned that the newly formed United Arab Republic was waging psychological warfare on a large scale, broadcasting more than 500 hours of propaganda a week, which represented the most potent weapon of indirect aggression against France's interests in Algeria, targeting an illiterate population that was very 'vulnerable' and easily manipulated with words.[72]

In addition to the relaying of transmissions, which Fanon describes, a number of other strategies were used to avoid being jammed: the RALC and other anticolonial radio stations broadcast at different times and on different days; they interrupted broadcasting, or stopped broadcasting altogether; they used different stations, changed channels, altered their programmes or toned down their rhetoric.[73] The most acerbic transmission of Radio Tétouan was replaced by Spanish programmes and its anticolonial discourses became attenuated, which made the task of jamming the radio obsolete.[74]

The RALC, having had the transmission of its programmes interrupted from 5 September 1958, resumed broadcasting on 12 July 1959; it started transmitting simultaneously on four frequencies and had at its disposal transmitters which allowed it to operate synchronously on many different frequencies with slippages.[75] The GCR did not have enough jamming devices to cover all the frequencies on which the RALC operated and therefore had to ask the RTF to intervene. The activities of the RALC challenged the GCR's capacity to scramble all the other nationalist radios simultaneously; with limited resources, the GCR had to allow other nationalist radios – like 'La Voix des Arabes' or the 'sister' station of the RALC in Tunis – to operate freely. La Croix's team might have partially restricted the RALC but could not silence its Tunisian twin 'sibling' which was clearly audible in colloquial Arabic.[76]

With the development of transistor devices, medium wave transmitters posed a challenge for jamming. Although the massive and virulent anticolonial attacks from the Middle East could not be ignored, it was the transmitters of Moroccan and Tunisian radios which represented the greatest concern for the GCR. Morocco developed a formidable radiophonic capability; Tunisia was planning to install a medium wave transmitter of 300 kW, and further develop its short wave broadcasts.[77] Tunisia, Morocco and Egypt amassed a substantial arsenal of radiophonic transmitters. All their programmes operated on several short waves simultaneously; some medium wave transmitters were programmed to broadcast on multiple frequencies, switching from one frequency to another almost instantaneously. As La Croix explains, because short and medium waves were synchronous, jamming the short waves was ineffective unless the synchronous medium waves were also scrambled with the same level of efficiency.[78] Moreover, all the programmes were broadcast simultaneously, meaning jamming required coordinated coverage across both wavebands. The sheer volume of anticolonial transmissions on short and medium waves was overwhelming the GCR. Medium waves operated on fixed frequencies, and the transmitters provided by RTF were inadequate for the task.[79] The GCR lacked the capacity to deploy the necessary number of transmitters simultaneously to combat the numerous powerful transmitters operating together from different countries. As Fanon's 'This Is the Voice of Algeria' makes abundantly clear, the jamming operation was ineffective.[80]

In his letter to the prime minister, La Croix underplays the GCR's difficulty in scrambling nationalist radios operating on short and medium wave. However, he goes on in his report to highlight the dramatic upsurge in radio transmission involving Algeria, and the threat which Egypt and other Arab countries posed to French interest.[81] Significantly, the acquisition of powerful equipment seemed to be part of the 'arms race' in anticolonial struggle and in the Cold War. The communist radio stations intensified their propaganda. Radio Moscow found attentive ears in Algeria. The Arabic section amplified its propaganda against France for instituting in Algeria an 'order of terror and collective extermination'.[82] Radio Prague, Radio Sofia and Radio Tirana ventriloquised Radio Moscow's anti-French propaganda. On 16 October 1957, Radio Prague transmitted a new programme entitled 'La Civilisation française en Algérie'.[83] The radio stations of the communist bloc – Moscow, Prague, Sofia, Tirana and German Democratic Republic[84]

– broached the issue of decolonisation, with Algeria occupying centre stage. Radio Moscow remained the most aggressive in its denunciation of France for 'attack[ing] a defenceless civilian population, while starvation and death reigned in the internment camps'.[85] Radio Moscow encouraged African people 'to engage without further delay in a general campaign of liberation, "imperative of our time", despite the impotent rage of the followers of prolonged colonisation, such as Soustelle'.[86] Radio Moscow's pronouncements were loud and clear in condemning France's dying colonialism. To this cacophony of anticolonial propaganda, Radio Pékin added its piercing voice, inciting African people to free themselves from the yoke of oppression. Radio Pékin's programmes in French were clearly audible in Africa; their coverage doubling from 1 ½ to 3 hours daily, from 18:30 to 20:30 and from 21:30 to 22:30.[87] Radio Pékin 'spoke tirelessly about France's "atrocious crimes" in Algeria' and about 'the "farce" of the referendum'.[88] Pékin hailed Algerian people for being at the forefront of Africa's decolonisation.[89] The GCR, faced with a number of powerful transmitters broadcasting from the communist bloc, Middle East and Africa, was outmanoeuvred.

One of the most remarkable features of this growing movement in the Middle East and North Africa was voluntary or fortuitous coalitions of radio broadcasters which generated a great deal of propaganda against France. The directors of various radio stations agreed to coordinate their radio broadcasts to make them a powerful weapon in the struggle for liberation of Algeria.[90] Despite the GCR's attempts to silence the 'Voice of Free Algeria', Radio nationale marocaine and Radio Tunis worked together to provide coverage and ensure that their broadcast reached Algeria's borders and beyond: Radio Tunis transmitting to the east and the Radio nationale marocaine to the west of Algeria. This coalition – supported by broadcasts from Cairo, Baghdad, Damascus, Libya and Amman – complicated La Croix's task. The transmitters of 'La Voix des Arabes' were so powerful that La Croix and his team at the GCR had to abandon a large-scale strategy of jamming to concentrate on the Tunisian radio programmes.

The RALC's 'frequency hopping' frustrated the GCR's in its task of jamming: resources were not available at the times when this slippery medium operated and disseminated its programmes.[91] Arab radio stations – Rabat, Tétouan, Tanger, Tunis, Cairo, Damascus, Baghdad – were transmitting programmes all day, from 4:00 in the morning to well beyond midnight; there were effectively no gaps in the programming which operated on no less than 16 frequencies and which, unsurprisingly, challenged the capacity of the GCR's jamming service. The role played by RTF in jamming nationalist radio programmes was passive, in the sense that it was always executed under the orders of the prime minister or the GCR (answerable to the latter). RTF did not have the resources to meet the demands of the GCR's jamming operation; besides, this operation went against the spirit of its actual function which was to broadcast rather than disrupt transmission.[92]

'In short', writes Colonel Guy Robert, Acting Director of the GCR, 'we are witnessing a very rapid development in the number of subversive broadcasts. It is certain that the means are not commensurate with the demands.'[93] In their attack against France, foreign radio stations deployed instruments which were continually evolving; jamming their programmes became a very difficult operation for the GCR. The lack of sufficient means to scramble transmission had political implications. 'La Voix des Arabes' had a large audience among the indigenous population, drawn by the variety of its programmes and by the content of its various forums. Moroccan radio programmes were audible and well received in the Oran region. Among all the radio stations, Tunisian radiophonic broadcasts enjoyed great popularity in the eastern part of Algeria. On the other hand, the RALC was, according to Colonel Robert, probably the least listened to because it was the more heavily jammed.[94] Nonetheless, this does not mean that it was inaudible. As Fanon shows in 'This Is the Voice of Algeria', its voice was captured by other means. Fanon's assertion that jamming had the opposite outcome to what was intended must be read against this historical background. Not only did it mobilise the Algerian populations but it also galvanised all Arab radio stations against French colonialism and its repressive instruments. Simply put, jamming catalysed these radio stations to broadcast on behalf of the RALC in its absence, representing by proxy that which was silenced

To counter the GCR's jamming strategy, frequency hopping with relaying programmes were adopted by nationalist radio stations. As Fanon avers: 'Tracts were distributed telling the Algerians to keep tuned in for a period of two or three hours. In the course of a single broadcast a second station, broadcasting over a different wave-length, would relay the first jammed station.'[95] In addition to the issue of transmission which represented a battleground, a whole sociology has to be considered for determining the reception of the RALC programmes. The significance of this battle of the waves must be sought not at the level of electromagnetism, that is, the physics of jamming or frequency hopping, but at the level of interpretative politics. This politics, constituted by listening to the radio as a group activity, was a quasi-religious activity, a sort of ceremonial rite. 'The listener, enrolled in the battle of the waves, had to figure out the tactics of the enemy, and in an almost physical way circumvent the strategy of the adversary.'[96]

It is instructive to reiterate that the RALC operated on different frequencies; reception required, as Fanon explains, an operator/interpreter whose ear would be glued to the radio receiver tuning in to its frequency range and capturing its elusive voice, which the GCR sought to scramble and make inaudible. The news did not flow from the radio receiver to the ears of its listeners, but was received and mediated via this operator/interpreter and their meaning 'negotiated' with the listeners at the end of the broadcast.

Listening to the RALC pertained to the realm of 'mythology', in the Barthesian sense: it mobilised its listeners by motivating their commitment to be 'at one with the nation in its struggle'; it re-enacted the grand narrative of the revolution by recapturing and reliving its great pages of history as they were written on the battlefield. Notwithstanding the interruption of the RALC, its listeners would convey to their neighbours a reconstructed view of this narrative, one whose content was half-empty and half-full: empty by dint of the silencing devices of the GCR, full through the work of 'reconstructing' the news and the supplementary economy which compensated for this silencing. The supplement was either provided by the broadcasts of other nationalist radio stations or via this reconstructed view, which was conveyed via the 'téléphone arabe' – a pejorative expression which means 'hearsay', 'gossip', whispering and spreading rumours, and creative narrative. Such work, which pertains to reconstructive interpretation, was in Fanon's view crucial in sustaining the revolution:

Because of a silence on this or that fact which, if prolonged, might prove upsetting and dangerous for the people's unity, the whole nation would snatch fragments of sentences in the course of a broadcast and attach to them a decisive meaning. Imperfectly heard, obscured by an incessant jamming, forced to change wave lengths two or three times in the course of a broadcast, the Voice of Fighting Algeria could hardly ever be heard from beginning to end. It was a choppy, broken voice. From one village to the next, from one shack to the next, the Voice of Algeria would recount new things, tell of more and more glorious battles, picture vividly the collapse of the occupying power. The enemy lost its density, and at the level of the consciousness of the occupied, experienced a series of essential setbacks. Thus the Voice of Algeria, which for months led the life of a fugitive, which was tracked by the adversary's powerful jamming networks, and whose 'word' was often inaudible, nourished the citizen's faith in the Revolution.[97]

Paradoxically, the jamming of the RALC operated in the opposite direction to its intended purpose, it worked only to consolidate its revolutionary propensity: it did not silence; in fact, it gave the RALC a more radical voice. 'This voice whose presence was felt, whose reality was sensed, assumed more and more weight in proportion to the number of jamming wave lengths broadcast by the specialized enemy stations.' Fanon establishes a correlation between the jamming of the RALC and the radicalisation of its listeners. The reception of the RALC's programmes, as a group activity, was not a passive exercise. As Fanon observes, every evening, from nine o'clock to midnight, huddled in large groups of sometimes hundreds, the Algerians would listen 'religiously' to 'The Voice of Free and Fighting Algeria' or 'The Voice of the Arabs'.

At the end of the evening, not hearing the Voice, the listener would sometimes leave the needle on a jammed wave-length or one that simply produced static, and would announce that the voice of the combatants was here. For an hour the room would be filled with the piercing, excruciating din of the jamming. Behind each modulation, each active crackling, the Algerian would imagine not only words, but concrete battles. The war of the sound waves, in the gourbi, re-enacts for the benefit of the citizen the armed clash of his people and colonialism. As a general rule, it is the Voice of Algeria that wins out. The enemy stations, once the broadcast is completed, abandon their work of sabotage. The military music of warring Algeria that concludes the broadcast can then freely fill the lungs and the heads of the faithful. These few brazen notes reward three hours of daily hope and have played a fundamental role for months in the training and strengthening of the Algerian national consciousness.[98]

Jamming made the RALC conspicuous by its *absence*. Effectively, its silencing threw into sharp relief its very *presence*. This presence as absence was, according to Fanon, the articulation of a state of being, a phenomenology which was fundamentally political; this sort of absent presence constituted the condition of thought and political experience for Algerians in their combat against French colonialism. In structuralist terms, the oxymoron – absent presence – seemingly defaulted on signification, with the suspension of language; by jamming, occupying the frequencies on which the RALC transmitted and cancelling its signal, the sign seemed to lag behind signification as the signified was completely overtaken by its signifier, presence was covered over and supplanted by absence to the extent that it created a nebula, 'a din of excruciating noise', an interference. In political terms, this interference which was heard as 'static' was signifying; this buzzing, parasitic, noise expressed the voice of the revolution, 'present "in the air" in isolated pieces, but not objectively'.[99] This radio noise was created by jamming devices of the GCR, generated by radio frequency interference aimed at stifling the 'Voice of Free Fighting Algeria'. Despite being 'often absent and physically inaudible', this voice conveyed a concrete structure of nationalistic feeling for the Algerians and 'became materialized in an irrefutable way'.[100] As Fanon explains, 'claiming to have heard the *Voice of Algeria* was, in a certain sense, distorting the truth, but it was above all the occasion to proclaim one's clandestine participation in the essence of the Revolution', which French colonialism sought to suppress. The GCR's jamming operations effectively 'emphasized the reality [of the revolution] and the intensity of the national expression'. They paradoxically gave credence to the RALC as the mouthpiece of the revolution and 'gave to the combat its maximum of reality'.[101]

Barthes's influence is perceptible in Fanon's work, published two years after *Mythologies* (1957). Conversant with semiology, *Studies in a Dying Colonialism* analyses the intersection of language, media and politics, positing that the medium is the message: the radiophonic message, as a medium, has a semiological content and a political function as well. As he pithily puts it:

> At another level, as a system of information, as a bearer of language, hence of message, the radio may be apprehended within the colonial situation in a special way. Radiophonic technique, the press, and in a general way the systems, messages, sign transmitters, exist in colonial society in accordance with a well-defined statute. Algerian society, the dominated society, never participates in this world of signs.[102]

The colonised's exclusion from the symbolic exchange, what Fanon dubs 'this world of signs', was not just self-imposed but systematically brought about by the colonial state. Historically, the settlers controlled and regulated the colonialist news, and maintained their hegemony in this 'world of signs'. Fanon identifies the radio as a phonological apparatus operating within a semiological system, as bearer of messages articulating meaning within a well-defined world of signs, a colonial world which rejected the natives. Referring to the Second World War BBC radio broadcast 'Ici la France', he chooses to interpret its daily programme 'Les Français parlent aux Français' negatively, not as the expression of resistance against Nazism, but as the manifestation of the insularity of colonial culture. As he explains, the native masses neither possessed radio receivers nor participated in this world of signs; Radio-Alger's programmes were never meant for the natives' consumption. The Algerians regarded the radio as an implement articulating colonial power and Radio-Alger as the mouthpiece of colonial society; 'with [their] own brand of humor', ironises Fanon, they perceived Radio-Alger as the voice of 'Frenchmen speaking to Frenchmen'.[103]

The Algerian Revolution overturned this perception and discernibly deconstructed this Manichaean world as it helped decolonise the radio and language as instruments of French colonialism. 'By means of the radio', argues Fanon, 'a technique rejected before 1954, the Algerian people decided to relaunch the Revolution.' The radio became 'indispensable', as 'the new Algeria on the march had decided to tell about itself and to make itself heard'. 'It was the radio', Fanon affirms, 'that enabled the Voice [RALC] to take root in the villages and on the hills. Having a radio seriously meant going to war.' With the creation of the RALC, the Algerians were committed to listening to the radio; purchasing a radio receiver invested them with the power 'to get the news concerning the formidable experience in progress in the country' and receive 'the first words of the nation'.[104]

Thanks to the radio, French was no longer considered the idiom of colonial oppression. The radio and the Algerian Revolution overturned the logocentrism of French and the ontological implications which it hitherto had for Algeria as a transcendent signifying system.[105] Broadcasting the pro- grammes of the RALC decolonised French and untethered it from its colonial anchorage; broadcasting in three languages – Arabic, Berber and French – 'unified the experience and gave it a universal dimension'.[106] The RALC appropriated French to articulate unequivocally 'the message of the Revo- lution'. 'Expressing oneself in French, understanding French, was no longer tantamount to treason.' Deployed by the RALC, 'conveying in a positive way the message of the Revolution, the French language also [became] an instru- ment of liberation'. In Black Skin, White Masks, Fanon insists on the absolute and unbending traits of French as an idiom of coloniality. To speak it, he argues, is to assume the occupier's culture. In 'This Is the Voice of Algeria', nuancing this view, he contends that the 1954 revolution threw into sharp relief the 'relative character' of the coloniser's language and cultural signs, thus problematising their hegemony.[107] Prior to 1954, the Algerian nationalists made a concerted effort to learn Arabic, which they considered as the language of the Algerian people. As Fanon states, 'speaking Arabic, refusing French as a language and as a means of cultural oppression, was a distinct and daily form of differentiation, of national existence.'[108] Arabic expressed the revolutionary will of the Algerian people; it was, in Fanon's words, 'the most effective means that the nation's being had of unveiling itself'.[109] At the Soummam Congress, which was held in August 1956 and culminated with setting up the National Council of the Algerian Revolution (CNRA), the FLN leadership made the conscious decision to discuss the proceedings in French; a decision which helped, at one and the same time, disseminate French and liberate it of its 'negative connotations'.[110] Simply put, the Algerian Revolution afforded French a 'universal dimension',[111] which colonialism failed to achieve. The wireless 'as a technique of disseminating news', and French 'as a basis for a possible communication became almost simultaneously accepted by the fighting nation'.[112]

The RALC created an 'imagined community'. If printing, according to Benedict Anderson, gave shape to modern nationalism in Europe, the radio played a decisive role in the process of decolonisation and nation-building: those listening to the RALC broadcasting in Berber, Arabic or French felt part of the nation that was in gestation. By tuning in to it clandestinely, Fanon argues, they were participating in the 'reality of the nation'. The title he initially proposed to Maspero for *Studies in a Dying Colonialism* draws its significance from such reality.

By mediating, the radio helped shape Algerian nationhood; this explains the vicissitudes of its modus operandi and of its reception. The real change of attitude vis-à-vis the radio took place at the end of 1956. Purchasing a radio was no longer considered 'the adoption of a modern technique for getting news, but the obtaining of access to the only means of entering into communication with the Revolution, of living with it'.[113] Better still:

> In making of the radio a primary means of resisting the increasingly overwhelming psychological and military pressures of the occupant, Algerian society made an autonomous decision to embrace the new technique and thus tune itself in on the new signaling systems brought into being by the Revolution.[114]

The listener who became actively involved in the battle of the waves knew how to counter the tactics of the enemy, not solely on the terrain of military strategy but also in the field of semiology. Constant jammings and interruptions hampered the RALC, which became inaudible to its listeners. A real creative work of reconstruction, Fanon contends, was needed to fill the gaps and silences caused by such intermissions. The battle of the waves demanded the solidarity of its listeners and was 're-fought in accordance with the deep aspirations and the unshakable faith of the group'.[115] The jamming of the RALC's programmes, broadcast 'on the run', paradoxically, worked only to strengthen the resolve of the revolution.

By the virtue of its decentred voice and its 'phantom-like character', the radio expressed the centrality of the cause; it forced the people to choose between the rhetoric of the coloniser ('the enemy's congenital lie') and that of the revolution. In the battle to win the hearts and minds, the RALC countered colonial propaganda with its revolutionary ideology, 'the people's own lie, which suddenly acquired a dimension of truth'. The wireless, argues Fanon, was, at one and the same time, the medium and the guarantor for this 'true lie'.[116] The war of words, or better still counter-propaganda, not only helped re-enact the armed struggle against French colonialism but also mobilised and strengthened national consciousness.

Fanon underscores the ideological instrumentalisation of the radio: like language, the radio was not a neutral instrument. Prior to 1954, because it was considered an organ of colonialism, its messages were rejected outright.[117] The Algerian war, nonetheless, changed the attitudes of the colonised Algerians vis-à-vis this intrusive agent that came from the outside to invade and disrupt the harmony of traditional modes of sociability. This 'foreign technique' was no longer perceived as an instrument of coloniality. 'The phenomena of the wireless and the receiver set', Fanon maintains, 'lost their coefficient of hostility, were stripped of their character of extraneousness, and became part of the coherent order of the nation in battle'.[118] A genuine work of deconstruction was taking place: the French language was adopted in order to subvert the hegemonic meanings which it had thus far articulated. Broadcasting its programmes in French, Fanon ironically notes, the RALC liberated the coloniser's language from its historical significations. Just like the radio, the French language was no longer demonised but was able to express the messages of truth awaited by the Nation.[119]

A GENDERED RADIO TRANSMISSION:
THE BATTLE OF THE WAVES AND THE VEIL

Radio France Cinq was set up in 1937 as a broadcasting service for the settlers in Algeria.[120] Technical difficulties hampered transmission; broadcasting was initially relayed from France. Radio studios were then established in Algiers, Oran and Constantine, broadcasting programmes in Arabic in 1940 and in Berber in 1948. At the pinnacle of the Algerian war, Radio-Alger became an instrument of propaganda, and the aim of these programmes, namely the ELAK (Emissions des langues arabes et kabyles), was to promote colonial propaganda. At the beginning of the war, the number of small transmitters increased and broadcasting time in French, Arabic and Kabyle went up to cover an estimated 255,000 radio sets.[121] In 1956, 50-watt transmitters were installed in Constantine and in Algiers; 100-watt transmitters in Blida and Oran. In 1958, the RTF put in place a tropospheric transmission system to relay programmes directly from Paris.[122]

The 'transistor revolution' of 1955–56 coincided with the outbreak of the Algerian war. The radio was deployed not only by the FLN as a tool of anti-colonial propaganda in its liberationist struggle but also by the French army as a weapon of psychological warfare. At the outbreak of the war, the radio was put under the control of the ministeries of Foreign Affairs, the Interior, Information, Defence and Algerian Affairs. From 1954, the purchasing of radio sets was subject to registration, and in August 1955, Soustelle imposed restrictions on the sale of batteries.[123] As we have seen, three contexts determined such governmental interference: the Cold War and the monitoring of news by the GCR; the rise of nationalism and anticolonial propaganda of Radio Cairo; and the setting up of 'La Voix de l'Algérie' on 12 December 1956.[124] Radiophonic programming was subject to control and censorship under the Special Powers Act, which was passed on 12 March of the same year. As Frédéric Brunnquell documents, these three contexts impacted on the directions of France's broadcasting overseas, namely the Emissions vers l'étranger (EVE) and the programming of ELAK.[125]

To be sure, it was not the radio as such that altered the perception of Algerians vis-à-vis Western technology, which was once used as a tool of colonial propaganda; on the contrary, it was the emergence of national consciousness that gave the radio a revolutionary voice and changed traditional attitudes towards this implement of modernity.[126] As Fanon explains:

> Before 1954, the receiving instrument, the radiophonic technique of long-distance communication of thought was not, in Algeria, a mere neutral object. Looked upon as a transmission belt of the colonialist power, as a means in the hands of the occupier by which to maintain his stranglehold on the nation, the radio was frowned upon. Before 1954, switching on the radio meant giving asylum to the occupier's words; it

meant allowing the colonizer's language to filter into the very heart of the house, the last of the supreme bastions of the national spirit. Before 1954, a radio in an Algerian house was the mark of Europeanization in progress, of vulnerability. It was the conscious opening to the influence of the dominator, to his pressure. It was the decision to give voice to the occupier. Having a radio meant accepting being besieged from within by the colonizer. It meant demonstrating that one chose cohabitation within the colonial framework. It meant, beyond any doubt, surrendering to the occupier.[127]

Fanon presents the battle of the waves as an extension of the battle of the veil, thus gendering and sexualising the radiophonic message. The veil delimited the space occupied by the coloniser and the colonised, the public sphere and the private one. While the colonised Algerians led a cloistered existence, the veil provided a barrier which protected their stultifying tradition from colonial modernity. Radio-Alger was considered as the voice of the occupier which represented the dominant views of colonial France. As an instrument of coloniality, it threatened the stability of the colonised society and traditional behaviour of sociability;[128] it mediated Western cultural models, which were considered incompatible with 'the strict, almost feudal type of patrilineal hierarchy, with its many moral taboos, that characterises the Algerian family'.[129] This intrusive implement was rejected by Algerians who upheld traditional family structures and types of sociability.[130]

The public and private were two clearly demarcated spheres. Radio wave transmission, travelling at great speed, confused the lines of demarcation. The wireless, as an invisible intruder and agent of effraction, violated these lines by bringing the outside inside, allowing the coloniser to penetrate the colonised home. As a vehicle, it transported the voice of the coloniser, taking it into the confines of traditional domesticity. As an instrument of propaganda, it carried disembodied voices across space, infiltrating enemy positions: its slippery signifiers could neither be controlled nor policed. This interfering implement blurred boundaries between public and private, between men and women, between coloniser and colonised, between urban centres of colonial power and local villages off the beaten track, leading thus far a segregated existence. The radio was the first to connect the local to the global; and, arguably, it was the first harbinger that announced the advent of the 'global village'. In colonial Algeria, it challenged traditional fixity and upset the lines of demarcation separating the sexes, lines which were represented by the veil. During the Algerian war, Fanon fears that the radio enables the coloniser 'to filter into the very heart of the house, the last of the supreme bastions of the national spirit'.[131]

As has been noted, the significance of the radio as an implement of propaganda was not lost on de Gaulle, and 'La Voix de la France libre' played a key role in the Resistance. It is worth reiterating that Fanon's radicalisation was influenced by 'La Voix de la France libre'. In his essay 'This Is the Voice of Algeria', he draws inspiration from 'Ici Londres' but repurposes radio, specifically La Voix de l'Algérie combattante, as a weapon against supporters of French Algeria who facilitated de Gaulle's return to power. Scales's reading of 'This Is the Voice of Algeria' overlooks the significance of the context of the 1958 putsch and the instrumentalisation of the radio and the veil as tools of psychological warfare.

In the putsch of May 1958, Marc Martin observes, the radio played a significant role in two clearly defined directions. First, it became literally the mouthpiece of the Comité du Salut Public and of the generals who seized power.[132] Radio-Alger, in this respect, became an instrument in the hands of the insurrectionists, thus ensuring govermentality in the colony. Second, Radio-Alger maintained open lines of communication with mainland France. The wireless was, in Martin's words, 'the essential, and at times exclusive, vehicle for the messages intended for it by the Algerian authorities, and a first-rate propaganda agent'.[133] Radio-Alger filled the political vacuum which the putsch created in mainland France. The tone of its insurrectionist voice was threatening and yet reassuring: it was one of the media used to organise the fraternisation demonstrations and announce the solution to the political impasse; it averted the political crisis and brought France back from the brink of civil war.[134] The radio became, to borrow Antoine Sabbagh's terminology, the 'echo chamber' of the putschists in May '58. It became an instrument of warfare, deployed by the army to mobilise the population in mainland France and in the colony, as well as to 'inform, educate and control' – in other words, to manipulate public opinion.[135]

In 1956, RTF changed its policy of broadcasting exclusively in French. The introduction of two additional channels on France 5, broadcasting in dialectical Arabic and Kabyle, was part of its policy of psychological warfare. In the 1958 putsch, Massu's paras mobilised France 5, which meanwhile changed its logo, adopting the name of France V – 'V' denoting victory of French Algeria.[136] Echoing Fanon, Antoine Sabbagh maintains that psychological warfare targeted the Algerian woman. As he puts it:

On the Arabic and Kabyle channels, educational programmes, the exaltation of Arab wisdom, the regular broadcasting of traditional tales, in short, the deliberately folkloristic tone of the programming, seem rather dull compared to the incendiary accents of The Voice of Free and Fighting Algeria [RALC] which then denounces the 'martyrdom of Djamila Bouhired' and the tortures inflicted on the Algerian people. The only major innovation in these programmes comes from the multiplication of women's magazines: a social magazine for women, a housewife's magazine, a Muslim woman's magazine. This sudden attention reflects the concerns of psychological action officers eager, at least on paper and on the airwaves, to convince Muslim women, the essential pivot of Algerian society, traditional and matriarchal.[137]

Taking his cue from Macey, MacMaster dismisses the 'revolutionary romanticism' of Fanon that 'entertained an exaggerated radical optimism as to the potential of pro-independence radio to forge a new Algerian national and political consciousness'.[138] MacMaster underplays the impact the radio had on the Algerian people, especially on the liberation of women.

It should be kept in mind that listening to the radio was frequently a group or quasi-public process that was mediated by other women, kin and villagers and where there existed support for the FLN, or deep hostility to the occupying armed forces, French propaganda would have been either subjected to withering criticism, switched off or re-tuned to nationalist wavelengths. Algerian women listening at home were also highly selective as to what they chose to hear, and French research showed that the majority of women (59.3 per cent) preferred to listen to music and songs, rather than to news or current affairs (18.6 per cent). It seems unlikely that French radio broadcasts had any transformative effect on the emancipation of Algerian women, although the spread of the transistor radio into the isolated villages of the interior, in the absence of other means of mass communication, undoubtedly provided them with an important window on the rapidly changing events of the War of Independence.[139]

Listening to the wireless was a group activity, as Mokeddem shows in Les Hommes qui marchent, re-enacting Fanon's 'revolutionary romanticism'; in rural areas, Algerians huddled around the radio – the 'Tisf (pidgin French Algerian for 'TSF' which stands for 'Télégraphie Sans Fil' or wireless telegraphy/radio) – to capture news of the revolution.[140] Nonetheless, to debunk

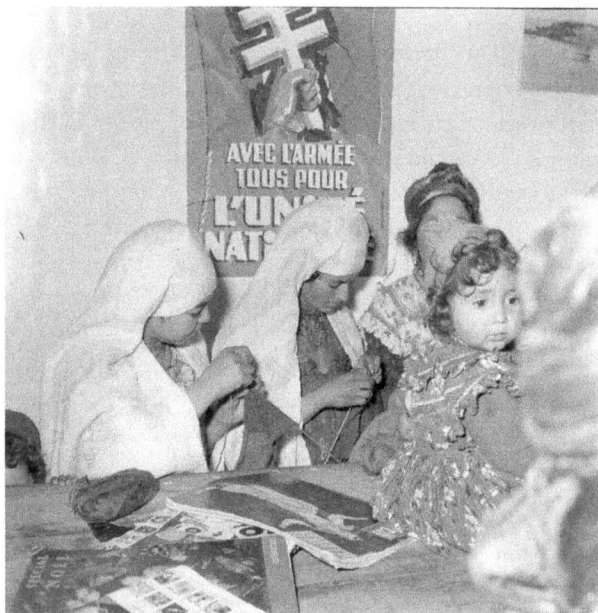

Photos 6 and 7. Women's Circle at Palestro offering sewing classes, run by rural social and health workers (ASSRA), PFAT (female Army personnel), and SAS officers. (© ECPAD)

this revolutionary romanticism, MacMaster uses a photograph depicting a group of Algerian women knitting and listening to the radio. Indeed, listening to the wireless was a 'quasi-public process', but in this instance, it was not mediated by a matriarchal figure, as MacMaster intimates. Rather it was organised and controlled by the Mouvement de solidarité féminine, working in tandem with the Fifth Bureau, during the fraternalisation demonstrations of May 1958. Visible to all is the propaganda paraphernalia on the wall and table: the Cross of Lorraine, symbol of both French Resistance and the putsch that brought de Gaulle to power; a hygiene guide, reflecting the dimensions of colonial nosopolitics; French magazines, notably the Spécial Noël issue, indicating the seasonal timing; and the radio at the table's centre – seemingly pulling back the veil on a private domestic scene, disrobing Algerian women. MacMaster is keen to emphasise the difficulty in assessing 'the impact of the mass media in changing basic attitudes or opinions'.[141] However, just as Scales does, he overlooks the gendering of the radio in his critique of Fanon: the battle of the waves was nothing but an extension of the battle of the veil, a battle in which the French attempted to conquer the last bastions that protected Algerian culture and society against French colonialism.

An analysis of Radio-Alger's coverage of the unveiling and burning of the veil ceremonies reveals its role in staging and propagandising these events. Radio-Alger and the Mouvement de solidarité féminine facilitated the ceremonies, operating at the intersection of noso- and biopolitics to infiltrate the domestic sphere. Through its broadcasts, Radio-Alger repeatedly enacted the unveiling of Algerian women, while the Mouvement de solidarité féminine served as a key instrument of psychological warfare. This sort of warfare reached its peak in the Battle of Algiers and continued thereafter via radio programmes such as Radio-Alger's 'Magazine de la femme' or Ici Alger's 'Courrier des auditrices', urging Algerian women to jettison the veil and espouse modernity.[142] A number of letters sent to Nadhyra, the presenter of 'Magazine de la femme', were published in Ici Alger; letters 'with different nuances [which] express the same point of view: education, modernism, equality'. In these letters, 'Muslim women ... are claiming their rights to education and life', and Radio-Alger emphasises 'the essential role that our wives, sisters and daughters can play in the construction of the new Algeria'. It also celebrates the 'awakening of all those who, shaking up traditions and customs, affirm their individual freedoms and contribute to building a 'modern society in various fields of life'.[143] A similar view is expressed in a petition sent to Radio Casbah, which called on Algerian women to jettison the garb of tradition which smothered them in their corporeality and impeded their education and progress.[144]

The women involved in these ceremonies were wives of ex-servicemen, or recruits from the slums of Algiers mobilised by the officers of the Section administrative urbaine and the Mouvement de solidarité féminine. Rejecting the propaganda claim that hundreds of Algerian women participated in the demonstrations, El Moudjahid contends that the very few who were involved were coerced by the army.[145] To amplify this message, 'La Voix des Arabes' and 'La Voix de l'Algérie arabe soeur' maintained that those who demonstrated were forcibly transported from the neighbouring villages of Algiers, Oran, Constantine and Bône.[146] Fanon reiterates El Moudjahid's position that those who participated in the unveiling ceremonies were, by and large, recruits from the lumpenproletariat: the destitutes and prostitutes, domestic servants, the hordes of vagrants and unemployed who existed at the margins of productive process and inhabited the slums of Algiers.[147]

Radio-Alger was not a neutral and passive transmitter of the events but was implicated in their organisation, calling on Birmandreis's inhabitants to demonstrate en masse.[148] On 19 May, after broadcasting Sid Cara's declaration, Radio-Alger issued a communiqué, 'Madame Massu parle aux femmes d'Algérie', to mobilise Algerian women and coordinate the fraternisation demonstration with a meet time of 5:30 pm at the Tagarins, where trucks would be waiting to take them to the Forum. Through the microphone of Radio-Alger, Algerian women were instructed 'to make [their] voice heard to ask to live in the new Algeria, in French progress and prosperity'.[149] Radio-Alger provided a commentary on the events that had taken place the previous evening at the Forum, which culminated in the unveiling ceremony and the burning of the veil.[150] On 18 May, it also presented a reportage on the fraternisation demonstrations which took place in the afternoon of the same day. At the Forum, Soustelle, Dr Sid Cara and Generals Jouhaud, Gilles, Allard, Massu and Salan were in attendance.

In this broadcast, Soustelle highlighted the importance of fraternal ties among those gathered at the Forum under the tricolour flag, emphasising unity without discrimination. He contended that detractors and doubters need only look at photographs or listen to the airwaves to grasp the historical significance of these events. Radio-Alger, re-enacting these events, detailed how Algerian women emerged out of a white sea of veiled faces to present Soustelle with a tricolour made out of their veils.[151] Speeches and declarations were delivered by Soustelle, Salan and Sid Cara; a statement was then made by a young Algerian girl to the Forum:

We, Muslim women ... realise how our traditional clothes, our existence of retreat ... distance us from our French sisters.... We want to firmly commit ourselves to the path of modernism and take advantage of the exalting era that Algeria is currently going through, to accentuate our development.[152]

This presentation, culminating with what Bourdieu calls the 'ceremonial rite' of unveiling, assumed a mythic dimension, as it obfuscated a hundred and thirty years of colonial discrimination and misogyny. By a coup de force, misogyny was deployed to service a feminist emancipatory discourse which was impregnated by colonial propaganda. In Sid Cara's and Soustelle's rhetoric, the tricolour emblematises at one and the same time Muslim women's liberation and their adherence to French imperiality. This propaganda, articulated in gendered terms, feminised and softened a bellicose putsch by exploiting the image of Algerian women. It employed an emancipatory discourse that purported to champion women's rights, while ultimately aiming to consolidate Franco-Algerian colonial relations.

In this regard, and as is evidenced by Sid Cara's declaration broadcast by Radio-Alger on May 19, the putsch was not a coup d'état but articulated a raison d'état which aimed at restoring France's sovereignty and colonial rule in Algeria. As Sid Cara intimates, the demonstrations were not 'gestures of hatred', 'outstretched fists', but expressions of fraternity, of friendship, of outpourings, of embraces between Europeans and Muslims': they were not 'demonstrations of revolt'; they were, on the contrary, a 'desperate appeal to the mother country'. In a significant reversal of politics, the putsch was not a coup against the French state, but came to signify the overthrow of Algeria's traditional patriarchy and sexual politics and targeted the Algerian woman who were considered as their matrix. Sid Cara concludes by reading a letter he received from a young Muslim girl from Algiers. Throwing into sharp relief the implication of the radio in the 'ceremonial of unveiling', the letter states: 'we are a large number of young Muslim girls who would like to reject the veil, but our parents refuse because of what people will say.... Give an order. We kindly ask you to broadcast this order on the radio ... so that our parents listen.'[153] In the new-found peace, Sid Cara is adamant that these young Muslim girls would evolve as French, if the parents listened. As an advocate of French Algeria, Sid Cara was entrusted to speak on their behalf, and thus came to supersede the unbending authority of the father. The putsch was effectively a coup against this figure epitomising patriarchy; it was also a coup against tradition which stood as an unsurmountable obstacle for integration. In this account, the radio was presented as an eloquent interlocutor for these silenced girls, an enabling mediator between father and daughter articulating the demise of patriarchy.

In the spirit of this mediation, Radio-Alger broadcast the unveiling ceremony of three 'Westernised' Algerian women organised on 20 May at the Forum. Lieutenant-Colonel Roger Trinquier presided over the ceremony during which these three young women proclaimed, by casting off their veils, the emancipation of Algerian women and announced the rapprochement of the latter with their European sisters.[154] Their pronouncements peddled the putschists' propaganda and colonialist rhetoric, emulating the infamous scenes of the burning of the veil which took place on 17 May at the Forum.

On 23 May, on the 13:00 news, Radio-Alger announced the arrival of generals Salan, Jouhaud, Massu at Mostaganem, following their visit to Oran; the three generals were accompanied by Soustelle, Sid Cara and Raymond Dronne. In Mostaganem, Massu, Salan and Soustelle addressed a crowd of 40,000 people; then, as per the ritual of the 'fraternisation' ceremony, a young girl, daughter and grand-daughter of ex-serving officers in the French army, was paraded in front of this crowd to express her support for French Algeria and advocate the emancipation of Algerian women. Emancipation was configured as an instance which was intimately interconnected with the maintenance of French Algeria, providing justification for the putsch as a raison d'état. Sid Cara applauded this new-found emancipation, intimacy and intermixing which were prohibited and rendered taboo by more than a century of French colonialism. In the discourse of Sid Cara, as well as that of the putschists, transmitted by Radio-Alger, a correlation was established between the future emancipation of Algerian women and the maintenance of French Algeria, between the latter and the safeguarding of the institutions of France's Fourth Republic, which were about to collapse. Simply put, the putsch was redefined, with some degree of agency, concurrently, as a raison d'état and as the *auto-da-fé* of Algerian tradition; the ceremonies of unveiling and the burning of the veil were presented as a call to de Gaulle to save the interests of the state in France and its colonial investments in French Algeria. The unveiled Algerian woman was cast in the symbolic figure of a new Marianne, the embodiment of the French Republic and its ideals of liberty, equality, fraternity.

The same ritual was re-enacted in Constantine on 26 May; Radio-Alger started broadcasting at 12:10 the fraternisation demonstrations which were overseen by General Nogues deputising for Salan. Sid Cara opened the ceremony by addressing the crowd. Then General Nogues read a statement written by Salan before allowing the Imam of Constantine to deliver a speech in Arabic. The Imam declared, 'Muslim men and women, you should know that we are free to exercise our religious practices in accordance with the principles of our religion', referring to principles that purportedly established equality between Muslim men and women. He debunked the myth of the veil, its 'imaginary' and 'exaggerated' forms which had 'nothing in common with the Muslim religion',[155] envisaging an important role for women in the social revolution which was taking place, and which could not be accomplished without France's political and cultural institutions. Following the Imam's pronouncements on the compatibility of Islam and French cultural institutions, Soustelle presented to the crowd a young Muslim girl, Miss Hamidé, the daughter of a prominent doctor in Constantine, who was asked to read a statement reaffirming the Imam's views.[156] At the applause of the crowd, Miss Hamidé took off her veil and threw it over the balcony of the podium. In Radio-Alger's reportage, this symbolic gesture not only consolidated the total and complete equality of Algerian women with their sisters of all faiths but was also an endorsement of French Algeria. What evidence can be gleaned from this sequence of events and from these voyeuristic and sexualised scenes which were broadcast by Radio-Alger?

The fraternisation demonstrations all culminated with unveiling ceremonies which reproduced the libidinous economy of French colonialism. Radio-Alger mediated this economy through its sound frequencies. Similar to Geisor's voyeuristic photography, Radio-Alger enacted the phantasm of the 'erotics of ravishment' that sought to conquer the Algerian woman. The mise-à-nu was simultaneously re-enacted through radio frequencies as 'airing' and 'disclosure', laying bare, unveiling and exposing, as well as making public, unfolding, and unmasking. Indeed, as Soustelle intimates, the airwaves of Radio-Alger and photography provided documentary evidence authenticating the events of May 1958 and capturing the participation of Algerian women in the ceremonies. Unlike photography, whose signifiers, as Barthes might say, carried within themselves their own referents, the airwaves transmitted disembodied referents, sounds disconnected from their objective points of reference and emission. During May 1958, both photography and radio actively captured and articulated this mise-à-nu, aiming to demonstrate that the unfolding of events coincided with the unveiling of Algerian women. These ceremonies interpellated Algerian women by initiating a process through which they would encounter French cultural identity. 'Frenchness' was presented to them for public acceptance and endorsement, reflecting the colonial power dynamics at play.

While photography froze the subjects of these events, radio maintained their dynamism, transporting them from the clamour of public spaces to the intimacy of domestic settings. Radio transmission blurred – or rather, violated – the boundaries between these spheres by introducing the coloniser's voice into the confines of traditional domesticity. Photography immortalised the act of unveiling in static images, centralising Algerian women in these events. In contrast, radio transmission functioned as a self-reflexive embedding, a *mise en abyme* that re-enacted the process of interpellation for all Algerian women. It revealed to them the (in)visibility of their secluded existence and invited their participation in the unveiling scenes. The unveiling ceremony, as the climax of these events, represented a dual violation of Algerian women in Radio-Alger's reportage. The initial violation occurred through the public, coercive act of unveiling, while the broadcast itself constituted a secondary violation through its re-enactment. Photography captured this moment as a fixed point in time and space, whereas radio, through its frequencies, disseminated the event to a broader audience, extending its reach and impact.

From this extended account on the radio's instrumentalisation during the Algerian war, we can discern several key insights. First, the radio played an active role in the events of May 1958, serving as an important device in organising and reporting on the unfolding situation. It functioned as a tool for instruction and mobilisation, particularly for women, mediating and re-enacting the mise-en-scène of unveiling and the burning of their veils, thus becoming a performative agent in the colonial spectacle. Second, it is crucial to acknowledge the inadequacies of two critical perspectives: MacMaster's critique of Fanon's 'revolutionary romanticism', arguing that Fanon hyperbolised the radio's potential to forge Algerian consciousness; and Scales's rebuttal of Fanon for overlooking the pre-existing auditory culture of Algerians in the 1930s and 1940s. Both overlook Fanon's nuanced portrayal of the radio as an ambivalent medium. Fanon underscores its dual function as an implement of colonial power and a voice for revolutionary resistance. He highlights its capacity to infiltrate Algerian homes and perpetuate colonial narratives, while also articulating and disseminating anticolonial sentiment. By recognising this duality, Fanon offers a comprehensive understanding of the radio's role in the Algerian struggle for independence. Third, psychological action extended the field of warfare, encompassing the 'battle of the airwaves' as the battle of the veil. Fanon emphasises the radio's gendered nature as an instrument of colonial intrusion into the domestic sphere, an aspect Scales overlooks. Fanon argues that radio technology penetrated private spaces, directly addressing women; he also cautions against its potency as a tool of colonial influence. This gendered dimension reveals the radio's dual role in both reinforcing and challenging traditional social structures within Algerian society. Last but not least, the radio made loud pronouncements on the emancipation of Algerian women, instructing and encouraging them to participate in the May 1958 events and the reconstruction of a new French Algeria. It announced itself as the harbinger of colonial modernity and emancipation. However, as we will see in Chapter 6, it was implicated as a retrograde and blunt instrument of torture. It bequeathed French psychological warfare the infamous *gégène*, which means 'questioning' in familiar and military vocabulary.

4

Republic of Cousins or Citizens?

French colonisation profoundly reshaped Algerian society, economy and politics, thereby transforming the prevalent mode of production. Marx's analysis of the Sénatus-consulte of 1863 and the Warnier Law of 1873 demonstrates how these colonial laws facilitated the systematic dismantling of traditional land ownership structures by expropriating native Algerians' land and precipitating the parcelisation of collective property.[1] Pre-colonial Algerian society was governed by gerontocracy, with the *aarch* (extended family) forming the basis of social and economic organisation. Homesteads were indivisible, as was collective land ownership, which passed down through generations. Marx observed that only the extended family was the subject of law defining land tenure, with the principle of land indivisibility surviving centuries of Arab and Turkish domination. French colonial laws aimed to dismantle the extended family and tribe as sociological units and destabilise their economy. This process of disintegration, driven by nineteenth-century bourgeois ideals of individual property rights, sought to break tribal resistance and facilitate colonial settlements. The Sénatus-consulte initiated the parcelisation of collective property, while the Warnier Law completed this process by exposing communal lands to market speculation. These laws were part of a broader social engineering programme that: triggered the breakdown of traditional economic, political and cultural structures; destabilised the foundations of a society based on blood relations and land indivisibility; facilitated the expropriation of indigenous property; and promoted colonial settlements. The colonial legal framework fundamentally altered Algerian society, weakening tribal resistance and paving the way for the imposition of French rule and capitalist economic structures.

In *The Algerians*, Bourdieu's observations further support this analysis, noting that the imposition of French judicial and administrative laws disrupted the social structures of colonised Algeria. Property laws, including the Cantonment of 1856–57, the Sénatus-consulte and the Warnier Law, were designed to destroy traditional economic and social structures. Bourdieu, citing A. de Broglie, a staunch proponent of the Sénatus-consulte, argues that this legislation had two primary objectives: first, to convert tribal lands into private property, making them available for European settlers, and, second, to dismantle tribal structures, which were viewed as impediments to colonial 'pacification'.[2] The consequences of these policies were devastating for the tribes. As an elder of the Ouled Rechaich tribe lamented: '[The French] killed our young men; they forced us to make a war contribution when they occupied our territories. All that was nothing; wounds eventually heal. But the setting up of private property and the authorisation given to each individual to sell his share of the land means the death sentence for the tribe.'[3] Whether openly acknowledged as an 'engine of war' or disguised under assimilationist ideology, these policies consistently prioritised European interests, weakening the foundation of indigenous culture through property laws, land sequestrations, expropriations, forestry regulations, and pasture land restrictions.[4] These policies enabled the alienation of common/tribal property, dispossessing the native population and uprooting them, forcing many to join the ranks of the lumpenproletariat. The rural population struggled to subsist, leading to rapid urbanisation. This process began with the famines of 1866–68 and 1893, and reached its peak after 1930, as poverty drove Algerian peasants from the countryside to colonial urban centres. The disintegration of organic communities, along with detribalisation and the rural exodus, produced the 'mass man' – uprooted, lacking tradition, values, and social ties, and existing outside legal structures and productive exchange.[5] This process weakened family unity, resulting in instability and overcrowding in unsanitary conditions, especially in cities. Echoing Marx's observation that collective property and homesteads in pre-colonial Algeria were inalienable, Bourdieu asserts that the extensive legal protections surrounding the agnatic group's property reflected the strong interconnections and integrity of the patrimony, the unity of the extended family, and the authority of the family head. French colonial laws in Algeria, particularly the Sénatus-consulte and the Warnier Law, weakened these interconnections, caused breaches in the system of collective property, and accelerated the disintegration of the family unit. By instituting property alienability, he argues, these laws dismantled traditional structures, dispossessed tribes, and undermined anticolonial resistance. Both Marx and Bourdieu highlight the intricate interplay of legal and political factors in shaping colonial Algeria's economy and society.

The extended family, the basic yet most fundamental social cell where diverse elements converged, was replaced by single-family units. Traditional society – comprised of 'interlocking communities' represented by 'concentric circles of allegiances', each with its own name, property and honour[6] – disintegrated into isolated individuals, leading to the disappearance of their sustaining traditions. The extended family stretched beyond the nuclear family, uniting multiple generations of agnates under a single patriarch whose unquestioned authority assigned each household and bachelor their place within the community. The mother, assisting her husband in managing family provisions, represented paternal authority within female society, earning her the moniker 'pillar of the community'.[7] The family was a fundamental unit – economic, political, and religious. It served as the foundational component of the entire system: the primary group, structural model for all groupings, and indivisible societal atom. The family assigned each member distinct roles and responsibilities. As the cornerstone of a way of life and tradition, it provided firm foundations and was steadfastly committed to preservation. Embedded within a network of shared interests, the family regarded the maintenance of coherence and stability as its prime objective, even at the expense of individual aspirations.

Tillion emphasises the significance of land (*arthe*) and women's honour (*irthe*) in colonised Algerian society, where elders managed the patrimony. These interrelated concepts defined what was forbidden to outsiders, with the *haram* signifying this prohibition. In traditional Algerian society, the primary concerns were safeguarding women and land from foreign encroachment. The tribes 'kept themselves to themselves' to maintain the principle of inalienable collective property, vital to their existence. These tribes were endogamous, and their endogamy had an economic edge. Tillion argues that endogamy served as a defence mechanism against the Koranic Revolution, which, by granting inheritance rights to women, threatened to undermine collective property and potentially lead to tribal disintegration. Before French colonisation, these tribes maintained a gendered spatial organisation that clearly demarcated public and private spheres. This arrangement allowed women to work and socialise freely among themselves without encountering men outside their family, so the issue of veiling did not initially arise.

It is important to emphasise that French colonialism systematically dismantled Algeria's long-standing principle of land indivisibility – a principle that had endured through centuries of Arab and Ottoman rule. The property laws enacted in 1856–57, 1863 and 1873 catalysed the disintegration of traditional tribal structures, fundamentally altering Algeria's socioeconomic fabric. The implementation of French colonial property laws led to widespread dispossession of Algerian tribes, forcing them to seek work in urban areas or mainland France. During periods of famine, masses of displaced vagrant-fellahs migrated to urban centres – the hubs of colonial power – in search of public charity. Tillion elaborates on this phenomenon in *Algeria: The Realities,*[8] and briefly addresses it in *The Republic of Cousins*, noting:

> [D]uring this period the rural exodus has further escalated and peasants are invading the suburbs and shanty towns by their thousands. The two phenomena have opposite results: on the one hand, town-dwellers are becoming citizens, to the greatest advantage of their country; on the other, we see haughty nomads, proud landowners, becoming 'vagrants'.[9]

French colonialism detribalised traditional society without fostering any conception of or respect for individual autonomy. Tillion observes that women's debasement was most severe in suburban areas. She argues that these intermediate and transitional spaces between rural and urban environments inflicted the most significant harm on women's status and rights.

> It is here, in these intermediate zones, that the greatest damage will be caused. Not in the traditional endogamous society, where marriage is *really* an affair between cousins; not in the intellectual society of the town, where the notion of 'human individual' has achieved some substance: but at every level lying between the two.[10]

The endogamous society, governed by gerontocracy, while denying individuals – especially women – inheritance rights, provided for them equitably within its familial and communal framework. Boys were treated as cousins and brothers, girls as sisters and cousins, and both sexes were cared for and supported by the economic and social structures that maintained the extended family. Tillion aptly dubbed this system the 'Republic of Cousins'.[11] French colonialism, through its systematic expropriation of native Algerians, precipitated the collapse of these traditional structures. Reframing Tillion's argument in Althusserian terms: the 'Republic of Citizens', ostensibly replacing the 'Republic of Cousins', interpellated native Algerians without truly individuating them. Instead, it subjugated them, consigning them to a state of stateless subjecthood. Tillion contended that the resultant social dislocation left women in a particularly vulnerable position, as they found themselves untethered from their traditional support systems yet simultaneously excluded from the full benefits of the new colonial order. This transition left them in a precarious legal position: subject to French laws but denied the sovereignty of citizenship. Women bore the brunt of this change, stripped of their status as 'cousins' within traditional structures, yet not recognised as full 'citizens' under the new system. This liminal state exacerbated their vulnerability and marginalisation in both the evolving colonial society and their own communities.

'The maximum degree of alienation, for women', argues Tillion, 'is encountered in mutant populations, ones detribalised by recent sedentarisation or urbanisation.'[12] To rephrase Tillion's assertion, insofar as the veil was a sociological manifestation of sedentarisation and urbanisation, one could say that it was also a key aspect of French colonialism. Quoting Bourdieu's *Le Déracinement*, she explains that women lived cloistered in cities because 'there is no longer any separate space for each social unit: the male space and the female space overlap.'[13] Urbanisation pulverised tribal society, displacing but not entirely overturning old structures. This process dichotomised colonial space and generated a Manichaean economy within the colony, characterised by 'two societies coexist[ing] side by side [...] mutually opposed, but conjoined.'[14] This coexistence of traditional and modern societal structures created a complex landscape where women's rights and roles were caught between conflicting social and cultural paradigms.

The closed, insular nature of colonial-era Algerian society and its retentive culture must be understood as a manifestation of colonial history and a reflexive response to colonial intrusion. Tillion's analysis highlights the complex interplay between tradition and modernity in shaping gender relations amid rapid social change, leading to the coexistence of conflicting societal norms and an incomplete evolution of endogamous practices. However, her theorising lacks clarity regarding the '*unfinished*' transformation of endogamy.[15] It is important to note that with colonisation and the parcelisation of land, endogamy lost its primary economic function and evolved to serve different purposes. No longer solely guarding inalienable family holdings, endogamy underwent a fundamental change in response to the expropriation, impoverishment and breakdown of extended families. It became a mechanism to protect against colonial intrusion by safeguarding women, thus acquiring a new cultural and political significance. This critique of endogamy's anticolonial role does not endorse its regressive impact on Algerian women and their marginalisation. Rather, it highlights Tillion's view that the veil, while stemming from urbanisation and detribalisation, paradoxically embodied colonial modernity and became a symbol of resistance against it.

Colonial laws in Algeria expropriated land and alienated the native population, creating a segregated state. Excluded from political citizenship, the colonised retreated to the private sphere, where religion and sexuality became crucial to preserving their cultural identity. This colonial imposition led to the ossification of social and traditional structures, establishing a stark division between family and society, symbolised by the veil. The pre-existing segregation of private and public spheres, rooted in endogamous sexual politics, was further exacerbated by colonial rule. Consequently, the veil acquired multifaceted significance, demarcating not only gendered spaces but also the boundary between coloniser and colonised. Colonialism disrupted but did not entirely dismantle endogamy, which traditionally regulated sexuality, maintained cultural identities, and ensured the transmission of cultural practices. Instead, it hardened endogamous structures and fostered colonial traditionalism. While land expropriation weakened the extended family economically, it did not erode endogamous practices, which remained a bulwark against French interference. In sum, colonialism fragmented family landholdings and social structures, weakening extended families, impoverishing their members and intensifying natalist tendencies. In response, Algerian society withdrew into the private sphere, using family life and religion as strongholds for resistance and cultural preservation. Understanding the impact of colonialism on endogamy is key to comprehending broader processes of cultural change and resistance in colonial Algeria. This complex interplay of colonialism and tradition shaped the trajectory of Algerian society and history, leaving a lasting impact on its social fabric and cultural identity.

Tillion argues that the urban cultural phenomenon resulting from detribalisation, caused by colonial expropriation, gave rise to a new personality type struggling to survive in urban environments. Crucially, this phenomenon separated male society and women. Women's status deteriorated further in suburban areas, which served as an intermediate space between rural and city life. While Tillion uses terms like 'detribalisation' and 'urbanisation' to discuss tribal disintegration, she fails to explicitly attribute this breakdown to colonialism or the implementation of specific laws. Her analysis lacks a direct acknowledgment of the colonial policies and legal frameworks that were instrumental in dismantling traditional tribal structures.

To understand how colonialism established an 'iron curtain'[16] between family and society, it is crucial to recognise that the alienation of women was not due to native culture's inability to adjust to urbanisation, as Tillion suggests. Instead, French colonialism, not Islamic laws, ultimately disintegrated a society built upon homogeneous family holdings. The Algerian society's tendency to 'keep itself to itself' and 'not communicate' was not a result of prevailing endogamous economic relations.[17] Rather, this behaviour was a response to the intrusive colonial gaze, prompting the society to shield itself from external scrutiny. The determining factors of this *retentive* culture lie in French colonial history and politics. Simply put, the 'Republic of Citizens' imposed by colonialism to replace the old structures governing the 'society of cousins' paradoxically led to its claustration. It erected this 'iron curtain', with the veil representing this disjunction between family and society. While the endogamous sexual politics of this society had already segregated private and public spaces, colonialism further complicated their interfacing. In colonial times, the veil acquired additional significance beyond its role as a signifier of patriarchy. It came to define not only the space occupied by men and women but also that separating coloniser from colonised. This divide clearly demarcated the public and private spheres and determined sexuality. Family life and religion served as spaces where culture was preserved and the colonial conflict was contested.

Like Tillion, Bourdieu presents the Algerian war as the outcome of 'the colonial policy and the clash of opposing civilizations'. This Manichaeanism was merely a manifestation of a society pulled in different directions by 'the hidden or open tensions that existed between the dominant European society and the dominated Algerian society'.[18] Unlike Tillion, Bourdieu attributes this Manichaeanism to the colonial system, which drove a wedge between these two antagonistic societies. Like Sartre and Fanon, Bourdieu contends that the Algerian war highlighted the internal logic of the colonial system, whose violence created scandalous inequalities and maintained colonial dominance over the natives.[19] However, colonial force was met with both symbolic and strategic resistance. This resistance was fuelled by 'the feelings of revolt and resentment aroused against this increase in social inequality and discrimination'.[20] Cultural institutions, particularly family and religion, deeply rooted in tradition, articulated this resistance. Fanon conveys this symbolic and strategic resistance in his discussion of the Algerian family and the historical dynamism of the veil. Drawing inspiration from Fanon, Tillion observes that the wearing of the veil was dwindling in cities while it was 'on the rise' in the countryside.[21] For Tillion, veiling and unveiling signified either women's marginalisation or their social mobility and embourgeoisement. She notes, 'the middle-class woman who [became] a great lady nowadays often signal[ed] this advance by discarding her veil'.[22] This observation appears to contradict her argument that the veil was tied to urbanisation, as it was in Algeria's cities that the veil was adopted, while rural women did not cover their faces. However, Tillion also notes signs of a reversal, with the veil declining in cities and more women adopting it in villages.[23] My project is not to expose this contradiction at the core of her thesis but to situate it historically within the context of Algeria's war of independence, specifically within Bourdieu's *The Algerians* and Fanon's 'Algeria Unveiled'. Echoing Fanon, Tillion writes, 'Algeria, where during the Seven Year War the veil played various strategic roles, is still going through a process of self-examination.'[24] Like Fanon, Tillion is adamant that women played a significant role in the Revolution, which she views as 'the work of modernist, not retrograde elements'.[25] She contends that in both urban and rural areas of Algeria, the veil gained symbolic importance in the struggle for independence.[26]

THE ALGERIAN FAMILY

Throughout the nineteenth and early twentieth centuries, colonialism attempted, with relative success, to break up the extended family in Algeria. Consequently, the couple emerged as the most significant social and cultural unit. The Algerian war altered the dynamics of conjugal relations, which had previously been based on women's subordination and confinement to domestic roles. After the 1954 revolution, traditional and cultural institutions that once defined the spaces occupied by men and women, and by husbands and wives, no longer held sway. As Fanon explains:

> The couple is no longer shut in upon itself. It no longer finds its end in itself. It is no longer the result of the natural instinct of perpetuation of the species, nor the institutionalized means of satisfying one's sexuality. The couple becomes the basic cell of the commonwealth, the fertile nucleus of the nation. The Algerian couple, in becoming a link in the revolutionary organization, is transformed into a unit of existence. *The mingling of fighting experience with conjugal life deepens the relations between husband and wife and cements their union. There is a simultaneous and effervescent emergence of the citizen, the patriot, and the modern spouse.*[27]

In his study of the Algerian family, Fanon argues that sexuality is a site marked by the colonial past, and that only revolutionary praxis could liberate the Algerian people from both the embrace of tradition and the shackles of colonialism, enabling them to enter the stage of world history. His observations on the changing dynamics of couples are significant in two respects. First, they illuminate the impact of French colonialism on the extended family. To maintain hegemony, colonialism attempted to control what Louis Althusser, the French Algerian cultural critic, terms the Ideological State Apparatuses (ISAs), specifically the family and religion of colonised Algerians. Second, Fanon's remarks highlight that these ideological sites became highly contested, paradoxically serving as both reactionary and revolutionary forces within Algerian society. To resist French colonialism, these ISAs were transformed into agencies of political resistance. Essentially, the colonial encounter played out at the intersection of private and public space, with the veil symbolising the materiality of this intersection. The tradition of veiling, although retrograde, functioned as a defence mechanism against colonial intrusion. 'We have seen', Fanon observes, 'the transformation of the Algerian woman taking place through her revolutionary commitment and her instrumentalization of the veil.'[28] This radical transformation affected not only family life but also the very constitution of Algerian society, contributing to the emancipation of Algerian women.

Fanon neither glorified the stultifying traditions of colonised Algeria nor eulogised the instrumentalisation of the veil. He denounced the cloistered existence of Algerian women and the nefarious effects French colonialism had had on the colonised tradition by reifying it into an ensemble of 'automatic gestures and archaic beliefs'.[29] He asserted that the freedom of the individual and the liberation of women should accompany decolonisation: the liberation of Algerian society was intrinsically linked to a sexual revolution and the emancipation of Algerian women from retrograde traditions.

The Algerian Revolution profoundly affected family structures and gender dynamics. The struggle for independence and French colonial repression caused severe trauma, often disrupting patriarchal authority. Fathers were frequently arrested, tortured, or killed in front of their children, leaving deep psychological scars. As a result, the traditionally cohesive Algerian family began to fragment, with individuals forced to confront new challenges and make independent decisions. The once-stable values guiding family life became ineffective in the rapidly changing social and political landscape. Women took on roles previously reserved for men, while children, exposed to the harsh realities of war, matured faster than their peers in more stable times. Despite these hardships, the Algerian family displayed remarkable resilience, remaining a crucial source of support and solidarity during the independence struggle.

The revolution also profoundly impacted the father–son relationship. Prior to 1954, nationalist activity introduced contradictions into the family structure, but the father's absolute authority as the epitome of colonial traditionalism remained intact. However, during the armed struggle, this authority was challenged as sons assumed autonomy and embraced the revolutionary cause. To defeat colonialism and build a new nation, Algerians had to undergo self-discovery and renewal. The group could no longer rely on the father to determine values; instead, individuals sought them as circumstances dictated. The Algerian family, previously structured, found itself in flux as the revolution unfolded. With a vague understanding of the emerging world, fathers felt disarmed and anxious in the face of their sons' revolutionary actions. Algerian society had to adapt to the radical mutations as gerontocracy was being dismantled with its old and stultifying structures and values. As Fanon writes, 'In the course of the multiple episodes of the war, the people came to realize that if they wished to bring a new world to birth they would have to create a new Algerian society from top to bottom.'[30] Fanon associates the father figure with tradition and the colonial 'universe of infinite waiting and resignation', while the son represents the revolutionary changes sweeping through colonial Algeria. Fanon insists that the demise of the father figure was concomitant with the collapse of the 'old paternal assurance'.[31] Having lost his standing, the father had to follow in the footsteps of his son, joining him on a new path of revolutionary praxis to effect change. The Algerian war curbed the once-absolute authority of the father, bringing about the 'defeat of the father' and changing the relationship between father and son.[32] This moment was, in more ways than one, Oedipal: the son displaced and replaced the father. Implicitly and explicitly, Fanon suggests that the revolution dealt a blow to this figure of gerontocracy. However, a critical question remains: did the revolution truly overturn patriarchy, or did it merely reshape its manifestations? While the traditional father figure lost authority, it is crucial to examine whether patriarchal structures were fundamentally dismantled or simply reconfigured within the new revolutionary context. This nuanced understanding is essential for comprehending the long-term implications of the revolution on Algerian family dynamics and gender relations.

If the son was 'emasculated' by tradition, the daughter was kept in a perpetual state of infancy, always considered a minor. At puberty, she was married off – a practice motivated not solely by economic considerations, but by the desire to avoid acquiring 'a new woman without status, a child-woman, in the house'.[33] While European women experienced three clearly defined periods before reaching maturity and entering adult life – childhood, puberty, and womanhood – their Algerian counterparts, according to Fanon, 'kn[ew] only two stages – childhood-puberty, and marriage'.[34] The

Algerian war fundamentally altered the dynamics of relationships between individuals and the extended family, between men and women, and between fathers and daughters. In the fight against colonialism, the old values governing sexual relations had to be rethought: women could no longer be silenced and kept in a state of perpetual minority. The Algerian woman could no longer be confined to a colonial state of domesticity; the war liberated her from her cloistered life.

The revolution in gender and sexual politics became an extension of the Algerian Revolution itself. As Fanon succinctly puts it: 'The unveiled Algerian woman, who assumed an increasingly important place in revolutionary action, developed her personality, discovered the exalting realm of responsibility. The freedom of the Algerian people from then on became identified with woman's liberation, with her entry into history.'[35] This transformation challenged deeply ingrained societal norms and patriarchal structures. By stepping out of traditional roles and engaging in revolutionary activities, women began to redefine their place in Algerian society. However, it is crucial to note that while the revolution provided opportunities for women's empowerment, the extent and permanence of these changes in post-independence Algeria remained a complex issue. The interplay between revolutionary ideals and deeply rooted cultural practices continued to shape the evolving status of women in Algerian society long after the war's end.

However, questions about endogamous morality and rectitude were rendered obsolete by the political developments occasioned by the war. 'The Algerian girl who was emerging into the agitated arena of history', Fanon argues, 'was inviting her father to undergo a kind of mutation, to wrench himself free of himself.'[36] The revolution did away with traditional values, which were 'sterile' and 'infantil[ising]'. Fanon is adamant that the conduct of militant girls followed patterns that transcended 'traditional standards'.[37] Alluding to their involvement in the Battle of Algiers, he goes on to add:

This woman who, in the avenues of Algiers or of Constantine, would carry the grenades or the submachine-gun chargers, this woman who tomorrow would be outraged, violated, tortured, could not put herself back into her former state of mind and relive her behavior of the past; this woman who was writing the heroic pages of Algerian history was, in so doing, bursting the bounds of the narrow world in which she had lived without responsibility, and was at the same time participating in the destruction of colonialism and in the birth of a new woman.[38]

Fanon argues that women's participation radically altered gender attitudes, replacing the 'woman-for-marriage' ideal with the 'woman-in-the-Revolution' concept. The revolutionary struggle imposed new dynamics on traditional household roles, radicalising couples in their armed resistance against French colonialism. United militant couples emerged as robust units of the commonwealth, collaborating against the oppressive regime. Notably, the 'individual' and the 'couple' – sociological constructs born from colonial fragmentation of extended families – developed as rediscovered, willed foundations of the nascent nation. However, it is crucial to avoid a one-sided interpretation. The war compelled the entire Algerian population to engage fully in the anticolonial struggle. In regroupment camps, women organised FLN cells, exchanged experiences of repression, and often joined the Armée de libération nationale (ALN). Fanon maintains that massive population displacements profoundly disturbed the social fabric. He details the hardships endured by civilians under brutal pacification measures, describing destroyed villages, fleeing men, and the disappearance of traditional mourning rituals as deaths became frequent and violent. He asserts that the war's dislocation of Algerian society led the people to hold France responsible for all inflicted wounds until independence was achieved.

In 'The Algerian Family', Fanon expands on one of the key themes he discusses in the first chapter of *Studies in a Dying Colonialism*, 'Algeria Unveiled': the historical dynamism of the veil. It is obvious that he wrote to protest against the rape, torture and violation of the Algerian woman as part of the psychological warfare undertaken by the Fifth Bureau to break the unity of the Algerian family and of the revolution. The intensification of the war, with the pacification policy undertaken by the French army, namely the policy of scorched earth and the resettlement of Algerian families in so-called regroupment camps, led to the displacement of more than one third of the population. Tens of thousands were forced to seek refuge in Tunisia and Morocco. The policy precipitated the physical fragmentation of Algerian society and the dislocation of the family. Nonetheless, the war created stronger bonds between its members. Paradoxically, in its attempt to break the will of the Algerian people and destroy their resistance, French colonialism strengthened their resolve. Fanon is adamant that 'this physically dispersed people is realising its unity and founding in suffering a spiritual community which constitutes the most solid bastion of the Algerian Revolution'.[39]

PACIFICATION AND CARE

In the mid-1860s, a locust invasion, combined with drought and typhus, devastated Algeria. Several precursor events aggravated the problem: in autumn 1863, a massive fire ravaged forests in the Constantine region; in spring 1864, swarms of locusts appeared, carried by persistent sirocco winds; political unrest against the French, followed by repressions, worsened the situation and, in 1865, new fires engulfed all coastal forests from Tunisia to Morocco. Extreme drought prevented seed germination in some areas. The disaster worsened when locusts invaded again in April 1866, transforming scarcity into calamitous famine. An earthquake on 2 January 1867, and a cholera epidemic in June, compounded the famine. Cholera primarily affected the indigenous population, killing an estimated 86,791.[40] In autumn 1867, starving people marched across Algeria, surrounding towns. Typhus spread rapidly, with contagious individuals ruthlessly excluded from cities. In Oran alone, typhus killed 2,743 out of 35,000 inhabitants.[41] 1867 became known as 'the year of death'.[42]

The administration turned a blind eye to the plight of the indigenous population, officially denying the famine and typhus. It is estimated that about 1 million people in Algeria, a third of its native population, died due to famine, diseases, the violent conquest and the repression of the 1871 El-Mokrani revolt.[43] The catastrophe raises questions about colonial responsibility. Spared from starvation, Europeans made little effort to aid indigenous people, with some even refusing to advance grain for seeding. Clergy members provided relief, establishing hospices and founding orphanages. Historians like Annie Rey-Goldzeiguer strongly blame France, citing the repression of the 1864 uprising and the military governors' failure to grasp the situation's gravity.[44] The colonial power proved incapable of mitigating the disaster. Poor transportation infrastructure and the destruction of traditional structures hindered aid efforts. Despite the devastation, a message of hope emerged in the demographic recovery that followed, defying predictions of the extinction of Algerian Arabs. The population nearly doubled from 2,931,000 in 1866 to 5,158,000 in 1906.

I begin this final section of the chapter with a brief historical account of the devastating famine in Algeria during 1867–8, drawing from Pierre Darmon's 'L'année de la mort'. I reference the famine to contextualise not only the forces that led to the breakdown of traditional social and economic structures sustaining the extended family, and thereby motivated urbanisation, but also the contradictory workings of colonial biopolitics. This context is crucial for understanding the development of healthcare and assistance institutions, as outlined in Chapter 1. Moreover, this contextualisation helps us frame the establishment of the Sections administratives spécialisées (SAS) as a medico-administrative unit and draws parallels between pacification efforts in the nineteenth century and during the Algerian war.

What insights can we glean from the detailed account in Chapter 1 regarding the role of healthcare and assistance in the conquest and colonisation of Algeria? Chapter 1 details the complex and often contradictory role of healthcare in the colonial context, serving simultaneously as a means of assistance and a mechanism of control. This historical context is highly pertinent to Fanon's *Studies in a Dying Colonialism*, particularly in its exploration of the interplay between gender, medicine and colonialism. As has been pointed out, the economy of care – especially colonial hygiene – helped institute and maintain the Manichaeanism that divided colonial society. Care was not merely a medico-administrative service; it functioned as an almost exclusively military operation, crucial in both the conquest of Algeria and the maintenance of colonial domination. The *bureaux arabes*, established by Bugeaud in the early 1840s, administered this care alongside one of the most devastating tactics of warfare: the *razzia*. After the failure and abandonment of the *bureaux arabes*, Cambon employed care to mitigate the pernicious effects of colonial policies. These policies promoted settlements, expropriated land, uprooted and displaced the native population, broke down family unity, and ultimately led to the fragmentation of Algerian society. At the height of the Algerian war, Soustelle and Lacoste pursued a strategy similar to Cambon's. This historical continuity underscores the enduring role of healthcare as a tool of colonial power, a theme that resonates strongly with Fanon's analysis in *Studies in a Dying Colonialism*.

Soustelle was appointed Governor-General on 26 January 1955, just days before the collapse of Mendès-France's government on 5 February. Upon his arrival in Algeria on 15 February, assisted by Tillion, he visited the Aurès region. It became apparent to Soustelle that poor administration of rural regions in what were hitherto called the '*communes mixtes*', and the lack of intelligence, hampered the success of French military operations. This visit brought to mind those of Cambon, Chellier and Soulié in the same region, who had previously administered care, provided assistance and helped alleviate the dire conditions of the native population suffering from famines and diseases in the late nineteenth and early twentieth centuries. The SAS were established by Soustelle in September 1955 to remedy the poor administration that had created a chasm between central government representatives and the colonised territories, seen as one of the causes of the widespread rebellion. The SAS, conceived as the cornerstone of France's pacification policy, revived the tradition of the *bureaux arabes*. Officially established in 1844 and tasked with administering the *communes mixtes*, the *bureaux arabes* provided care, policed tribes, ensured tax collection and executed summary justice. Their officers, simultaneously soldiers, health-carers, informers, administrators, judges and executioners, carried out comprehensive policing: surveilling all aspects of public life, mobilising economic resources for colonisation, and administering justice and health.[45] The establishment of civilian rule in Algeria in 1870 ended this institution (except in the Southern Algerian Territories, which remained under military rule) that had ensured permanent contact with the population. The demise of the *bureaux arabes* coincided with a period of economic hardship between 1866 and 1868, marked by a massive rural exodus as Algerians faced famines and epidemics, alongside settlers gaining control of the civilian government.[46] Oblivious to the failures of the *bureaux arabes*, Lacoste praised the SAS for continuing their tradition.[47]

The SAS emulated the *bureaux arabes* not only in administration but also in medical and social assistance ostensibly brought to assist deprived rural populations.[48] They oversaw agricultural work, administered health services, provided education, and built infrastructure to reconnect remote areas to colonisation centres. Basic health and education were the two main foci of each resettlement camp, which typically included a dispensary, school, social centre, *café maure*, and grocery shop.[49] The SAS (and their urban counterparts, the Sections administratives urbaines [SAU]) constituted the central plank of colonial biopolitics during the decolonisation period. A crucial element of this biopolitical strategy was the purported emancipation of Algerian women, primarily promoted through home economics programmes at women's centres.

It would be misleading to view the SAS as mere 'charity and welfare offices' (Bureaux de bienfaisance et d'assistance), working for the benefit and betterment of the native population. Much like the *bureaux arabes*, they were apparatuses of colonial control and domination. From 1956 to 1959, the colonial territory was strategically demarcated into three zones: 'pacified' areas, zones in open conflict, and no-go areas.[50] In zones where the ALN established its bases, the rural population was forcibly displaced. This pacification process re-activated the massive waves of rural-to-urban migration of the late nineteenth and early twentieth centuries, as well as the rural exodus of the 1920s and 1940s. These movements had previously driven the dispossessed rural population to the outskirts of city centres, where the first *bidonvilles* (slums) were erected. This exodus gave rise to what Fanon termed the *lumpenproletariat*, a class subsisting at the margins of colonial society and its economic processes. These areas became hotspots for epidemics due to poor sanitation, but also fertile ground for germinating anticolonial politics. Pacification, in its attempt to clear sites of ALN resistance, merely displaced the issue elsewhere. Initially, before the creation of the so-called 'regroupment centres', the uprooted rural population either resettled in neighbouring towns and villages or moved to the *bidonvilles*. These slums became eyesores in the cities and posed a serious threat to the edifice of French colonialism.

The policy of resettlement became a key military strategy in pacification efforts between 1958 and 1959. In 1959, the Inspection générale des regroupements de la population (IGRP) was established to monitor and contain the threat posed by the proliferation of resettlement centres and to end chaotic resettlements that exacerbated the problem of *bidonvilles*.[51] The IGRP reported on resettlement activities, including the number of people involved, housing, schooling, medical, and economic resources. In 1955, under the command of General Parlange, the first SAS and resettlement camp were set up in the Aurès region. In 1959, the Challe plan initiated the systematic clearing of the population from military zones of operation and implemented an official policy of resettlement with the creation of the IGRP, led by General Parlange.[52] As Fanon notes, the Challe plan aimed to 'cut the [Algerian army of liberation] off from the people' by alienating it from its support base, namely the rural population. Fanon laments that 'the French authorities have recently officially recognised the existence of one million displaced, regrouped Algerians'. According to IGRP reports, by 1961, 2,380 centres contained 1,868,545 resettled people. Michel Cornaton estimated that 2,350,000 people, representing one-third of the rural population and more than one-fourth of the entire Algerian population, were uprooted and displaced from their villages.[53] The pacification and resettlement policies led to the dislocation of Algerian society and the obliteration of its economic and social structures, as documented by Bourdieu and Sayad in their study.[54]

The pacification strategy relied heavily on intelligence gathered by the SAS to exert control over the rural population. In the countryside, the SAS played a role akin to that of the SAU in managing the overcrowded neighbourhoods and shantytowns of major cities. Both entities were strategically deployed to infiltrate, control, and alienate the ALN from the rural and urban populations. The forced resettlements had traumatic effects on the population and disastrous consequences for the rural economy. General Salan hailed the pacification strategy as a success, claiming it contained four-fifths of the population and maintained security. However, this so-called success came at an enormous human cost. The pacification strategy re-enacted the unspeakable violence of Algeria's colonial conquest, perpetrating atrocities against the civilian population, including murder, rape, expropriation, and the displacement of entire communities. As Mohamed Harbi lamented, the entire country was effectively transformed into a massive concentration camp.[55]

The strategies employed by the SAS to support the French army in uprooting the rural population were far from benevolent. SAS officers, wielding special powers, blurred the lines between military and civilian institutions. Although ostensibly tasked with 'instructing, caring, advising', and 'serving' the native population, they primarily functioned as extensions of the army, furthering its strategic interests. The SAS, akin to the first aid stations, mobile units of the 1920s and 1930s, and the 'auxiliary' hospitals and infirmaries established by Cambon and Jonnart, were not purely medical institutions aimed at caring for the deprived indigenous population. Their work extended beyond clinical practice, embodying aspects of *médicine de colonisation*. In 'Medicine and Colonialism', Fanon decries this nosopolitics, condemning not only medicine's role as an ideological apparatus promoting colonialism but also its blatant instrumentalisation by the army as a weapon of war. As French colonialism entered its final stages, the SAS became a crucial tool of colonial biopolitics. Their role in resettling and controlling the Algerian population exemplified the complex interplay between medical care, administrative control, and military strategy in the dying days of French colonial rule.

Throughout Algeria's colonisation, biopolitics worked consistently to optimise the conditions of life and work for European settlers while severely curtailing those of the native population. The military strategies adopted during this period gave rise to a nosopolitics that devastated Algerian society. Biopolitics, defined as the administration and management of life, sought to ensure public health and accumulate wealth. Nosopolitics, as an instrument of biopolitics, optimised life and work through health policies. In democratic France, biopolitics and nosopolitics ostensibly functioned positively.

However, in colonial Algeria, these processes were manipulated to serve colonial interests. In Algeria, biopolitics and nosopolitics assumed dual functions. On the one hand, they optimised the conditions of life and work for European settlers by expropriating the indigenous population. On the other, they became tools of colonial oppression, bringing poverty, famine and disease to native society. Fanon decried this politics of life and health, highlighting its complicity with colonialism. He and the publication *El Moudjahid* condemned the 'forbidden zones' – areas demarcated by the French army after 'clearing' and resettling the rural population. Fanon described these no-go areas as zones of 'forbidden life' and the regroupment centres as 'camps of slow death'.[56] The entire population was at the mercy of the army, which exercised the power of life and death over them.

On 11 April 1959, in an interview with the newspaper *La Croix* following his return from Algeria, where he visited the 'regroupment centres', Mgr Jean Rodhain, General Secretary of the Catholic Relief Service, dismissed claims that French methods of regrouping were unrelated to what are known as reservations.[57] On 18 April, *Le Monde* published a report revealing the appalling conditions of these centres, which represented – economically, socially and psychologically – one of the most painful, previously untold aspects of the Algerian war.[58] At the request of Paul Delouvrier, General Delegate of the French Government in Algeria from December 1958 to November 1960, six investigators inspected fifteen centres in Orléansville, Tiaret and Blida. Michel Rocard consequently wrote a report condemning the regroupment camps where 2 million peasants were allegedly 'herded'. After spending several months travelling across Algeria, he discovered that thousands of people were at risk of starvation, with the authorities seemingly indifferent to their plight. Rocard estimated that 200,000 people, mostly children, had died from hunger. On 17 February 1959, he submitted his report to Paul Delouvrier. After being passed to senior officials and leaked from a ministerial office, the report was published on 17 April 1959 in *France-Observateur*, and the following day in *Le Monde*, causing considerable embarrassment to both Rocard, the author, and Delouvrier, as well as to the French authorities.

The conclusions of the report were damning: the conditions of those who had been relocated were dire and urgent action was needed to provide them with basic sustenance. From the outset, the report states that these wretched centres were created by military authorities to carry out the 'closure' or 'cleaning' of areas where pacification was in progress.[59] The report estimates that by 1958, 1 million people had been displaced to these centres, with nearly two-thirds of the resettlements occurring in the previous year, 1957. It also anticipates an increase in resettlements in 1959, as SAS officers and military commanders employed them as a tactic for containing and managing a 'troublesome' population. Each centre accommodated more than 800 people, comprising between 100 and 150 families, primarily women and children. The report specifies that the number of children

Photo 8. Fifth Bureau propaganda tract captures regroupment centres as sites of abject deprivation and slow death. The tract targeting Algerian women says: 'Inhabitants of the Douars: What will you eat this winter? Do you believe the *fellaghas* will be able to supply your douar … and feed your children?'.

was significantly high, representing, in some instances, three-quarters of the resettled population.[60] Hygiene in the centres was deplorable. In *Studies in a Dying Colonialism*, Fanon alludes to the disturbing findings of the report, stating:

> One million hostages behind barbed wires, and now the French themselves sound the alarm: 'Medication no longer has any effect on these regrouped people, so great is their physiological deterioration.' What then? Colonialism is fighting to strengthen its domination and human and economic exploitation.[61]

Fanon powerfully conveys the grim realities of colonialism; his words serve as a stark reminder of the human cost exacted by this oppressive system and its bio- and nosopolitical practices.

According to the report, the French policy of 'regroupment' led to the collapse of traditional economic structures, forcing resettled individuals to abandon their grain reserves kept in the *matmoura*, described as 'both a guarantee and an essential symbol of the family head's social prestige'.[62] The report, emphasising the gravity of the situation, states: 'The abandonment or confiscation of the *matmoura* signifies that the head of the family [could] no longer feed his family.'[63] This collapse resulted in the loss of family autonomy and self-sufficiency, with significant consequences for social standing, livelihood and dignity. The report estimates that 200,000 individuals found themselves in a precarious situation, without resources of their own. These displaced people received irregular and meagre rations, sometimes amounting to a mere 11 kilograms of barley per adult per month. This pitiful allocation was particularly challenging for households with young children. Distributions of food, clothes, medicine and health-related aid were disrupted intermittently, leaving vulnerable families without critical resources. In some locations, distributions ceased for as long as a month and a half. [64] The resettlement policies pursued by the French army led to the widespread impoverishment of the rural population, who lost both land and livestock. The assistance provided by the SAS was often insufficient and delayed. As *Le Monde* reported on 24 July 1959: 'The population lived on semolina distributed by the Administration. Each resettled person is given 120g of semolina a day.'[65] Similarly, *Témoignage chrétien* reported in June 1959 that the consequences of this assistance resulted in the utter dehumanisation of the natives, who were left in a state of complete dependency on the French army and SAS command.[66]

Following the report's publication in *Le Monde*, *El Moudjahid* responded with two articles: 'Colonialist Barbarity' on 24 April and 'Pacification at an Impasse: The Regroupment Camps' on 10 May 1959. These articles, likely authored by Frantz Fanon, were written concurrently with *Studies in a Dying Colonialism*. Drawing on the report's findings, the articles vehemently denounced the regroupment centres as sites of abject poverty. They equated the French 'pacification' strategy to the brutal *razzia* tactics of the past, highlighting how civilian populations were targeted in retaliation for ALN incursions. Echoing themes from *Studies in a Dying Colonialism*, the articles condemned the forced displacement of 1 million Algerian civilians. To fully appreciate the significance of these two articles, it is crucial to consider them

يا نساء الجزائر

المتنة الغاشمة
خلت دياركم بلا رجال
و أولادكم بالجوع

Photo 9. Fifth Bureau propaganda tract exploits women's fears, blames 'barbaric rebellion' for family breakdown and hardship. The text says: Women of Algeria / the barbaric rebellion / is for you / the house without men / fear and misery / hungry children.

alongside other contemporaneous pieces that explored themes central to *Studies in a Dying Colonialism*. On 1 November, *El Moudjahid* published excerpts from the chapter 'The Algerian Family', which traced the experiences of Algerian families amidst the intense resistance against pacification efforts. Two weeks later, on 16 November, excerpts from 'Algeria Unveiled' appeared under the title 'Algerian Girls and Women in the Revolution'. 'Colonialist Barbarity' and 'Pacification at an Impasse' employ a similar idiom to *Studies in a Dying Colonialism*, vividly describing the upheavals brought by the revolution to Algerian society and families. They emphasise how the war served as a catalyst in radicalising the Algerian people, particularly women, as they confronted the challenges of decolonisation.

While editorial work in *El Moudjahid* was collective, as Cherki notes, 'Colonialist Barbarity' and 'Pacification at an Impasse' distinctly echo Fanon's voice. These articles present the regroupment centres as cells of organised resistance and highlight the crucial role of women in the struggle, mirroring themes in *Studies in a Dying Colonialism*. Both the articles and Fanon's book critically evaluate the French army's resettlement policy, which aimed to isolate the Algerian population from the ALN. They argue that the tactic of 'cloistering' over 1 million people paradoxically consolidated the struggle and radicalised the population. The articles assert that within the camps, repression gave rise to national consciousness, contrary to the colonisers' intentions. While exposing the appalling conditions in the regroupment camps and assessing the strategic aims of isolation, the *El Moudjahid* pieces contend that colonialism's goals were not achieved. Instead, they argue that the highest forms of political consciousness emerged within the Algerian family structure under these harsh circumstances.[67] These articles appear to reinforce key themes from *Studies in a Dying Colonialism*, particularly in their nuanced understanding of Algerian women's roles and the use of media to challenge colonial power. Discernible intertextual references to chapters like 'Algeria Unveiled' and 'This is the Voice of Free Algeria' invoke women's participation in the revolution and highlight how the voice of free Algeria infiltrated and subverted the colonial regime.

The regroupment camps served as sites of confinement for women and children, their imprisonment described as a form of 'claustration'.[68] The language used in these articles to depict this containment invokes Orientalist imagery, but in a subversive manner. These camps are portrayed as obscene 'gynaecea' of pacification, representing the cloistering of the entire rural population, mainly women and children. Paradoxically, despite being centres of misery and alienation, these camps became crucibles of liberation. Fanon's account transforms the grim reality of 'concentration-camp Algeria'[69] into a narrative of emerging freedom. He posits that from this cloistered and interned Algeria, a new nation would arise – an Algeria unveiled and revolutionised. This juxtaposition of confinement and liberation creates a powerful narrative arc. The very spaces intended to suppress the Algerian population become, in Fanon's analysis, the birthplaces of a new national consciousness. The transformation from oppression to emancipation within these confined spaces underscores the resilience and revolutionary potential of the Algerian people, particularly women.

In 'concentration-camp Algeria', the displaced population consisted mainly of women and children, confined to areas surrounded by barbed wire near military posts and SAS offices. This internment stemmed from auxiliary institutions of 'care' that quarantined and segregated the native population. Describing confinement in regroupment camps as 'claustration' evokes the nosopolitics of Cambon, Soulié, and Chellier, who claimed to 'liberate' Algerian women from the 'gynaecea'. These institutions viewed cultural traditions as sources of disease and morbidity. In their drive for colonial hygiene, they equated Algerian women's 'backward' traditions with communicable diseases, treating both as interrelated problems. This description also recalls the emancipatory rhetoric of the Women's Solidarity Movement (MSF), which condemned Algerian women's traditions as obstacles to colonial progress. However, this rhetoric often clashed with political realities, particularly in the harsh conditions of regroupment camps, where women's confinement directly contradicted the alleged goals of liberation. As discussed in Chapter 1, the health propaganda campaign led by Cambon and executed by Chellier reinforced French sovereignty by targeting the domestic and social lives of Algerian women. Following the 13 May 1958 crisis, the MSF continued this campaign, ostensibly to emancipate Muslim women but actually to undermine nationalist sentiment and strengthen French control. The MSF's medico-administrative programme was a key part of a wider strategy to assert control over Algerian society, particularly by targeting women's roles and spaces. While publicly advocating the liberation of Algerian women, the MSF's actions consistently violated their basic human rights.

The French regroupment camps yielded mixed results in isolating the ALN from rural populations. While most internees remained loyal to the independence movement, the French successfully recruited some for the *harka*. On 4 February 1958, Lacoste outlined a three-phase approach to pacification and administration in a letter to the *Inspecteurs généraux de l'administration en mission extraordinaire* (IGAMEs) and Prefects, emphasising the importance of SAS chiefs in civic and social action, youth programmes, and education. This three-phase strategy was a key aspect of the counter-insurgency and psychological action based on a destruction/reconstruction approach. Lacoste described it as a 'comprehensive strategy' combining military, administrative, and social efforts to maintain French control in Algeria. In this strategy, *harkas* and women were assigned important roles in pacification efforts. *Goums* and *harkas*, units of native Algerian soldiers recruited to serve under French officers, were instrumental in the SAS's efforts to regain control of populations in regions affected or threatened by FLN activities. These indigenous units supported the SAS mission by helping to reconnect with local populations, restore their confidence, reintroduce them to administrative processes, and rebuild respect for the French presence. The ultimate goal was to bring these populations back into the French community. By leveraging these native units, the SAS aimed to bridge the gap between the French administration and the Algerian population, countering the influence of the FLN while promoting French political legitimacy.

Photo 10. The Catinat Women's Self-Defence Group, formed in January 1959, consisted of 18 Algerian women trained and equipped by the Catinat SAS officer to protect and monitor the *douar*. (© ECPAD)

In the so-called '*douars en autodéfense*', under SAS command, *harkis* were recruited to protect these areas from FLN incursions; Algerian women were armed – or rather weaponised[70] – as they became targets of the French army's propaganda war. A notable example was the mobilisation of the Catinat women.[71] In December 1959, photographer Léonec Kierzkowski from the French army Cinematographic Service in Algeria reported that a group of *auto-défense féminine*, comprising twelve armed women, was allegedly formed by SAS officer Lieutenant Ontrup. Patrick Buisson claims that the intention was to extend the *harka* to include women. The photographic images of Algerian women donning the French army uniform – the symbol par excellence of political assimilation and cultural conversion – demonstrate that French army lieutenants like Ontrup could not only unveil them but also recruit them to the *harka*, just as the FLN recruited women to the service of the revolution. As the battleground shifted, the strategy crystallised around the figure of the Algerian woman, re-enacting the unveiling ceremonies of May 1958 and countering the historical dynamism of veiling in the Battle of Algiers. However, the SAS's attempts to instil rudimentary home economics and social hygiene in Algerian women[72] and recruit them to the *harka* were key tactics in a fierce conflict with the *Organisation politico-administrative* (OPA/ALN) over control of the rural population, which became a crucial element in the war.

The OPA/ALN perceived the resettlement centres and the associated social actions – such as education, health and assistance – as serious threats to the revolution. To thwart the SAS initiatives and propaganda efforts, the OPA itself provided economic aid and medical assistance, and dedicated an editorial in *El Moudjahid* entitled 'Journal d'une maquisarde' to celebrate the contributions of Algerian women to the revolution. Fanon's *Studies in a Dying Colonialism*, situated within this context, captures the conflict between the SAS and the OPA by exploring the centrality of Algerian women in the revolution, the ramifications of France's resettlement policies, psychological warfare, and the complicity of medicine and colonialism.

The SAS posed a serious challenge to the FLN by deploying its detachments against the Algerian insurgents in its counter-insurgency programmes. Additionally, functioning as a medico-administrative entity, the SAS used the rhetoric of women's emancipation and gender and sexual politics as levers in the pacification process. However, the OPA/ALN's primary concern was the high proportion of women and children in the camps. They feared sexual violence as a French tactic to divide Algerian society, with reports of women being exploited and girls recruited as *harkis*. The OPA/ALN viewed control over women and families as crucial to their claims of sovereignty. Consequently, the camps became battlegrounds not just for military control, but for issues of women's sexuality and family structures. While not achieving widespread political conversion, the camps created significant problems for the Algerian independence movement, particularly in controlling and protecting women and families. The OPA/ALN 'placed a priority on women as an important site for their own claims to sovereignty. Apart from the logistical challenges posed by the camps, which cut off a significant supply line, they were on the front lines of a larger battle concerned with women's sexuality and the family'.[73]

Colonialism was not satisfied with merely expropriating land; it also targeted native traditions and social structures that protected indigenous people from colonial intrusion, undertaking their systematic destruction. It was not just the soil – the land, the inalienable family holdings – that was occupied; it was the cultural essence, as represented by the Algerian woman, that became the subject of contestation. As Fanon affirms in the appendix to 'Algeria Unveiled':

> French colonialism has settled itself in the very centre of the Algerian individual and has undertaken a sustained work of cleanup, of expulsion of self, of rationally pursued mutilation.

> There is not occupation of territory, on the one hand, and independence of persons on the other. It is the country as a whole, its history, its daily pulsation that are contested, disfigured, in the hope of a final destruction.[74]

Published in 1957 and reissued in 1959 in *Studies in a Dying Colonialism*, the appendix[75] engages with the legislative programme undertaken by the colonial administration to overhaul Algerian society and its traditional cultural institutions, which posed an obstacle to French colonisation. The Algerian woman as a 'sociological case study' preoccupied scholars in sociology, ethnology, and experts in Islam and Islamic jurisprudence. Referring to debates in the French National Assembly on the emancipation of Algerian women, Fanon contends that this sociological case had political implications. Most politicians in the Assembly concurred that Algerian women 'dream of being free', but were oppressed by 'a retrograde and ferocious patriarchy'. He argues that these politicians demanded an improvement in women's status as 'the only means of disarming the rebellion'.[76] Fanon rejects the colonial mythology surrounding the cloistering of Algerian women – 'their alleged confinement, lack of importance, humility, and silent existence bordering on quasi-absence'.[77] He also challenges the demonisation of 'Moslem society' as having 'made no place for her, amputating her personality, allowing her neither development nor maturity, maintaining her in a perpetual infantilism'.[78] Instead, Fanon argues that the retreat into domestic space was not a 'hatred of the sun or the streets or spectacles', nor 'a flight from the world', but an act of anticolonial resistance. He writes, 'This withdrawal, this rejection of an imposed structure, this falling back upon the fertile kernel that a restricted but coherent existence represents, constituted for a long time the fundamental strength of the occupied.'[79] Fanon posits that this hardening of tradition, or 'sclerosis', was an anticolonial reflex occasioned by the expropriation of natives and their exclusion from politics. Algerian woman, acting as the last bastion resisting colonisation, kept alive the revolutionary spirit within the home. This retreat to the domestic space was, in fact, a revolutionary act in a state of latency, manifesting as colonial traditionalism but serving as a form of resistance.

5

The Uses of Medicine:
Colonial and Revolutionary

The Algerian war redefined the Geneva Convention, enabling nationalist parties, as non-state actors, to challenge colonial states' hegemony. These parties claimed violations of civil liberties and inalienable rights – ironically, by states that championed individual rights – and sought redress. One of the longest and bloodiest wars of decolonisation, the Algerian War of Independence was about the exercise of sovereignty; this military conflict was not purely military but manifested in competing claims regarding sovereignty, governmentality and the administration of care.[1] In *Studies in a Dying Colonialism*, Fanon examines the historical alliance between the medical establishment and the military, illustrating how medicine, once an instrument of colonial power, was transformed into a tool of resistance against French colonialism. As he opines, health became one of the battlegrounds in the Algerian war, crucially important in the construction of a new Algeria. Medicine was weaponised by the French army to quell FLN resistance, while the FLN deployed medicine to galvanise the masses for the Algerian cause.

Jennifer Johnson critiques scholars like Matthew Connelly for internationalising the Algerian conflict and neglecting Algerian archives, while also diverging from those who, like Fanon, emphasise colonial violence and torture. Instead, she adopts an Algerian perspective, shifting focus from battlefield atrocities to the role of healthcare institutions in the FLN's strategy during the Algerian war. Despite Fanon's clinical insights at Blida-Joinville hospital and commitment to the Algerian cause, Johnson dismisses him as an outsider, contending that his contributions were not integral to this strategy. She questions the integrity of 'his work [which] frequently lapses into Manichean generalizations'. While questioning Fanon's authority to represent Algerians, Johnson asserts that her study adopts the perspective of Algerian participants and prioritises their voices.[2] Nonetheless, I take issue with Johnson for overlooking in this study the centrality of Fanon's writing, especially 'Medicine and Colonialism'.

The French army, as well as the FLN, mobilised the institutions of welfare and healthcare to serve different conflicting ends. The colonial state instrumentalised these institutions as propaganda tools to win hearts and minds. Likewise, the FLN adopted these institutions in nation-building and the decolonisation of Algeria; they were used to rally the masses and to internationalise the conflict by seeking aid and diplomatic support from other countries. As I will have occasion to show, the SAS emerged as the primary vehicle for colonial propaganda: they constituted, in Johnson's words, 'the most comprehensive wartime initiative, [which] aimed to facilitate political rapprochement between the Algerian population and the colonial state'.[3] This rapprochement, for Fanon, meant colonial encroachment. The provision of healthcare, hygiene education, and domestic instruction to indigenous women by teams of doctors, nurses, and social workers served a dual purpose: while offering assistance, it also facilitated the gathering of intelligence critical to French military operations.

THE SAS'S MILITARISATION OF CARE AND WELFARE

It is misguided to think that the visits organised by the SAS were 'the first time state services penetrated the interior';[4] it was not Soustelle who conceived of the weaponisation of care by instituting the SAS, Cambon was the precursor. The brutal violence perpetrated by the French army against the civilian rural populations dispels the claim made by Johnson and Grégor Mathias that the institution of the SAS sought a resolution to the Algerian conflict 'through peaceful pacifiers, instructed to conquer with medicine rather than bullets'.[5] Pacification was a misnomer; the SAS unleashed untold violence: torture, rape and murder. Fanon's chapter 'Medicine and Colonialism' in Studies in a Dying Colonialism must be interpreted within this context, as a text articulating a dual strategy: while Fanon critiques the medical institution's complicity in colonial pacification and the instrumentalisation of care, he simultaneously posits it as crucial to both the revolution and the postcolonial reconstruction of Algerian society fragmented by colonialism.

In the late nineteenth century, Cambon utilised medical care and assistance to pacify the indigenous population. At the turn of the twentieth century, Jonnart employed a similar strategy to consolidate colonisation and serve European settler interests by protecting them from pandemics, facilitating their demographic growth, and enabling their hegemony over an expanding indigenous population. The healthcare system historically functioned as an extension of the military, serving as an apparatus of colonial governmentality. Care and assistance consistently followed repressive actions. For example, Cambon provided medical aid to mitigate the effects of native expropriation and suppression following the 1871 El-Mokrani uprising. Similarly, Soustelle proposed reforms to address the indigenous population's dire conditions in the wake of Paul Aussaresses's August 1955 repression. The SAS were introduced as one of the measures to bring relief of sorts. The subversive forces came from this population, and Soustelle's approach was twofold: to target and neutralise these forces and to win hearts and minds through propaganda and warfare. The decree of 26 September 1955 enabled Soustelle to create the SAS in order to 'recapture' the population in regions where the ALN was active and to protect regions at risk of being contaminated by the insurgency.[6]

The decree significantly derogated civilian powers to SAS officers, foreshadowing the Special Act of March 1956. This derogation was presented as a measure enabling the SAS officers to fulfil administrative functions that would serve the civilian population. In their duties, the SAS officers would be assisted by an accounting secretary, a *khodja* interpreter, a radio operator, a doctor and a nurse, and a *maghzen* acting as a police and protection force.[7] The SAS re-established the connection between the army and the administration of care. Like the *bureaux arabes*, the SAS were tasked with the 'control' and 'policing' of the population.[8] Care and assistance were deployed by these officers as two weapons of noso and biopolitics. Just as in the nineteenth century and during the colonial conquest, '[they] became potent symbols of colonial development to which the French could point as showcasing their commitment to Algeria'.[9] In *Studies in a Dying Colonialism*, Fanon debunks the beneficence of medicine and the mythology that the latter was a feature of progress by affirming that medicine was the weapon of colonial biopolitics which established and maintained colonial rule and devastated Algerian society.

The SAS, like the *bureaux arabes*, were conceived as the driving force of pacification, fulfilling a dual function: administering care in order to contain and control the population through infiltration. They aimed to consolidate *harka* and *supplétive* units by recruiting translators and women for the EMSI (Équipes médico-sociales itinérantes) to facilitate propaganda and psychological warfare. Lazreg observes that military strategists, recognising Algerian women's active involvement in the Battle of Algiers, decided to enlist them for propaganda and pacification efforts.[10] This approach, reminiscent of Cambon, Soullié and Chellier's strategies, targeted women and the family unit. Informed by quasi-medical and anthropological theories, it posited that women played a crucial role in preserving the cohesion and secluded nature of indigenous society.[11] Consequently, co-opting these women was seen as key to conquest and undermining traditions that resisted French colonial rule. This theorising echoes Chellier's ethnocentric views and Bourdieu's sociology of Algeria, which considers gender and colonial traditionalism as the last bastion of resistance against colonial intrusion.[12] Chellier's call for medicine to deploy women in conquering Algerians reverberated in General Paul Vanuxem's report: 'Psychological action aimed at Muslim women will only succeed if carried out by women.'[13] This calculated strategy weaponised gender dynamics and cultural sensitivities, instrumentalising women in the French colonial pacification of Algeria. In its strategising, the French army viewed the conquest of Algerian women as the penultimate stage before the destruction of the OPA, the resumption of civilian life, and the creation of a 'New Algeria'. However, this vision contrasted sharply with the one Fanon conceptualises in *Studies in a Dying Colonialism*.

Nafissa Sid Cara's appointment as Secretary of State for Social Affairs in Algeria, the first Muslim woman to hold a ministerial position, was key to this strategy. The EMSI were tasked with the 'conquest' of Algerian women through emancipation, a mission that was primarily *military* rather than socio-medical, as envisioned by Chellier at the turn of the century. Medical assistance was provided not just for care and cure, but to impose a 'French solution to the Algerian problem'.[14] The EMSI's true objective was not to assist the impoverished population, but to infiltrate it for intelligence gathering. Assistance was exchanged for information, and care for cultural conversion. Fanon captures the EMSI's propaganda, noting that distribution of aid was accompanied by criticism of 'retrograde customs' like veiling. Algerian women were led to believe their impoverishment stemmed from their gender, traditions, sexuality, poor hygiene, and inadequate home economics. Social and psychological hygiene were inextricably linked with ideological indoctrination.

In *douars* and *mechtas*, the EMSI's campaign against the veil was framed in terms of hygiene: women were instructed on unveiling, equating its removal with eliminating parasites like lice, ticks and flies.[15] The propaganda leaflet 'Voici l'image du fellaga', featuring a veiled grasshopper, encapsulated the psychological warfare that demonised traditional attire and sexuality as sources of backwardness, impoverishment and poor hygiene. The Algerian problem was consistently framed as a population issue. This propaganda characterised

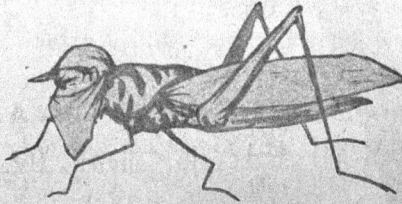

Voici l'image du fellaga :

**PARTOUT OU LE FELLAGA PASSE
IL NE RESTE PLUS RIEN !**
IL PREND **VOTRE ARGENT**
IL PREND **VOS FILS**
IL DÉTRUIT LES **ECOLES**
IL RUINE LES **DISPENSAIRES**
IL BRULE VOS **RÉCOLTES**
IL·COUPE LES POTEAUX DU **TÉLÉPHONE** ET DU **TÉLÉ-
GRAPHE**
SON PASSAGE SIGNIFIE :
    RUINE, DEUIL, LARMES, FAMINE ET **MISÈRE**
VOUS LUTTEZ CONTRE LES SAUTERELLES

**LUTTEZ AUSSI CONTRE LE FELLAGA
LA SAUTERELLE D'AUJOURD'HUI**
Rangez-vous résolument aux côtés de
L'ARMÉE DE PACIFICATION

Photo 11. Fifth Bureau propaganda leaflet 'Voici l'image du
fellaga'. The text says: This is the image of the fellaga: / Wherever
the fellaga passes, nothing remains! / He takes your money / He
takes your sons / He destroys schools / He ruins dispensaries / He
burns your crops / He cuts telephone and telegraph poles / His
passage means: / Ruin, mourning, tears, famine and misery / You
fight against locusts / Fight also against the fellaga / The locust of
today / Resolutely stand alongside / The Pacification Army.

Algerian women as proliferating locusts, posing an economic threat to
colonial society. Inculcating new home economics was not merely a military
tactic but a significant instance of colonial biopolitics. The imagery in this
propaganda leaflet was designed to establish a conceptual bond between
FLN terrorism and the devastating plague of locusts and famines that
ravaged Algeria in the nineteenth century. Unveiling Algerian women was

part of a broader strategy to extract them from traditional family structures and redefine their roles within a new social order, ultimately aiming to dismantle and supplant traditional society. The new social order was mediated through various forms of psychological action. In 'circles féminines', women's social gatherings and home economics instruction functioned as conduits for this propaganda. As Chapter 3 elucidates, the radio played a pivotal role, broadcasting programmes that demonised the veil.[16] It is instructive to note that the radio, a generator of this propaganda, acted on women's corporeality. Significantly, this medium, which was employed to disseminate colonial feminist rhetoric, was also utilised in interrogations, disturbingly focusing on women's genitalia.

CONDEMNATION OF MEDICAL PERSONNEL AND VIOLATION OF FUNDAMENTAL RIGHTS AND FREEDOMS

The Algerian Red Crescent (Croissant-Rouge algérien – CRA) emerged as a crucial humanitarian response during Algeria's war, facing unique challenges due to the absence of a recognised government and the external location of the Comité de Coordination et d'Exécution (CCE). Established in January 1957 by FLN, the CRA served a dual purpose: providing medical and humanitarian aid and challenging colonial hegemony through international advocacy. The CRA's structure was intricately integrated into the FLN-ALN's pyramidal organisation, operating within the social services branch. This integration enabled effective functioning at all levels of the revolutionary organisation, maintaining coordination under the FLN's central leadership. To gain de facto recognition and address urgent humanitarian needs, the CRA initially operated anonymously within Algeria. The CCE later established an official CRA to represent Algeria internationally, facilitating the receipt of aid. The CRA's headquarters were based legally in Tangier, with its secretariat moved to Rabat for geopolitical reasons, and additional offices were established in Geneva and Cairo to engage with international bodies and manage donations.

At its inception, the CRA faced the monumental task of addressing the needs of over 360,000 refugees, a number that approached 1 million by the conflict's later stages. The organisation initiated training programmes for rescuers and nurses, recruited Algerian doctors, and served as an auxiliary to the Algerian liberation army (ALN). Despite operational challenges, the CRA successfully built relationships with international Red Cross and Red Crescent societies, securing support from entities such as the Oxford Committee for Famine Relief (renamed Oxfam in 1960) and various Muslim organisations globally. Moreover, the CRA received crucial support from the International Committee of the Red Cross (ICRC), which played a vital role in addressing the humanitarian crisis. The ICRC conducted visits to Morocco and Tunisia, and brought international attention to the plight of Algerian refugees at the 19th International Conference of Red Cross Societies in 1957. This intervention significantly strengthened the CRA's efforts and heightened international awareness of the urgent humanitarian crisis in the region. The CRA worked closely with the ICRC, monitoring human rights in detention centres and addressing refugee needs. Key figures like Dr Bentami, the CRA's delegate to the ICRC in Geneva, and Mr Benbahmed, heading the Middle East delegation, were instrumental in establishing international relations and managing aid distribution. Crucially, the CRA was established to counteract the SAS's use of healthcare as a tool for propaganda and civilian pacification. Beyond providing care, the CRA collaborated with humanitarian organisations to expose the weaponisation of medicine and healthcare by French officials like Soustelle and Lacoste. This dual focus on humanitarian aid and advocacy underscored the CRA's role in challenging colonial hegemony. The FLN's decision to create a rival health system in 1957 further emphasised the importance of healthcare in the independence struggle. The CRA's work with other Red Crescent organisations and international bodies not only sought financial and material assistance but also aimed to internationalise the Algerian conflict by raising awareness in other countries. The CRA's formation and activities were deeply intertwined with Algeria's struggle for independence, serving as a pivotal chapter in the history of human rights.

As Johnson affirms, the Algerian war raised serious questions about 'the meaning of humanitarianism and human rights' and became an acid test of the universality and political independence of newly formed institutions, such as the United Nations (1945), the Universal Declaration of Human Rights (1948), the Genocide Convention (1948), the Fourth Geneva Convention (1949), and the European Convention for the Protection of Human Rights and Fundamental Freedoms (1953). The rhetoric promoted by these institutions, championing human rights and fundamental freedoms, was actually at odds with European colonial interests. During the wave of decolonisation that swept across Africa and other Third World countries, the Algerian case challenged prevailing rhetoric and highlighted inherent contradictions. In their struggle for independence, Johnson affirms, Algerians adopted the universal language of humanitarianism and fundamental rights and 'juggled the provision of medicine and healthcare, aid, and political representation at the International Committee of the Red Cross and the United Nations'. It was this language that enabled the FLN to achieve political victory in the war by convincing the international community of the legitimacy of their cause and challenging their colonial oppressors' hegemony in a way they could not match on the battlefield.[17]

The CRA served two critical functions: countering the SAS's use of healthcare for propaganda and pacification, and through collaboration with international organisations like the ICRC, exposing the French militarisation of medicine. The CRA also highlighted the persecution of medical personnel aiding Algerian combatants. Having examined the SAS's role, I will now address the weaponisation of medical care and pharmaceuticals, as well as the prosecution of medical staff treating wounded Algerians. In *Studies in a Dying Colonialism*, written in connection with these two critical functions, Fanon is adept at employing this language of humanitarianism to bring about Algeria's decolonisation.

The French colonial administration implemented measures that severely compromised medical ethics and practice. It enacted stringent regulations on medication sales and compelled doctors to report patients, fundamentally undermining medical professionals' ability to fulfil their duties. The repression of medical personnel was severe and widespread. In Algiers alone, out of 25 Algerian doctors, 12 abandoned their practices, 5 went missing, 7 were arrested, and 1 was assassinated. Notable cases of medical persecution include Dr Zemirli, sentenced to hard labour for a prescription found on a rebel, and Dr Chatz of Benisaf, who faced dubious charges. Prominent figures like Dr Nefissa Hamoud, Dr Sadek Hadjeres and Frantz Fanon were among those penalised for providing medical treatment to wounded FLN combatants. Before delving into specific cases, it is important to note that these instances exemplify the broader systematic targeting of healthcare workers across Algeria, with many medical professionals enduring inhumane detention, exile or execution simply for treating Algerian patients.[18]

The decree of 24 October 1955, published in the *Official Journal of Algeria*, imposed strict import controls on various chemicals, drugs and medical supplies. Decrees issued by Soustelle and Lacoste prohibited the sale of chemical and pharmaceutical products, severely impacting wounded ALN combatants. On 12 May 1957, a decree issued by the Prefect of Algiers required healthcare establishments to report injured patients to police authorities, effectively breaching medical confidentiality. These measures had a profound impact on the medical community, with Mustapha Makaci estimating that approximately 90 per cent of medical personnel were forced to leave the country to avoid persecution. France's actions in Algeria violated several international conventions and ethical principles. The Geneva Conventions, which France had helped establish, were contravened multiple times. Medical neutrality and the universal right to treatment regardless of racial, political, or religious affiliation were undermined, and medical confidentiality was breached by requiring healthcare providers to report patients to authorities.

In response to these measures, the FLN established the Service de Santé (Health Service), also known as the Algerian Red Crescent (Le Croissant-rouge algérien), which General Salan acknowledged as one of the FLN's most effective propaganda efforts.[19] In its issue of 4 May 1957, *Le Concours médical* highlighted the ethical dilemmas faced by doctors in Algeria, drawing attention to the conflict between medical ethics and colonial policies. These policies severely compromised medical ethics and practice, violating international law and undermining the fundamental principles of healthcare provision. This systematic persecution of medical professionals had far-reaching consequences for both the medical community and the broader population of Algeria.

The French authorities' arrest, internment and execution of medical personnel significantly impacted rules of engagement, laws of war, medical neutrality and protection of medical staff in armed conflicts. On 11 March 1958, Dr Reda Zemirli's sentencing to eight years of hard labour highlighted these issues. The FLN's denunciation of this case received widespread support and spurred international opposition to the prosecution of medical personnel in the conflict, garnering support from Red Crescent societies in Egypt, Tunisia, Jordan and Syria, as well as Red Cross organisations in Lebanon, Chile, Colombia, Canada, Germany, Sweden, Norway and Bulgaria. Moreover, the case prompted serious concerns for the ICRC, compelling its intervention.

At the 19th International Conference in New Delhi, the ICRC proposed a resolution to expand Article 3 of the 1949 Geneva Conventions. This resolution sought to ensure non-discriminatory treatment of the injured, protection for medical practitioners, respect for patient confidentiality, and the unrestricted circulation of medicines for therapeutic purposes. This proposal was a direct response to repressive measures against medical personnel and pharmacists, particularly those implemented through Soustelle and Lacoste's decrees.

On 23 April 1958, following Dr Zemirli's sentencing, Henri Langlais of the Bureau de liaison avec l'Algérie informed the ICRC of several related cases. Jeannine Belkhodja was sentenced to five years of hard labour on 21 June 1957, for FLN cell membership and explosive device manufacturing. Gilberte Bory, a midwife, received a two-year hard labour sentence on 3 April 1957, for failing to report and abetting FLN members. Michel Martini was given a five-year sentence on 25 April 1957, for providing assistance to the FLN. Dr Jean Massebœuf of Ténès received a 20-year sentence on 24 September 1957, for allegedly supplying weapons to the FLN. Two cases resulted in fatalities: Alaoua Bendjelloul, a pharmacist in Constantine, was arrested on 15 April 1956, following the alleged discovery of explosives at his residence, and subsequently killed during an alleged escape attempt. Similarly, Dr Benaouda Benzerdjeb, arrested on 17 January 1956 for tract distribution, also died while in custody. Other cases were brought to the attention of the ICRC. Three nurses were arrested and sentenced to five years of hard labour. Drs Boudjema, Schatz and Pastor were also arrested and faced a similar fate. Dr Mostapha Laliam received a harsher sentence of 20 years.[20] On 6 March 1958, Dr Ismaïl Dahlouk Mahfoud was apprehended and sentenced to five years of hard labour on 2 March 1959.

In his report to ICRC, Langlais explained that these doctors were prosecuted and convicted not for carrying out their medical work: 'the exercise of their profession in favour of the "rebels" was not mentioned at any time during their trial; they were simply accused either of acts of terrorism or of participation in an association of criminals.'[21] On 28 April 1958, in response to a telegram from the Syrian Red Crescent regarding the arrest and imprisonment of Dr Zemirli, the president of the French Red Cross reiterated Langlais's view, that 'no conviction [had] ever been pronounced by French courts, both military and civil, against doctors for allegedly treating rebels'. 'It happens', he added:

> that the French authorities arrest and bring individuals to trial for acts of rebellion (participation in criminal associations, endangering the external security of the state, harbouring and transporting terrorists, etc.). It also happens that, among these individuals, there are doctors. Their status as doctors cannot and must not exempt them from respecting the laws and observing both military and civilian regulations.[22]

However, evidence contradicts claims by Langlais and the president of the French Red Cross regarding the treatment of medical professionals who aided wounded FLN combatants. Many, including Zemirli, were arrested on flimsy evidence, tried in military courts, and harshly sentenced. Some cases never reached trial; instead, individuals like Benzerdjeb and Bendjelloul were apprehended, questioned and summarily executed. Langlais's report glosses over the controversy surrounding Benzerdjeb's case, merely noting that an investigation against an unnamed person by the Algiers Public Prosecutor's Office was dismissed on 11 August 1956. This simplification obscures the broader issue: the army's hijacking of the legal system to weaponise medicine and pharmaceuticals through harsh sentencing and summary executions of doctors and pharmacists.

In a letter dated 28 May 1959, Dr Bentami informed the ICRC about the case of Dahlouk Mahfoud but crucially highlighted the public executions of FLN members and the display of dead bodies, as reported by the French press.[23] In a telex to the ICRC, the president of the CRA, Mostefa Benbahmed, reported that on 11 November of that same year, 47 young Algerians, including Dr Hafid Boudjemaa, were arrested in Djidjelli and mutilated before their execution. Benbahmed lamented that France's brutal military actions not only thwarted the CRA and ICRC's efforts to humanise the war, but also severely hindered negotiations for the release of French soldiers held captive by the ALN. He urged the ICRC to investigate the case and take necessary action.[24] Hocène Boukli, like Benbahmed and Dr Bentami, linked the prosecution of medical personnel to the executions of captured Algerian combatants by the French army. In his letter to J. de Preux, ICRC delegate in Tunis, Boukli drew attention to cases of prosecuted medical personnel (namely Drs Zemirli and Laliam) alongside those of armed combatants condemned to death, such as Amar Ammari, Mohamed Khennof and Larbi Berkar.[25] This juxtaposition underscored the French army's violation of international law. French authorities refused to acknowledge the Algerian conflict as a war, denying captured enemy combatants prisoner of war (POW) status. There were no POW camps, but 'state prisons, penitentiaries, detention centres, screening and clearing camps, and military tribunals passing death sentences on captured Algerian soldiers'.[26] Boukli demonstrated France's violation of humanitarian principles on two accounts through its mistreatment of medical personnel and also of those who should have been recognised as POWs.

In his resignation letter to Lacoste, when he decided to leave the French medical service due to its complicity with murderous colonialism and to advocate for the FLN's Service de santé, Fanon eloquently denounced this violation, ironically noting that it had been elevated to a legislative principle. Fanon provided assistance to wounded combatants, much like Drs Laliam and Benzerdjeb; his ward at the Blida-Joinville became, according to Cherki, a 'hornet nest for *fellagas*' and FLN operatives.[27] As many commentators contend, the expulsion order issued by Lacoste to Fanon instructing him to leave Algeria in two days was a reprieve from torture and imprisonment, literally a stay of execution. The prosecution of medical personnel, the violation of human rights and fundamental freedoms, and the weaponisation of medical care as a tool of colonial propaganda and biopolitics provide an interpretative context for *Studies in a Dying Colonialism*. These factors offer insights into the political environment in which Fanon worked and the dangers he faced as a doctor providing medical assistance to FLN combatants.

Johnson rightly asserts that, during their struggle for independence, Algerians strategically employed the universal language of humanitarianism and fundamental rights. Through diplomacy, the FLN achieved political victory and challenged French colonial hegemony in ways unattainable through military means alone. Contrary to Johnson's hasty dismissal of Fanon's work, I argue that Fanon skilfully employed this language as a strategic tool to achieve victory. His grasp of linguistic power dynamics in colonial contexts allowed him to leverage language effectively in the struggle for liberation. Johnson's critique of Fanon's work as prone to Manichaean generalisations overlooks his significant contributions, particularly in 'Medicine and Colonialism'. By underestimating Fanon's centrality to anticolonial strategy, her analysis fails to fully appreciate the nuanced insights he provided on the intersection of medicine, politics and decolonisation. Furthermore, she fails to consider Fanon's 'Medicine and Colonialism' within the historical context that saw the CRA play a dual role in the Algerian struggle for independence: countering the SAS's use of healthcare for propaganda and pacification, while also exposing the militarisation of medicine through collaboration with international organisations like the ICRC.

The CRA highlighted the persecution of medical personnel aiding Algerian combatants. Fanon's *Studies in a Dying Colonialism*, written in this context, served as a critique of French militarisation of care and welfare and advocated for medicine as a crucial institution in Algeria's decolonisation. Johnson's analysis overlooks Fanon's personal experience as a victim of this militarisation and persecution for treating Algerians. Fanon's work was not merely theoretical; it was grounded in the very real threats of torture, hard labour, or execution that he and numerous other medical professionals faced. Fanon's critique of the complicity between French colonialism and medicine was informed by first-hand experience and observation. His involvement in the Algerian independence movement was characterised by direct support for the FLN, providing clandestine medical aid and shelter to fighters. His vocal opposition to French colonial policies led to his expulsion from Algeria. Subsequently, he joined the FLN's external delegation in Tunisia, continuing his medical work while becoming a key figure in the movement's propaganda efforts. Notably, his involvement with *El Moudjahid*, the FLN's official newspaper, allowed him to play a crucial role in shaping and disseminating the FLN's message to domestic and international audiences during the Algerian war. The following section describes how Fanon demonstrates the inextricable link between medical practice, political resistance and decolonisation. This intersectionality, often underappreciated in broader analyses such as Johnson's, underscores Fanon's enduring significance in the discourse on colonial medicine and liberation struggles.

MEDICINE, COLONIALISM AND DECOLONISATION

Medicine, one of the central planks of the narrative of progress and development, consolidated France's colonisation of Algeria. In 'Medicine and Colonialism', Fanon refers to the role played by medicine in facilitating the colonial conquest in the nineteenth century, but pays it scant attention. He chooses, instead, to explore the intersection of medicine and colonialism during the Algerian war through two perspectives: one informed by his experience as a doctor at Blida-Joinville hospital, and the other as an FLN militant who, rather than rejecting medicine, mobilises it for the revolution. Before examining this ambivalence, which marks the moments of *before* and *after* the revolution, and which also structures his other chapters on the radio and the veil, it is important to clarify that 'Medicine and Colonialism' draws on two other works, namely 'North African Syndrome' and *Black Skin White Masks*, and offers a clear critique of the Algiers School of Psychiatry. Led by Professor Antoine Porot at Blida hospital, this school was criticised for deploying 'an intellectual violence that was in every sense the equal of colonialism's dehumanising legal and social structure, a savagery concomitant with the brutality required to police Algeria's Manichean world'.[28]

Medicine, epidemiology and hygiene were, historically, implicated in establishing French colonialism in Algeria. Some scholars argue that Algeria's conquest should be attributed not to Bugeaud, but to the epidemiologist Alphonse Laveran, whose discovery of the malaria parasite significantly impacted French colonisation efforts. Because of this historical complicity,

Photo 12. Mobile units providing free medical assistance (AMG) for the inhabitants of Zemmoura at the medical post of the 72nd Artillery Group. (© ECPAD)

writes Fanon, 'it [was] impossible to create the physical and the psychological conditions for learning about hygiene or the assimilation of concepts concerning epidemic diseases'.[29] Insofar as the natives were concerned, Fanon intimates, matters relating to epidemiology and hygiene were not considered important in the fight against diseases, but were perceived as factors in their colonisation. Such complicity was in plain view in the coercive administration of care carried out by mobile medical units. As Fanon affirms:

> The compulsory visit by the doctor to the *douar* is preceded by the assembling of the population through the agency of the police authorities. The doctor who arrives in this atmosphere of general constraint is never a native doctor but always a doctor belonging to the dominant society and very often to the army.
>
> The statistics on sanitary improvements are not interpreted by the native as progress in the fight against illness, in general, but as fresh proof of the extension of the occupier's hold on the country. When the French

authorities show visitors through the Tizi-Ouzou sanitorium or the operating units of the Mustapha hospital in Algiers, this has for the native just
one meaning: 'This is what we have done for the people of this country;
this country owes us everything; were it not for us, there would be no
country.'[30]

The colonial narrative mythologises settlers as pioneers in the making of
French Algeria, portraying soldiers, physicians, hygienists, and epidemiologists as key agents of progress and colonisation. This ideological construct
legitimises the colonial enterprise while obscuring its inherent violence. By
emphasising scientific and military contributions, the narrative reframes
colonialism as a civilising mission, thus eliding the systemic oppression and
cultural erasure intrinsic to colonial domination. Hospitals were often touted
as inventions of progress and sanitary improvements, but this progress came
at a high cost. As noted earlier, the natives were made to pay 'heavy taxes'
in the forms of expropriation and *razzias*, which engendered famine and
its sequelae of plagues and contagious diseases. The devastating famine of
1867–8, also known as the 'year of death', was a direct consequence of colonial
'progress' and 'development'. Medical assistance to the natives was, in fact,
an initiative of colonial governmentality aimed at imposing confinement on
impoverished indigenous populations, who were seen as carriers of contagious diseases that threatened French colonisation. As discussed in Chapter
1, indigenous populations historically eschewed these hospitals, which were
frequently staffed by military physicians wearing uniforms identical to those
of soldiers who had pillaged villages, confiscated grain and livestock, razed
homes, and perpetrated sexual violence. The natives distrusted and rejected
the medical technology used by the coloniser to justify occupation.

In normal circumstances, the doctor–patient relationship is built on trust:
the patient allows the doctor to examine them with the hope to relieve their
suffering and restore peace in their body.[31] However, the colonial situation
undermined this trust and distorted the doctor–patient relationship. The
patient was 'diffident' in the presence of the doctor and rejected the medical
technology brought by the coloniser. Their rejection of medical treatment
– their attachment to traditional empirics – was not a refusal of life but a
greater passivity before that 'close and contagious death'. In other words,
their refuge in tradition and their fatalism were determined by their objective conditions as colonised and expropriated subjects. For the colonised
patient, life is not 'a flowering or development of an essential productive-
ness'; rather, it is endured 'as a permanent struggle against an omnipresent

death'. 'This ever-menacing death is experienced as endemic famine, unemployment, a high death rate, an inferiority complex, and the absence of any hope for the future'; life had the appearance of 'incomplete death'.[32] Fanon's description of the objective conditions of the colonised people's life as an 'ever-menacing death' captures the workings of colonial biopolitics.

The colonial situation imparted a psychology of resentment and disavowal in the colonised, who 'exert[ed] considerable effort to keep away from the colonial world, not to expose himself to any action of the conqueror'.[33] Colonialism established a relation of subordination in all aspects of cultural life. This subordination was politically expressed through the economic, technical, and administrative frameworks imposed by colonialism, which supplanted traditional practices and maintained the colonised under colonial hegemony. In terms that echo his study of the complex of disavowal and resentful behaviour in *Black Skin, White Masks*, Fanon analyses the power relations that structure medical discourse. Just as in his theorising of language, Fanon argues that medical discourse was not neutral but had to be inscribed within the framework of cultural domination, as it articulated the dimensions of the colonial world. For the colonised, espousing Western medicine was tantamount to integration and assimilation; it meant accepting the terms of colonial subordination. By refusing to adopt medicine as a Western technology, Algerians simultaneously rejected their cultural subordination and sought refuge in tradition.

Like Memmi, Fanon outlines the portrait of the colonised who jettisoned Western cultural models only to find shelter in a stultifying tradition. Turin provides an analysis similar to Fanon's, asserting that medical discourse failed to persuade native Algerians, who rejected its therapeutics outright. In Fanon's study of the interplay between medicine and colonialism, the rejection of Western technologies and the colonial framework within which these operated is expressed in terms of colonial traditionalism. As observed in Chapter 2, he identifies the same colonial traditionalism at work in his discussion of the veil and the radio. From the nineteenth century until the Algerian war, medical technology was rejected by Algerians; the crux of Fanon's argument is that the war changed their attitude in the fight against colonialism. Medicine, which hitherto had acted in complicity with colonialism, was adopted by Algerians to defy the latter's hegemonic rule. Before examining the transformative role of medicine in the Algerian liberation struggle, it is imperative to first analyse Fanon's critique of how medical practices were deployed to reinforce French colonial dominance. This exploration will provide crucial context for understanding the subsequent shift in the function of healthcare during the independence movement.

Decrying the complicity of medicine and colonialism, Fanon contends that the doctor is, first and foremost, a settler. Dr Warnier epitomises the 'colonial doctors' who were socially defined not by their profession but by their investment in colonial settlements as landowners: 'the owner[s] of mills, wine cellars, or orange groves'. Medicine was considered a supplementary practice that provided additional income. Alluding to Dr Warnier and the eponymous law of 1873 that expropriated the natives, Fanon writes: 'In the colonies, the doctor is an integral part of colonization.'[34] Dr Warnier's influential role in shaping Algeria's legislative programme led to widespread expropriation of native land, culminating in the 1863 Sénatus-consulte and the subsequent Warnier Law. These laws had devastating consequences for the indigenous population, resulting in poverty, famine and disease. Colonial law and medicine worked hand in hand as potent tools to consolidate colonial power and facilitate settlement. Cambon's initiative to provide basic medical care sought to mitigate the harmful effects of expropriation on both natives and settlers. This medical programme operated alongside the broader colonial project, addressing immediate health concerns while reinforcing colonial control. The interplay between legislative expropriation and medical intervention illustrates the duplicitous strategies used by colonial authorities to maintain power and manage the fallout from their policies. Ultimately, medicine not only addressed health crises but also legitimised and sustained the colonial presence in Algeria, consolidating the colonial enterprise and supporting settlement efforts.

Ventriloquising the views of Cambon, Jonnart, Soulié and Chellier on the role played by doctors in consolidating France's colonial enterprise in Algeria, Fanon takes a trenchant view, arguing that every physician harboured a colonialist, a pioneer and an adventurer.[35] Economically, the doctor benefited from the colonial regime to the extent that, in moments of heightened tension, as was the case during the Algerian war, 'very often he assumes the role of militia chief organizer of "counter-terrorist" raids', and that '[i]n a period of crisis the cowboy pulls out his revolver and his instruments of torture'.[36] Such a trenchant view responds to two concerns regarding the weaponisation of medical technology. First, and as has been argued, the colonial administration imposed restrictions on the sale of pharmaceutical supplies to ALN wounded combatants, significantly impacting their medical care during the conflict. Pharmacists were prohibited from dispensing critical medical supplies, including antibiotics like penicillin and streptomycin, as well as anti-tetanus treatments, alcohol, and even cotton, without a prescription and without noting down the patient's personal details.[37]

Furthermore, medical practitioners were mandated to report patients presenting with suspicious wounds to the authorities. These measures effectively restricted access to essential medical care for Algerians, particularly those involved in the resistance movement. Second, doctors were implicated in the torture of Algerian people. The weaponisation of healthcare and its instrumentalisation in torture exemplify how the medical system was subverted to serve the colonial regime's interests, undermining its purported mission of addressing the Algerian population's health needs.

Nonetheless, Fanon avoids generalisation, noting that several doctors were subsequently prosecuted for defying Soustelle's and Lacoste's directives and assisting ALN combatants, while, in many cases, colonising doctors acted in complicity with the colonial establishment. When called upon to provide a medico-legal examination, they would always conclude that 'there was no evidence to suggest that the accused had been tortured'.[38] At inquests, they would testify to the legal authorities that no foul play took place, that the deceased did not succumb to torture, or that their death was not occasioned by summary execution. Fanon laments that 'doctors, attached to various torture centers, intervene[d] after every session in order to put the tortured back into condition for new sessions'. Massive doses of vitamins and heart stimulants were administered, during and after questioning to the tortured suspects, to keep them 'hovering between life and death'. 'Ten times the doctor intervenes', Fanon decries, 'ten times he gives the prisoner back to the pack of torturers'. Rather than upholding medical ethics and the Hippocratic oath, these doctors betrayed their professional responsibilities to serve the interests of the colonial power. As he writes:

In the European medical corps in Algeria, and especially in the military health corps, such things are common. Professional morality, medical ethics, self-respect and respect for others, have given way to the most uncivilized, the most degrading, the most perverse kinds of behavior. Finally, attention must be called to the habit formed by certain psychiatrists of flying to the aid of the police. There are, for instance, psychiatrists in Algiers, known to numerous prisoners, who have given electric shock treatments to the accused and have questioned them during the waking phase, which is characterized by a certain confusion, a relaxation of resistance, a disappearance of the person's defenses. When by chance these men are liberated because the doctor, despite this barbarous treatment, was able to obtain no information, what is brought to us is a personality in shreds. The work of rehabilitating the man is then extremely difficult. This is only one of the numerous crimes of which French colonialism in Algeria has made itself guilty.[39]

Alluding to Fanon's 'Medicine and Colonialism', Branche argues that during the Algerian war, the medical establishment was powerless to denounce or prevent torture. She describes an 'economy of care' that violated both medical practice and ethics, echoing Fanon's observations. Doctors treated torture victims not to heal, but to sustain them for further interrogation.[40] Medical interventions were timed to maximise the efficacy of questioning and violence, keeping victims alive for information extraction while prolonging their suffering. This practice contravened medical ethics and undermined the fundamental role of doctors to ensure 'cure' – etymologically rooted in 'care', meaning remedy, recovery, and restoration of health. Some doctors, in an attempt to avoid complicity in torture and violation of deontological codes, opted to administer pentothal and collaborate with the military to extract information.

In 'Medicine and Colonialism', Fanon's primary objective was not to provide a historical account of the medical establishment's complicity with the colonial regime or its institutional consolidation. Nor did he intend to dwell on medical doctors' involvement in administering torture. While he makes brief references to these complicities, his interest lies beyond them, focusing on the mobilisation of medicine that Algerians had previously rejected during the colonial period. Like 'Algeria Unveiled' and 'This is the Voice of Free Algeria', 'Medicine and Colonialism' follows the same historical dynamism: before the revolution, medicine was complicit with colonialism and Algerians rejected it; the revolution changed their attitude. Drawing parallels to the changing attitudes towards the veil and radio, Fanon argues that similar transformations were occurring regarding medicine. He emphatically states that 'radically new types of behavior in various aspects of the private and public life of the Algerian[s]' were emerging.[41] Fanon contends that the Algerian war broke the chains of colonialism and moderated previously extreme attitudes towards medicine (as well as sartorial habits and Western technologies like the radio and medicine). Before the Algerian war, visiting a doctor, administrator, constable, or mayor were considered equivalent actions for Algerians, as they were all seen as representatives of the colonial regime.[42] Rather than focusing solely on the medical establishment's complicity with colonialism, Fanon's analysis centres on the intersectionality of medicine and Algerian nationalism. Crucially, he sees the changing attitudes towards medicine as a reflection of the broader sociopolitical transformations occurring during the Algerian war.

As has been noted, the French colonial authorities weaponised pharmaceutical products by imposing an embargo on anti-tetanus vaccine, antibiotics, cotton and alcohol. These products – prohibited to Algerians – were transformed into weapons to deny care and cure, and thereby liquidate those suspected of supporting the revolution, just as radio sets and batteries were withdrawn from the market to silence the Voice of Combatant and Free Algeria (La Voix de l'Algérie combattante). In response, it became paramount for the revolutionary movement to counter the colonial authorities by setting up a welfare system to care for Algerians and a broadcasting network to keep them informed. Just as tradesmen supplied radio receivers to Algerians, Algerian pharmacists, doctors, and nurses provided medical supplies to the wounded combatant.[43] Fanon shows how the colonial regime weaponised medicine and other technologies in its efforts to suppress the Algerian nationalist movement. In turn, the revolutionaries sought to reclaim and repurpose these same tools to support the welfare and communication needs of the Algerian people, undermining the colonial authorities' control. Fanon's analysis highlights the dialectical relationship between the colonial state's efforts to deny Algerians access to essential medical supplies and the revolutionary movement's determination to provide care and sustenance to the population. This struggle over the provision and distribution of medicine became a key battleground in the broader conflict for Algerian independence.

The colonial context profoundly influenced the dynamics between native doctors and their patients. Colonialism not only strained doctor–patient relations but also positioned doctors as representatives of the occupying power. Even when the doctor was from the colonised population, this ambivalence persisted. The native doctor, seen as adopting the conqueror's techniques and mannerisms, symbolised the potential for any colonised individual to become a professional like an engineer, lawyer, or doctor. However, this also created a rift, as the native doctor was often viewed as having become acculturated, that is, as having transcended the psychological and emotional confines of the colonised group, leading to a perception of their alignment with the oppressors. Native doctors faced dual challenges: scepticism from their community and a need to assert their place in a rational, Westernised medical framework, often resulting in a rejection of traditional practices.

For Fanon, the native doctor internalised the neuroses he adumbrates in *Black Skin, White Masks* of the acculturated who turned against their native culture. Consequently, native doctors who treated Algerian patients reflected broader colonial tensions. This scenario illustrates the broader struggles of colonised intellectuals before Algeria's liberation, highlighting the complex interplay of identity, power and resistance in colonial medical practice. Building on Fanon's analysis, Makaci contends that the perception of Algerian doctors during the colonial period and the War of Independence was characterised by a complex interplay of conflicting sentiments.[44] The native population's view of these doctors was marked by profound ambivalence, stemming from the medical establishment's historical complicity with the colonial military apparatus during the conquest. On the one hand, there was a sense of compassion and respect for Algerian doctors who resisted colonial domination during the war. They were often seen as educated elites who could advocate for the rights and wellbeing of their compatriots. Conversely, this positive sentiment was offset by an unwarranted disparagement rooted in two primary factors: a deeply ingrained inferiority complex fostered by colonial rule, and a problematic legacy bequeathed by earlier cohorts of Algerian physicians. The colonial legacy significantly impacted the perception of Algerian doctors. Early generations of Algerian physicians, often from privileged backgrounds, frequently used their medical credentials primarily for political advancement rather than focusing on healthcare provision. This created a legacy of distrust among the general population, who viewed these doctors as complicit with the colonial system, or self-serving rather than dedicated to public health. This complex stigma posed a significant challenge for the new generation of Algerian physicians. However, it was ultimately overcome through their unanimous and active participation in the national liberation struggle. By aligning themselves with the independence movement and providing crucial medical support to their fellow Algerians, these physicians were able to rebuild trust and establish themselves as integral members of the resistance. This shift in perception played a crucial role in rehabilitating the image of Algerian doctors and integrating them fully into the fabric of the emerging independent nation.

Confronted with the weaponisation of medicine by the colonial authorities, the FLN had to set up a public health system capable of replacing the periodic and coercive visits organised by the SAS.[45] Fanon ironically remarks that this new system did not have to 'launch a "psychological approach program for the purpose of winning over the underdeveloped population".'[46] Like the radio, medical technology lost its extraneousness, its foreign characteristics, and was put at the service of the revolution. 'The problems of hygiene and prevention of disease', Fanon affirms, 'were approached in a remarkably creative atmosphere.'[47] This system came to supplant old superstitions inherent within maraboutism and traditional empirics. Fanon argues that the revolution freed the Algerians from colonial traditionalism and facilitated the decolonisation of medicine, as the Algerian people chose to 'take their destiny into their own hands [and] assimilate the most modern forms of technology at an extraordinary rate.'[48] The FLN's strategic reclaiming of medicine was crucial in Algeria's independence struggle. By establishing an alternative public health system, the FLN subverted the colonial weaponisation of medicine and repurposed it for liberation. This dual-purpose approach addressed immediate health needs while advancing political objectives. Transforming medicine from a tool of colonial control into a vehicle for self-determination, the FLN delegitimised French rule and garnered support for independence. This reappropriation exemplifies how the FLN leveraged social services to undermine colonial authority and assert Algerian autonomy.

6

Torture and Gender: Interrogation, Resettlement and Pacification

In his letter to his brother, dated 13 October 1837, de Saint-Arnaud reflects on the brutal French colonial assault on the city of Constantine. 'The bayonet', he writes, 'left none alive. No prisoners were taken.'[1] His chilling description continues: 'Not a cry of pain escaped the dying; death was given or received with a rage of despair that clenched teeth and sent cries back into the depths of the soul.… I fixed my gaze on many of those terrible yet poetic faces of the dying, which reminded me of the beautiful painting of the Battle of Austerlitz.'[2] The blood-bought conquest, seemingly justified in the eyes of the French army, laid the groundwork for the three-day reign of looting and disorder at the city. De Saint-Arnaud asserts that attempting to stop it would have been madness.[3] He recounts a tragic scene in which about two hundred women and children perished in treacherous ravines, their bodies scattered across the surrounding rocks. Emulating Gérard, de Saint-Arnaud crafts a singular history painting that glorifies French bravery while obscuring their atrocities. He effectively whitewashes the brutal reality of the conquest, concluding his portrayal with the imperative: 'Let us draw a thick veil and not tarnish our glory or our memories.'[4]

Nearly 120 years later, in March 1959, similar atrocities occurred in the department of Constantine. Ferhat Abbas reported French troops massacred Algerian civilians, mostly women and children, in a cave near Batna.[5] In response, the colonial authorities and the commander-in-chief of the French army denied claims of 112 civilian deaths by asphyxiating grenades. Instead, they stated that an operation in Mac-Mahon neutralised 32 rebels and freed 40 captive Muslim youths, while later eliminating 28 rebels in the Aurès.[6] The incident at Terchioui echoed previous massacres of Algerian civilians sheltering in caves, such as those perpetrated by Pélissier and de Saint-Arnaud at the Dahra over a century earlier. This atrocity starkly reveals the true face of French 'pacification' efforts in Algeria, exposing the brutal violence that historically sustained colonialism.

I begin this chapter by discussing de Saint-Arnaud's description of violence in the colonial conquest so as to connect it with the violence enacted during the War of Independence. The 'Rapport sur le moral des tirailleurs pour 1956' provides a disturbing perspective on the violence perpetrated against the civilian population, particularly women and children.[7] In the report, the reference to Bugeaud, a nineteenth-century French general infamous for his brutal tactics – continued by his proponents Pélissier and de Saint-Arnaud during the conquest of Algeria – signals a continuity of military repression that dehumanises both the Algerian people and the very concept of warfare itself.

The report presents a harrowing account of a military strategy rooted in fear and terror, explicitly targeting women as a central element of control. It stipulates that the only way to make [the population] yield is 'to attack their interests: their women first',[8] revealing a disturbingly gendered logic that positions women as both symbols of the enemy's power and as vulnerable means of undermining Algerian resistance. Women are not viewed as collateral damage; they are seen as central to the rebellion's cohesion, and their violation becomes a key tactic to quash resistance.

The pacification of the rebellion is framed in biopolitical terms as 'cutting out the gangrene',[9] a metaphor suggesting that violence against the populace – especially women – is necessary for the colonial project's 'health'. The strategic targeting of women's bodies aimed to destroy material resistance but also to break cultural and psychological resilience. Women's bodies became the battlefield for colonial conquest, with rape, torture and murder inherently concealed within the broader pacification strategy.

The report advocates for the colonial tactic of collective punishment, subjecting entire families to violence for retribution and control. These actions were not merely punitive; they were designed to break the community's spirit, demonstrating how colonialism weaponised the family unit to fracture Algerian society from within. The systematic repression outlined in the report, with its explicit focus on gendered violence, is presented as a tool of 'discipline' meant to instil fear and perpetuate control. The targeting of women in French military strategy during the Algerian war speaks to a broader pattern of violence, in which gendered bodies were used to dismantle the resistance and morale of the colonised population. Such violence was institutionalised and justified not only as a strategic military objective but as a necessary component of the colonial project. These gendered dimensions of violence, embedded in the structure of military power and colonial biopolitics, demand closer scrutiny in this chapter.

PACIFICATION: A DESTRUCTIVE
AND RECONSTRUCTIVE STRATEGY

On 7 January 1957, the Algerian war reached a critical juncture when General Massu was granted police powers, triggering the Battle of Algiers. The conflict shifted from rural areas, where the ALN operated, to urban centres, targeting the politico-administrative organisation (OPA), the FLN's civilian arm. Emergency laws empowered the French army with extraordinary authority, superseding normal police functions. Lacoste identified the OPA as the revolution's core, believing its destruction essential for pacification.[10] The Fifth and Second Bureaus, responsible respectively for conducting psychological operations and exploiting information through the Centre de renseignement et d'action and the Détachement opérationnel de protection (DOP), played crucial roles in undermining the OPA's influence. Interrogation emerged as a pivotal intelligence-gathering tactic, the defining aspect of the war. In military parlance, 'doing intelligence' became a euphemism for torture.[11] The special powers granted to Massu and his paratroopers, ostensibly to preserve state authority, ultimately subverted it. These measures, intended to maintain control in Algeria, paradoxically weakened the democratic foundations of the French Republic, undermining France's democratic state and its principles.

During the Battle of Algiers, the French military took control of the legal system from civilian authorities. As the FLN operated covertly among the civilian population, Roger Trinquier's urban protection forces (Dispositif de protection urbaine – DPU) began targeting and questioning civilians to identify FLN suspects. Rather than handing suspects over to the police for legal prosecution, the military detained them without charge. On 29 January 1957, a decision was made to create a detention centre in Algiers with a capacity for 20,000 internees. The Paul-Cazelles camp was established on 6 February for this purpose. The army circumvented the legal system by placing suspects under 'house arrest' (*assignation à résidence*), allowing indefinite detention and interrogation without charge. On 6 April 1957, the Socialist Federation of Algiers reported concerns that 20,000 Algerians were being held in clandestine camps. In addition to Paul-Cazelles, Ben-Aknoun and Beni-Messous, four transit camps were created to facilitate detentions. From January to September 1957, Paul Teitgen, Police Prefect of Algiers, signed 24,000 house arrest orders, offering no legal protections. This systematic circumvention of legal procedures and the establishment of extrajudicial detention facilities represented a significant erosion of civil liberties and due process, highlighting the extent to which military operations during the Battle of Algiers undermined democratic principles and the rule of law. Referring to this erosion, Fanon writes: 'French colonialism since 1954 has wanted nothing other than to break the will of the people, to destroy its resistance, to liquidate its hopes. For five years it has avoided no extremist tactic, whether of terror or of torture.'[12]

Fanon laments the rapid multiplication of internment centres across Algeria in 1955–56, noting that French colonial tactics aimed to divide and fragment the Algerian people, particularly families, making cohesion impossible. He also deplores that tens of thousands of Algerian men were interned in centres like Lodi, Paul-Cazelles, and Berrouaghia, where fathers and husbands were held captive for years. Algerian women were suddenly deprived of their husbands and forced to find ways to feed their children. Detainees were often transferred to Beni-Messous and Paul-Cazelles after weeks of detention and interrogation without legal counsel. Torture was systematically used in numerous clandestine centres, including villas, military barracks, schools and Moorish baths. The decree of 11 April 1957 regarding house arrest marked a pivotal turning point, militarising the legal system in a manner that undermined France's civilian rule of law. Consequently, the Fourth Republic began to crumble as it failed to reconcile legality with political expediency.

At the Centre de tri et de transit (CTT), a zone where law and due process were suspended, detainees often disappeared after questioning as they transited through the DOPs. This violation was tolerated in the state's interests. The war evolved from a counter-insurrectionary action against guerrillas into a military operation targeting the civilian population. As civilian FLN members fled Algiers' repression, the operation expanded to the countryside. The SAS were deployed to quell FLN resistance and win civilian support for the French cause. The strategy aimed to dismantle the FLN's politico-administrative infrastructure through massive raids, arrests, interrogations and intelligence gathering in urban and rural areas. In this subversive 'war of information', the radio became the most potent weapon – a key instrument for propaganda dissemination and intelligence acquisition during interrogations. The 'intelligence chain' had key antennae to accelerate its functioning: DOP teams with interrogators and prisoner-informants, alongside Second Bureau liaison officers, managed intelligence flow, directed research and cross-checked results. These officers led operations, effectively creating a mobile Second Bureau. This intelligence chain drove the ongoing struggle in Algeria.[13] General Huet, emphasising that intelligence constituted the 'nervous system of the struggle', employed neurological metaphors.[14] He described the SAS and psychological operations as vital organs sourcing information by monitoring and infiltrating the population.

To counter guerrilla warfare, the territory was reconfigured for strategic control. Certain areas were deemed no-go zones, considered FLN bases. Inhabitants of these areas were forcibly relocated, and their homes were destroyed. The SAS led pacification efforts in these regions. Although intended to represent a more 'benevolent' approach, the SAS was implicated, along with the army, in forcibly displacing large segments of the rural population. Under the guise of providing assistance, they controlled and policed these displaced civilians. As seen in Chapters 1 and 4, a seamless line connected the SAS to other institutions of care, like the *bureaux arabes*, established in the nineteenth century to control the population and ensure colonial conquest.

The SAS was established to mitigate the effects of France's 'muscular approach' to the Algerian war, similar to the forceful tactics used during the nineteenth-century pacification of Algeria. As Colonel Montagnac stated, the goal was to 'destroy everything that crawls at our feet like dogs'.[15] The brutal pacification carried out by Montagnac coincided with the establishement of the *bureaux arabes* to soften the impact. Similarly, Cambon implemented institutions of care to alleviate the suffering of expropriated natives affected by repressive collective punishment laws after the El-Mokrani uprising in 1871. Likewise, the SAS provided a biopolitical framework, promoting the positive aspects of the French presence among the repressed and displaced population. The Algerian war re-enacted the nineteenth-century pacification, replaying the history of *razzias*, rape and destruction of native rural habitats. Concepts of 'collective responsibility' and 'punishment' reappeared, denying natives individuality, civic justice, and basic legal rights and protection. These notions presumed their guilt, lumping all natives together, and were manifestations of colonial and state racism. They constituted a 'legal monstrosity'[16] that ostensibly justified the French army's use of violence and torture. Collective responsibility and punishment were strategies used to colonise and dominate during the conquest and to suppress insurgency in the Algerian war. These strategies empowered the French army to arrest, torture and carry out summary executions, targeting the civilian population to 'pacify' and 'win [them] over' while quelling FLN resistance. However, these repressive measures only fuelled further resentment and opposition to French rule.

Community resettlements served as collective punishment, causing hardship and ongoing torment by disrupting social structures and forcibly relocating entire communities. This displacement subjugated and controlled the population, undermining FLN resistance and establishing a social order favouring French colonial interests. The CTT, SAS and other centres[17] implemented a strategy to eradicate the insurgency and establish a neocolonial 'French Algeria'. While the CTT focused on interrogating individual suspects, the SAS concentrated on resettling entire rural communities. Both aimed to pacify suspects, sever their ties with the insurgency, recruit them into the *harka* and integrate them into the army's envisioned neocolonial French Algeria. Torture broke down individuals' bodies and psyches, while psychological tactics coerced them into accepting the neocolonial order. This process of 'resettling' the body sought to reshape individuals to fit a new regime of coloniality.

Michel Cornaton argues that the primary objective of the resettlements was to ensure military security in difficult-to-control areas rather than to destroy social and economic structures, as was the case during the period of conquest.[18] However, a closer analysis reveals that resettlements were, in fact, used during the colonial conquest to pacify and control native populations.[19] Pacification, conceived as a military programme to dismantle and reconstruct Algerian society, employed a dual strategy.[20] It involved co-opting Algerians into the *harka* to turn local populations against ALN combatants and the liberation movement, while simultaneously uprooting and displacing entire rural communities to sever the ALN from its support bases. This strategy aimed to cripple the ALN's organisational structure and weaken its ties to the rural masses. The tactic of resettling rural civilian populations began in 'no-go areas' in 1955 and later expanded to all regions outside military control. The regroupement policies can be understood within the historical context of the *razzia* strategy as a weapon of war: the destruction of harvests, theft of grain and livestock, expropriation of land and burning of entire *douars* were intended to dismantle Algerian society and obliterate its economic and social foundations. These same tactics were re-enacted under the regroupement policies. Algerian writer Mouloud Feraoun offers a poignant assessment of the impact of the Challe Plan on both the ALN and the rural population: 'The maquis seems out of sorts,' he writes, 'suffering in our djebels.'[21]

The counter-insurgency war rested on two interconnected strategies: the destruction and then reconstruction of Algerian society. By uprooting and displacing the population, the French aimed to destroy the ALN's material support base, win the war, and facilitate the reconstruction of a new society into which this population would be reintegrated. Paradoxically, this war was waged against, for, and with the Algerian people,[22] unleashing systematic violence that engulfed the entire country. The methods employed by Massu and Salan to combat the subversive war plunged the army into a total war against civilians, violating fundamental individual rights and undermining French political and legal institutions. Their May 1958 putsch not only led to the demise of the Fourth Republic but also threatened to bring the war to France itself. Salan's decision to consolidate the civilian and military administration under his command marked a significant return to the *Indigénat* system, where the governor-general held absolute power and imposed exceptional rules maintained by a military regime. This move effectively returned Algeria to the conditions of its nineteenth-century conquest.

On 15 May 1958, when Salan called de Gaulle to power, two regimes emerged: one led by the army, effectively imposing a military dictatorship, and the other seeking to restore civilian government and the institutions of the defunct Fourth Republic. Intelligence operatives worked outside legal boundaries, employing torture – a practice widely known about and endorsed at the highest military levels despite its illegality. To crush the ALN and dismantle the FLN's politico-administrative structures embedded among civilians, the French army embarked on a plan that stifled the very population it aimed to embrace and win over.[23] With de Gaulle's return to power and the new constitution of the Fifth Republic reaffirming executive power, a commission was created to reinstate safeguards for individual rights and freedoms. However, and despite political claims that torture would no longer be tolerated, the French army continued to interrogate civilians and use torture to gather intelligence and suppress the Algerian rebellion, even under the new constitutional order of the Fifth Republic.

In December 1958, despite the apparent resumption of civilian government with General Salan's departure, repression paradoxically intensified, escalating into a full-scale war against civilian populations.[24] The repressive system installed by Salan persisted, operating outside civilian government jurisdiction. As Branche astutely observes, the Algerian war mirrored a colonising mission, re-enacting the violence of the nineteenth-century conquest.

During May 1958, the army and French settlers found common ground in advocating for 'French Algeria'. Settlers recognised that retaining French Algeria hinged on investing power in the army, with de Gaulle at the helm. The army revived its 1840s-era connection with the *bureaux arabes* to manage the native rural population. To conquer, pacify and win over the population, the army aimed to sever the ALN's association with the population. The army's brutal violence sought to break resistance while simultaneously winning hearts and minds – conflicting aims at the core of de Gaulle's politics. De Gaulle's approach to the Algerian crisis was twofold: military and political. He instructed General Challe to win the war on the ground, enabling political negotiations,[25] hence pursuing war and peace concurrently. De Gaulle's dual strategy served two purposes: it preserved the army's honour despite war crime violations while employing the raison d'état to conceal these offences. In retrospect, one could argue that he tacitly encouraged General Challe to prosecute the war with ruthless efficiency, thereby positioning himself to negotiate armistice terms that would shield against potential war crime accusations. The counter-revolutionary war against Algeria's rural population, resulting in war crimes and crimes against humanity, represented a final attempt to maintain French imperial power after the Indochina failure. Paradoxically, in serving state interests, the army undermined the state's governing principles. As Fanon argues, 'the whole French nation finds itself involved in the crime against a people and is today an accomplice in the murders and tortures that characterise the Algerian war'. 'Torture in Algeria', he affirms, 'is not an accident or error', but an inherent expression and means of the occupier–occupied relationship.[26]

It is crucial to debunk the argument that torture was the only way to quickly extract information to thwart 'terrorist' activities, as time was purportedly of the essence. Torture was not a singular activity; as Branche demonstrates, it was practised in groups and over extended periods to amplify its psychological effects. Moreover, torture always involved a witness to the ordeal, facilitating interrogation and information extraction. However, these witnesses could not testify about the torture, as they were subsequently made to disappear. The semantics of this operation are captured by François Lyotard in his discussion of the witness who is not a witness, because they cannot speak or seek redress for the damage they suffered before the law.[27] Those who survived the ordeal were left broken, or as Fanon described them, 'personalit[ies] in shreds', brought to him for treatment.[28]

Torture not only targeted those detained but also aimed to repress and pacify a third party: the FLN and the civilian population. It engendered symbolic violence, hidden from French public opinion but manifest in Algiers, reaffirming the colonial state's power against the FLN insurgency. Such symbolic violence fuelled what Fanon called 'the enormous circuit of "terrorism and counterterrorism",[29] ultimately culminating in the Battle of Algiers. As I will demonstrate below, this symbolic violence manifested in various forms, including public executions, forced unveiling of women and gang rapes conducted openly. These acts were not isolated incidents but components of a broader strategy to subjugate the Algerian population and crush its resistance.

Fanon points out that the French concern was solely the moral impact on the French psyche, overlooking the grave atrocities inflicted upon Algerians. The torture of Algerians and the rape of young girls were seen as threats to French honour, not as horrific crimes against humanity. Torture, Fanon argues, was a defining characteristic of the colonial state, and French soldiers in Algeria were compelled to become torturers. The Algerian struggle was not merely against torture, rape, and murder – though the French occupation was rife with such crimes. The Algerians understood that these atrocities were necessary to sustain the colonial structure through military occupation and powerful policing. Fanon contends that their demand was total liberation from French colonial rule. Their objective transcended condemning individual acts; it was a rejection of the entire dehumanising system that enabled and required such crimes.

Amid reports of French army torture, Mollet established a commission to protect human rights. In response to the backlash, General Salan condemned individual acts of violence against civilians, especially women and children, but, as commander-in-chief, his instructions to carry out 'muscular questioning'[30] led to these abuses, placing responsibility on him. His attempts to deflect blame by attributing the violence to rogue elements were unconvincing. As Fanon notes, such appalling practices were widespread and shockingly systematic.[31] French troops' conduct in Algeria exemplified a system of oppressive control, systematic racism and dehumanisation. Fanon asserts that torture was an inherent by-product of the entire colonial system, not isolated acts of devious individuals as Salan suggested.

Fanon deplores the French government's normalisation of torture – initially denying its existence and later claiming any instances were isolated, to be dealt with through internal measures. He insists that torture and massacres were grave crimes under public law that could not be concealed. When the ends justified any means, torture became rationalised as essential to the colonial system. In pursuing its goals through any available methods, Fanon argues, the colonial power detached ends from means, embracing torture as a valid instrument of control. He also criticises French intellectuals who condemned the dehumanising effects of the Algerian war on French youth, focused solely on the moral impact on the French psyche, ignoring the atrocities inflicted upon Algerians.[32]

Returning to Salan's duplicitous denial of systematic torture, the head of the commission investigating the issue of torture and missing persons held the army corps commanders responsible, not those following orders.[33] The ICRC unequivocally reported the systematic use of torture, contradicting Salan's denials and exposing pervasive human rights violations in the Algerian conflict. Torture, used to extract information, became synonymous with the war itself – where information was paramount. The Battle of Algiers is often dubbed 'the information war'.[34] Intelligence and psychological action became key determining factors; they constituted 'novel structural elements in the battle and its strategic operation'. The Officer of Information (OR), pivotal in the subversive war, was granted extraordinary powers to arrest, intern and interrogate.[35] In this 'psychological action', strategic operations and matters of justice became so intertwined that the course of justice was often obstructed or suspended.

Psychological action was hailed as a 'religion of intelligence', with the officers gathering it revered as its 'apostles'.[36] Intelligence had to be exploited immediately, and this new 'religion' installed torture as a mechanism to extract it. This 'religion' supplanted the absolutism of the *ancien régime*, where the sovereign, according to Foucault, had the power of life and death over their subjects. Torture became an instrument of colonial biopolitics, articulating this absolute power; it was instituted as an aspect of this 'religion', which held the right of life and death over individuals who were arrested, interrogated, incarcerated and liquidated. As Branche affirms, torture did not just mean denying individuals' freedom by arresting them; it authorised their execution. Summary executions, following the exploitation of information, were the *telos* of this 'religion' and the logical conclusion of the scrambling of the categories of the law. The 'religion of information' spread its new beliefs with 'good conscience', hijacking the legal powers of the state and weaponising justice to serve the army in the subversive war.[37]

THE MACHINERY OF REPRESSION:
TACTICS OF TERROR AND TORTURE

On 5, 13 and 14 March 1958, and 25 May 1959, *Le Monde* reported that the French army carried out summary executions. Similarly, in June 1959, *El Moudjahid* published reports of executions and mutilated bodies displayed in Tiaret, Le Clos Salembier, Malakoff, Alfredville and Béhagle.[38] These reports highlighted instances of human rights violations and atrocities committed by French forces against Algerian civilians and combatants.[39] The decree of April 1959 sought to restore the functions of the justice system and contain the army by re-establishing the state's monopoly over violence, explicitly forbidding summary executions.[40]

In November 1959, Colonel Argoud openly defied the state by calling for public executions, summary justice without due process and the display of mutilated bodies.[41] These practices, designed to terrorise the civilian population, brought the army into direct conflict with the newly founded Fifth Republic. Such terrorist acts posed an overt challenge to an already dysfunctional French state. Public executions and the display of FLN members' bodies were manifestations of a will-to-power, aimed at dominating, disciplining and punishing the population. These extrajudicial killings, along with those carried out by the French state, formed part of a broader disciplinary process to assert control and dominance over the Algerian people.

Summary executions and the public display of bodies were flagrant acts of terror and torture directed not only at the FLN organisation but also at the civilian population. Branche affirms that coercing family members to witness the interrogation or summary execution of relatives to extract information was a mise-en-scène of military power targeting civilians.[42] In the preface to *Studies in a Dying Colonialism*, Fanon cites the Swedish journalist Christina Lilliestierna's interview with refugees, recounting a harrowing incident where a seven-year-old boy was bound with steel wire and forced by a French lieutenant to witness the mistreatment and killing of his parents and sisters. This cruel act was intended to sear the memory of their torment and execution into the child's mind probably for as long as he lived. The Algerian Red Crescent documented numerous cases of Algerian civilians being summarily executed in front of their children. Fanon deplores this 'apocalyptic atmosphere' that generated state crimes and vengeful hatred – crimes defended by France, the self-proclaimed beacon of democracy – in its efforts to maintain colonial control.[43]

Justice administered by some high-ranking officers was swift and summary, lacking due process and aimed at subjugating the native population. For Aussaresses, it was a matter of arithmetic; due to the sheer number of those arrested and held in detention or at the CTTs, the justice system could not cope, leading to extrajudicial measures. To underscore the scale of the operation, it was estimated that in 1957, more than two thousand people were arrested every month. The institution of the CTT created a legal framework where the law was systematically violated. The strategies used in the Battle of Algiers were implemented across Algeria, leading the army to wage total war, not only against the FLN but also against civilian populations.[44] In the CTTs, the DOP conducted the interrogation of detainees, referred to as 'clients', with the assistance of interpreters and doctors. Doctors facilitated the interrogation, while interpreters not only acted as translators but also actively participated in the questioning. The methods employed ranged from verbal insults and death threats to beatings and the use of water and electricity. One of the key strategies was to undermine the confidence of the 'clients' and weaken their psychological resistance by acting on and breaking their corporeal schema. Torture, and the attendant physical violence it entailed, accomplished this goal.[45]

This violence had unsettling sexual overtones, compounding its brutality. Sexuality became a crucial battleground for psychological warfare. The instruments of interrogation targeted the body, focusing on reproductive organs, tragically transforming them into crucibles of suffering for both male and female victims. Several questions arise: why was so much attention focused on the reproductive organs? Were these acts manifestations of perverse Orientalist attitudes and sexuality? Or did they cut to the core of the colonial problem, namely the demographic dominance of the natives? Did they target the very aspect that engendered the native population against which the army was pitted? Was this form of torture intended to maim, emasculate and sterilise? Were they the solution to the Algerian 'problem'? Initially, the military chaplaincy rationalised certain illegal practices, such as torture, to avoid undermining the army. However, a clearer position was subsequently formulated in *Étude d'un comportement moral en face d'une guerre subversive*, which condemned interrogation methods that 'put suspects through the telephone' or involved water torture or rape targeting sexual organs to obtain information.[46]

Mouloud Feraoun bemoans 'the blind authority of [the French] army which tramples, dishonours, hits and kills'.[47] Yet, despite the army's physical and psychological assaults, it failed to sever the bonds between the ALN and the civilian population. In fact, as Feraoun affirms in his *Journal* at the beginning of 1959, it had the opposite effect; it cemented them. How could the French win hearts and minds when they were busy carrying out summary executions, displaying mutilated bodies, displacing entire villages and raping women? In his searing account, Fanon bears witness to the horrific brutalities inflicted upon Algerian women during the Algerian war. With haunting eloquence, he writes: 'Arrested, tortured, raped, shot down – [the Algerian women] testif[ied] to the violence of the occupier and to his inhumanity.'[48] Fanon's words cut to the core, giving voice to the unspeakable suffering and dehumanisation endured by these women at the hands of their oppressors.

The psychological tactics used during the Algerian war, both benevolent and violent, aimed to reconquer the population, with the rape of women serving as a recurring and symbolic method since the early days of colonial conquest over a century before.[49] Algerian women would cover their faces with mud or excrement to repel French soldiers.[50] Some war veterans claimed that Algerian women's veils and poor hygiene prevented soldiers from raping them. However, this issue was obfuscated and remained repressed, not only by the perpetrators but also by their victims. Cultural taboos further prevented victims from speaking about these atrocities. Feraoun provides a harrowing account of the untold sexual violence and rape that women experienced during the Algerian war. 'The soldiers', he bemoans, 'spent three nights at Taourirt-M, as if they were in a free brothel.'[51] Former conscript of the Algerian war and author of *Les Égorgeurs*, Benoît Rey offers a similar account, citing his commanding officer's instruction to soldiers: 'You could rape, but do it discreetly.'[52] British historian Alistair Horne, author of *A Savage War of Peace*, discusses the prevalence of rape perpetrated by French troops, particularly during the pacification of 'rebel' villages; these acts occurred concomitantly with the control of civilian populations.[53] Echoing these horrendous accounts, Frantz Fanon opines:

We must question the Algerian earth meter by meter, and measure the fragmentation of the Algerian family, the degree to which it finds itself scattered. A woman led away by soldiers who comes back a week later – it is unnecessary to question her to understand that she has been violated dozens of times. A husband taken away by the enemy who comes back with his body covered with contusions, more dead than alive, his mind stunned. Children scattered to the winds, innumerable orphans who roam about, haggard and famished. When a man welcomes his wife who has spent two weeks in a French camp ... he avoids looking at her and bows his head – when such things are a daily occurrence, it is not possible to imagine that the Algerian family can have remained intact and that hatred of colonialism has not swelled immeasurably ... In stirring up these men and women, colonialism has regrouped them beneath a single sign. Equally victims of the same tyranny, simultaneously identifying a single enemy, this physically dispersed people is realizing its unity and founding in suffering a spiritual community which constitutes the most solid bastion of the Algerian Revolution.[54]

From 1954 onwards, Fanon argues, the French regime's brutal tactics of terror and torture, intended to fragment Algerian society and crush resistance, ironically fostered a spiritual unity that propelled the Algerian Revolution. The very brutality designed to destroy Algerian society ultimately strengthened its struggle for freedom and justice. As thousands of Algerian men were interned, families were scattered, fleeing to Tunisia and Morocco. The widespread murder, rape and torture of Algerians by the French shocked the world and deeply disrupted family unity through fragmentation and dislocation.

Gender politics played a key role in the dual strategy to pacify the insurgency: (1) the destruction – in other words, violation – of the extended family and its cultural economy, and (2) the co-option of Algerian women. This psychological action targeted women as symbolic agents by 'unveiling' them, loosening their ties to traditional family life and endogamy. In *Studies in a Dying Colonialism*, Fanon assigns Algerian women a transformative role but cautions against the challenges they encountered in the face of the dislocation of the family unit. 'Algeria Unveiled' and the subsection 'Algeria Dispersed' in 'The Algerian Family', when read together, provide an incisive critique of how colonial violence disrupted Algerian family structures and inflicted suffering on women. This is not to suggest that Fanon idealised the role played by women in the revolution. In fact, he provides a blunt assessment of the hardships they faced, extending beyond the symbolic resistance portrayed in 'Algeria Unveiled'. Most critics romanticise this resistance through the act of veiling/unveiling, glossing over the actual suffering, rape, violence and brutal force which women endured. Ultimately, to provide a holistic reading of Fanon's work and articulate Algerian women's often brutal experiences, it is essential to reinterpret 'Algeria Unveiled' within its historical context and alongside the violence documented in the case studies in *The Wretched of the Earth*.

In June 1959, the Algerian Red Crescent published a booklet in French and English, entitled 'Les Réfugiés algériens'. While seeking material aid for refugees and victims of Challe's population resettlement policy, the Algerian Red Crescent highlighted issues of torture, summary executions and rape. It provided documentary photographic evidence of atrocities perpetrated by the French army, showing summarily executed civilians, sexualised torture and public rape in front of family members. One photograph illustrated what became known in French slang as the *tournante*: gang rape. Women and old men were kept restrained in separate areas by armed soldiers, while others took turns assaulting women and guarding the *mechta* or the *douar*.[55] On 20 February 1959, Feraoun documented the widespread violation of women in his *Journal*.[56] Soldiers descended on Aït Idir during the night. The next day, only twelve women admitted to being raped, while countless others hid behind the cover of silence. In one of Béni-Oucifs' villages, 56 illegitimate children were counted. Most attractive women were taken by the soldiers. Fatma witnessed her daughters and daughter-in-law being raped before her very eyes. Referring to Akli's daughter, a victim raped by soldiers, he states that 'the [Algerian] men have a hard time bearing the outrage done to the women'. Feraoun also recounts a more extreme case: a man known to his colleague H– committed suicide after being forcibly restrained and made to watch soldiers sexually abuse his wife, daughter and daughter-in-law.[57]

In *The Wretched of the Earth*, Fanon documents a similar case of rape and analyses the psychological trauma inflicted. In 'Colonial War and Mental Disorders', he discusses the case of B–'s impotence following his wife's rape by French soldiers after brutal interrogation. To fully understand this case study, it is important to familiarise the reader with the history of the trauma. B–, a 26-year-old former taxi driver, joined the FLN nationalist movement in 1955, transporting militants and weapons until French crackdowns forced him into the maquis. After two years of silence, his wife informed him of her dishonour at the hands of French soldiers, who had brutally interrogated and repeatedly raped her over a week, instructing her to relay their actions to B–. Though initially shaken, B– managed to suppress his immediate feelings, having heard similar accounts of Algerian women's torture. However, this personal tragedy struck at the core of his sense of honour and masculinity. While prioritising the larger struggle for liberation, B– grappled with the prospect of accepting his wife back into his life. His plight reflected the experiences of many Algerian soldiers who faced severe mental health issues upon learning of their wives' rape. Consumed by guilt, B– found himself impotent – a symbolic manifestation of his perceived emasculation.

His attempts at extra-marital affairs failed, which he initially attributed to physical exhaustion. During therapy sessions with Fanon, B– revealed disturbing impulses, such as wanting to tear up his daughter's photo. Fanon initially misdiagnosed these as unconscious incestuous impulses. However, further interviews and a dream in which B– saw a little cat rapidly rotting away, accompanied by unbearably 'evil' smells, led Fanon to reassess. B– confided to Fanon, 'That girl has something rotten about her', referring to his daughter. His insomnia worsened, and his anxiety heightened alarmingly. Finally, B– spoke about his wife, laughing bitterly, 'She's tasted the French.'[58] This revelation allowed Fanon to reconstruct the entire narrative. B– admitted that before every sexual attempt with other women, he thought of his wife. The psychological scars of her rape had shattered the foundations of his identity as a husband, father and man. As the independence struggle intensified, B–'s perspective gradually evolved. He became more willing to reconcile with his wife if national liberation was achieved, signalling a shift in priorities and recognition of the sacrifices endured by Algerian women. This narrative poignantly depicts the psychological trauma and internal conflicts faced by Algerian men during the anticolonial struggle, laying bare the complex interplay of honour, guilt and loyalty that shaped their responses to such harrowing experiences.

Ultimately, the evolution of B–'s perspective highlights not so much the ability to transcend personal anguish in the pursuit of a greater cause, but the sacrifices of women. Despite stigma and cultural taboos, B–'s wife spoke about being raped, about French soldiers violating her flesh. Her story exemplifies women's resilience and contributions. Fanon emphasises the importance of documenting and analysing the diverse roles women played during the struggle across cities, rural areas, enemy administrations, as informants, prisoners facing torture and in the judicial system. He calls for comprehensive coverage of women's multifaceted involvement and sacrifices during this revolutionary period. While men's contributions are well-documented, he argues that women played equally vital but largely unexplored roles across all spheres. To truly capture the full narrative, the multidimensional experiences of women in all circumstances must be explored. Only by meticulously documenting these diverse experiences can we appreciate women's central role in shaping the revolution's trajectory and victory. Their sacrifices deserve to be enshrined in the nation's history.

Cultural, historical and strategic factors shaped rape as an articulation of colonial conflict in Algeria. Motivated by the desire to possess and humiliate, rape functioned to maintain French colonial presence in Algerian women's bodies. Sexual violence targeted not just women, but Algerian men, families and society as a whole. The Algerian woman symbolised the last unconquered bastion of colonisation. Rape symbolically overcame this failure, replicating the expropriating economy of colonial conquest. It perversely maintained colonialism within women's bodies as a faltering historical fact. Torture took on a sexualised dimension, with rape and sexual assaults exercised on women's bodies 'in the material comfort of an occupying army, but with the symbolic dimension of conquering force.'[59] This brutal violence served to assert the coloniser's dominance over the intimate spheres of indigenous life. These sexual violations were doubly misogynistic, targeting both native women and colonised men. They stripped men of their masculine identity and authority while subjugating colonial subjects and rendering female bodies docile. This sort of misogyny weaponised rape and sexual assault to assert phallocentric power, reinforce colonial hegemony, and reconfigure power relations. Ultimately, these acts served to maintain domination through a perverse form of gendered violence.

THE GENDERED BATTLEFIELD: SEXUAL VIOLENCE AS BIOPOLITICAL WEAPON

After the Battle of Algiers, General Massu issued a directive addressing the FLN's effective deployment of women operatives in urban combat. In his *Journal*, Feraoun captures the escalating violence: 'The [FLN] mobilises women, and the soldiers start to arrest and torture women.'[60] The Algerian war descended into unspeakable atrocities, with violence, rape and sexual assaults becoming interrogation methods. Women were subjected to severe physical and sexual violence, with their bodies becoming targets for brutal acts of aggression. These acts, used as tools of oppression and control, transformed the female body into a battlefield for asserting dominance and inflicting terror. A harrowing example is the case of Djamila Boupacha, arrested in 1960 and subjected to horrific torture, including sexual assault with a bottle neck and toothbrush, and electric shocks that severely damaged her genitalia.[61] This intelligence-driven conflict saw the recruitment of various experts – linguists, psychologists, medical doctors, and interpreters – to aid in interrogations. Radio technology served a dual purpose: as a means of communication and information gathering, but also as an instrument of torture. Interpreters played a sinister role, assisting torturers by forcing suspects to speak during brutal questioning sessions. The Algerian war stands as a dark chapter in history, marked by heinous acts of violence and torture perpetrated against civilians, often with disturbing sexual undertones. The human body, particularly the genitals, became a battleground, with torture serving as a means to subjugate an entire population through unimaginably inhumane methods.[62]

Sexual reproduction is a biological necessity for human societies and is crucial for cultural reproduction. Althusser posits that societies must reproduce themselves both biologically and ideologically to sustain their means of production. He introduces the concepts of Ideological State Apparatuses (ISAs) and Repressive State Apparatus (RSA), which work together to reproduce dominant ideology and social structures. ISAs (such as family, religion, and education) primarily use ideology, while RSA overtly uses force. Althusser's theory of 'interpellation' explains how individuals become subjects through interaction with ISAs and compliance with RSA. This process occurs at the interface of public and private spheres, creating citizens who participate in political life. Critics argue that Althusser's theory is too formalistic and does not allow for change or resistance. However, his Algerian colonial background may explain this perspective. In colonial Algeria, there was one RSA (French) but two conflicting sets of ISAs: European/Catholic and Muslim/indigenous. Althusser's theory does not address the colonial anomaly where a single RSA coexists with two conflicting ISAs, leading to a disjunction between the private lives of the colonised and the public sphere. For the colonised Algerians – excluded from public life – family and religion became two crucial ISAs, both for individuation and for maintaining their cultural identity. In colonial contexts, Fanon argues, the family unit contrasts with that in 'normal' societies, where private life aligns more closely with national life.[63] In the colonial context, the colonised retreated to the private sphere to enact their cultural belonging, highlighting the complex relationship between identity, ideology and power in colonial societies.

As noted in Chapter 4, colonialism profoundly disrupted, but did not entirely dismantle, endogamy, which traditionally maintained distinct cultural identities, regulated sexuality, and ensured the intergenerational transmission of cultural practices. This disruption led to the hardening of endogamous structures and the emergence of colonial traditionalism. Colonial laws undermined traditional property systems, causing land alienation, fragmenting family structures, impoverishing communities and intensifying natalist tendencies. In response, Algerians retreated to the private sphere, leveraging family life and religion as bastions of resistance. The veil emerged as a potent symbol of cultural preservation, delineating boundaries between coloniser and colonised. Traditionally, endogamy served as a linchpin in cultural reproduction, but colonialism subverted its mechanisms, leading to substantial social, economic and cultural transformations. Understanding colonialism's impact on endogamy is crucial for comprehending broader processes of cultural change and resistance in colonial Algeria.

Colonial traditionalism posed a formidable barrier to French colonial advances. This resistance centred on Algerian women's sexuality, perceived as the final frontier of conquest and domination. French colonialism expropriated native Algerians, displaced them and occupied their land, but it could not hegemonise their culture. As both Fanon and Nora argue, Algerian women embodied this culture and its resistance to the colonising gaze. Likewise, Feraoun highlights the deep connection between women's bodies, sexuality and honour, contending that at the height of the Algerian war the public violation of women served to dishonour Algerian men. Pacification in the nineteenth century entailed a violation of the inextricable link between the *irthe/arthe*, constitutive of the foundational aspects of endogamy which resisted colonial intrusion. Initially, the economic structures that upheld endogamy were dislocated by alienating that which was not alienable: the family landholdings, the very materiality of *horma*. The alienation caused by colonialism led to a hardening of endogamous structures. The veil manifestly represented this hardening and came to symbolise the demarcation imposed by colonial Manichaeanism. Consequently, it instigated a 'battle' throughout the entire period of colonisation, with Algerian women as the primary targets. The assaults on women and land aimed at the mechanisms and agencies of biological and cultural reproduction of Algerian society. Colonial biopolitics was fundamentally a question of managing the native population and optimising the viability of the colonial project.

Colonial biopolitics aimed to dismantle the productive and reproductive processes of indigenous society, seeking its destruction. While managing the growing native population, the colonial assault on endogamy attacked its natalist tendencies – its very sexuality – which threatened the colonial project's viability. Torture, focusing on genitalia, targeted the reproductive apparatus that posed this threat, attempting to neutralise the native society's human potential. Summary executions served as another aspect of this biopolitical strategy. The public rape of women, like the public executions of men and display of mutilated bodies, manifested colonial authority over the body. These acts demonstrated the colonial state's will to annihilate the population, aiming to destroy and reconstruct indigenous society according to the repressive state's demands.

Fanon's 'Algeria Unveiled', which explores the veil's historical dynamism, significantly influenced Pontecorvo's film *The Battle of Algiers* (1966) and Alloula's book *The Colonial Harem* (1981), particularly in their examination of colonialism and gender politics. Alloula frames the colonial conflict in masculinist terms, arguing that the veiled Algerian woman became a target due to her perceived invisibility and inaccessibility. Unveiling her seemed like tacit revenge against an endogamous society that resisted the colonising gaze. Fanon contends that in the Europeans' erotic dreams, raping the Algerian woman follows her unveiling – a double deflowering that reveals the coloniser's relationship with the colonised. These dreams involve violent possession and near-murder, not of a single Algerian woman, but of multiple women in a gynaeceum or harem. These fantasies of violent possession represent a condensed symbol of colonial domination, articulating the desire to possess and dominate the entire colonised population. Raping the veiled Algerian woman embodies both cultural unveiling and sexual subjugation, with the colonised female body becoming a metaphor for the land and people to be seized. Caution is needed against purely Orientalist interpretations that risk obscuring the actual violence experienced by Algerian women. Balancing representational analysis with an understanding of lived experiences is crucial to fully grasp the gendered violence of colonialism. The violence against women was not merely a double deflowering as Fanon and Alloula intimated, but a triple violation. It was not only the rape of unveiling and the physical act women suffered in their corporeality, but also symbolically targeted men, the family, and society in its entirety. The public rape served to optimise the torture and defile the core value of *irthe* – the notion of men's honour invested in the body of women.

The French government commissioned a report in anticipation of the Ordinance of 4 February 1959, which aimed to reform the legal personal status of Algerian Muslims, to assess potential backlash. Captain L.P. Fauque authored this report, entitled *Stades d'évolution de la cellule familiale musulmane d'Algérie*. On 20 May of that year, the General Delegation of the Government in Algeria published it with limited distribution. Fauque echoes Fanon and Bourdieu in characterising colonial Algeria as a divided society and aligns with Tillion and Le Cour Grandmaison in depicting its endogamous populations as separate and fearful of racial intermixing. Despite 130 years of French colonisation, Fauque argues, Western influence only superficially permeated Algerian society, with reciprocal prohibitions maintaining European settlers and native Algerians as distinct communities. Fauque claims that education and social mobility sparked an awakening among Algerian women, seemingly at odds with Islamic tradition, creating a dilemma that forced Algerians to choose between 'de-Islamisation' or 'liberal interpretation of Koranic law'.[64] Fauque's report highlights tensions between modernisation and traditional Islamic values regarding women's roles. It exemplifies Lazreg's concept of 'military feminism', which weaponised women's emancipation for colonial control and pacification.[65] The proposed reform must be viewed in a context where the army brutally repressed the civilian population, especially women. The 1959 Ordinance aimed to reconfigure Algerian social structures by reforming traditional marriage and family laws, which the French perceived as obstacles to their colonial rule. However, Fauque's discourse starkly contrasts with the reality of colonial violence and misogyny, including the use of rape as a tool of oppression. It is important to interpret the reform as an integral part of the pacification strategy which consisted in dismantling the social structures of Algerian society.

It is also worth reiterating that this strategy was twofold: violent, aimed at crushing the FLN's organisational structure, and benevolent, focused on administering care and providing assistance to the impoverished native population. In the parlance of psychological action officers, it involved both *destruction* and *construction*.[66] Significantly, this action targeted Algerian women as prime agents to effect change, realise integration and pave the way for the reconstruction of 'New French Algeria'. To grasp the full ramifications of the violence that pacification engendered, it is crucial to analyse it intersectionally, considering military strategy, historical context and political implications. Understanding the gap between political rhetoric and realities on the ground requires a focus on the issue of population. Re-examining the views of Cambon and Chellier highlights how the colonial conflict was inherently a problem of population, intertwined with gender and sexual politics.

Cambon, aware of the native population's demographic dominance, staunchly opposed assimilation or integration. Such policies would have nullified the political and economic privileges of the 250,000 European settlers, who were a minority amidst over 4 million indigenous people in the 1890s. In Algeria, he argued, France encountered diverse populations intent on maintaining their distinct identities and lifestyles. This demographic anxiety persisted throughout Algeria's colonisation until decolonisation. By the time of the Algerian War of Independence in the 1950s, the population of approximately 10 million had a 10:1 ratio of natives to Europeans. A key factor motivating the rebellion was the Europeans' refusal to accept electoral parity, insisting that one European vote should not be worth less than nine Muslim votes. The demographic gap was the main obstacle to integration, which conflicted with the colonial regime the European settlers sought to maintain. From Cambon to Jonnart to Lacoste, the assimilation of the colonised represented a persistent challenge for the colonial state. Muslims' demography was the crux of the colonial problem, seemingly unresolvable without 'amputating' what defined and constituted the native population.

The events of 13 May 1958 did not precipitate an unexpected change in attitude regarding integration. Rather, they were part of a longer process. In a letter of 5 November 1956 to prefects and IGAME officials, Lacoste had already established a commission to overhaul laws concerning the personal legal status ('*statut personnel*') of Algerians.[67] The 1957 law, which introduced regulations to harmonise French and Islamic legislations, announced political reforms regarding women's emancipation, marriage and divorce. The reforms posed two significant challenges: one for mainland France and another for the colony. First, the integration of 9 million Muslim Algerians presented a substantial hurdle for French politics and its purported *laïcité*, which, contrary to claims, was neither culturally nor politically neutral. *Laïcité* functioned as a colonial mythology, used to disenfranchise those whose beliefs differed from Catholicism. Religion was a requirement for the naturalisation of native Algerians under the Sénatus-consulte law of 1865. This religious criterion persisted in the Jonnart Law of 1919, enacted after the 1905 Laïcité Law, as a condition for natives to attain French citizenship. Lacoste's reforms, ostensibly aimed at streamlining legal frameworks, effectively re-enacted the 1865 and 1919 laws by reaffirming the role of religion in politics. These reforms thus reinforced the connection between religion and politics, promoting a concept of naturalisation that sought to neutralise the cultural distinctiveness of the native population. Second, the assimilation of the indigenous population, which outnumbered the European settlers by a ratio of 10 to 1, threatened the loss of colonial privileges. This demographic reality posed an existential challenge to the colonial order, as full integration would inevitably lead to a shift in political power, undermining the very foundations of French colonial rule in Algeria.

These reforms, implemented after de Gaulle's return to power, reconfigured the main strategies for prosecuting the war. The battleground shifted from the theatre of war to targeting the family structure, Algerian women, and the personal status of Muslims. This significant shift, from warfare to psychological action, became central to France's 'subversive' and 'counter-revolutionary' war. The target was not just the *fellaghas* but the very elements that defined the native population – its identity, culture and traditions.

Ostensibly aimed at 'simplifying' laws governing indigenous society, these reforms primarily targeted Algerian women and family structures. However, the measures highlighted the primary challenge that had confronted French Algeria since its inception and sought to resolve the insurmountable demographic disparity between the European and indigenous populations by diminishing the latter, thereby neutralising their cultural potency.

While purporting to streamline legal frameworks, the reforms ultimately served to weaken the cultural resilience of the indigenous population. 'Integration' implied that Muslims must abandon their personal status to 'live under the same law [as the French], an indispensable condition for national unity',[68] ultimately neutralising native cultural norms. Women's emancipation had the same intended outcome: dismantling traditional society and family structures. This concept of emancipation starkly contrasted with the reality on the ground, which was marked by violence – torture, rape and summary execution of civilians. The rhetoric of emancipation highlighted the gap between political discourse and the harsh realities faced by the rural population, especially women, during pacification. The rapidly growing indigenous population presented another insurmountable challenge that could not be overlooked. The reforms, which sought to destroy Algerian society and rebuild it according to French laws and cultural norms, addressed this demographic issue by effecting the *mise-en-sac* of cultural difference. This sort of annihilation was tantamount to extermination by other means. The brutality of the war on the ground affirms the theses of historians like Le Cour Grandmaison that extermination was the endgame of French colonial conquest in Algeria. The four-decade conquest unleashed warfare designed to exterminate the native population,[69] as evidenced by the devastating famines during 1867–68. Yet colonisation stumbled over population challenges, defying claims that the 'degenerate' native population was doomed to vanish.[70] Amid the devastation, hope defied predictions of Algerian Arab extinction. The population nearly doubled, soaring from 2,931,000 in 1866 to 5,158,000 in 1906 and to over 9 million in the 1950s. Ultimately, colonisation faltered over demographic issues.

Additionally, as Chellier argues, religion and gender remained significant obstacles to the colonial agenda. She contends that indigenous women were more resistant to assimilation than men, asserting that French colonisation could not 'penetrate the gynaeceum' or conquer the domestic sphere. Echoing Chellier, Nora states that through conquest and settlement, 'the Muslim woman has safeguarded the unity of the family'.[71] French colonisation failed to penetrate the domestic and religious spheres – two domains that remained impervious to colonial influence. The veiled, inscrutable Algerian woman embodied Algeria's inviolable core, a sentinel guarding her society's culture. She personified the heart of the anticolonial struggle, preserving her people's cultural identity – an unbreakable link to a way of life the French could not dominate. Cixous captures this unbreachable core of resistance in her letter to Zohra Drif, an emblematic figure in the Battle of Algiers: 'The Casbah with its folds and powerful, poor people, its hunger, desires, and vaginality, was always for me the clandestine and revered sex of the City of Algiers. And it resisted rape.'[72]

The letter, intended for Zohra Drif but unsent, might also be redirected to her friend, Djemila Boupacha, who was tortured and raped. Vaginality symbolised both sexuality and population, serving as sources of anticolonial resistance despite poverty, and standing against the phallic power of the French army's subversive war. This vaginality was arrested, questioned, and liquidated, becoming the focus of psychological action and a strategic target in deconstructing and reconstructing native society. Fanon, like Cixous, portrays the veiled Algerian woman as Algeria's hidden, elusive face, personifying the Casbah and remaining inaccessible even when forcibly unveiled during the May 1958 'fraternisation ceremonies'. Fanon's chapters 'The Algerian Family' and 'Algeria Unveiled' should be read together as a protest against the Fifth and Second Bureaus' psychological warfare, which used rape, torture and violation of Algerian women to undermine the unity of both the Algerian family and the revolution.

The French army's pacification policy, that is, its scorched earth tactics and resettling Algerian families in 'regroupment camps', displaced over a third of the population. This policy, which fragmented Algerian society and dislocated families, was accompanied by legislation targeting the family and women's personal status. Military tactics and legal measures worked together to dismantle the two main obstacles to French colonialism: religion and gender politics. Despite efforts to break the Algerian family unit and society, Fanon argues that the war forged stronger bonds among Algerians. French colonialism's attempts to weaken resistance only strengthened their resolve. Fanon highlights this unity, asserting that the 'objectively dispersed people' found solidarity and formed a spiritual community, becoming the strongest bastion of the Algerian Revolution. Fanon clearly articulates two concerns: the psychological action to co-opt Algerian women with a view to targeting the population, and French soldiers' attempts to conquer the population by targeting Algerian women. At its core, the colonial conflict was fundamentally about population, shaped by gender and sexual politics.

Historically, antagonisms between indigenous populations and European settlers often centred on population dynamics and control of resources. The relative size and growth rate of the indigenous population compared to European settlers represented the core of the conflict. Controlling and shifting these population dynamics was a key strategic objective. As colonisation progressed, these conflicts extended beyond mere territorial disputes to encompass social and cultural domains. The French colonisation of Algeria in the nineteenth and twentieth centuries exemplifies how gender and sexuality became critical battlegrounds in colonial struggles. French colonial policies sought to undermine traditional Algerian society by redefining women's legal status, particularly in relation to marriage, divorce and emancipation from prevailing cultural and religious norms. Strategically, sexual violence committed by French forces was used as a tool of subjugation. Feraoun observes that rape became so widespread that the French could no longer claim moral superiority over the Algerians. 'Until now, social life, morals and customs', he writes, 'had the essential objective of jealously safeguarding the sexuality of women. [Algerians] considered this inalienable, and their honour was buried inside the vagina like a treasure more precious than life itself.' Commenting on the devastation wrought by colonial biopolitics, which kept Algerians in a state between life and death, he goes on to add: 'But now, they hold life dearer than their wives' vaginas.'[73]

In conclusion, Cixous's portrayal of the Casbah as 'vaginality' – symbolising overpopulation, poverty, and endemic diseases threatening European settlers – contextualises the events leading to the 'Battle of Algiers'. Threats from European mobsters to burn down the Casbah, a resistance hub, prompted Massu to launch the Battle of Algiers. He formed a team of two assistants to operate as a parallel, secret staff in the battle. Trinquier, known for his role in special services, was tasked with developing a counter-subversion plan and managing population control. Aussaresses, the second assistant, maintained constant communication with police and military command. While Trinquier provided intelligence, Aussaresses organised extrajudicial actions, working in prefecture offices by day and as chief torturer at the 'Tourelles' Villa by night. The Battle of Algiers unfolded nocturnally. Aussaresses described his 'dark' and 'secret' activities: organising arrests, sorting suspects, overseeing interrogations, imposing curfews, conducting summary executions and leaving mutilated bodies in streets to demonstrate government resolve.[74] His mission relieved other regimental units of these unpleasant tasks. In a biopolitical sense, 'cleaning' the Casbah was a matter of life and death. Aussaresses assumed a sovereign role, deciding fates, with serious cases deemed to pose significant threats not sur- viving. Torture was systematic, and those no longer needed by other units were sent to him for 'disposal'. In 'top secret' briefings to Massu, Salan and Lacoste, Aussaresses detailed arrests, torture and executions. Over 20,000 people (3 per cent of Algiers' population) were held in camps. He insisted summary executions were crucial for maintaining order, implicitly endorsed by the French government. Aussaresses believed these actions were effec- tively direct orders from Mollet's government, executed in the name of the French Republic.

Debunking the mythology of colonialism as a civilising mission is crucial. The entire history of colonial Algeria was characterised by brutal violence, theft, murder and rape, which collectively define the terms of colonial biopol- itics. In the name of the state, torture, summary executions and the rape of both land and women were sanctioned. 'Exploitation, tortures, raids, racism, collective liquidations, rational oppression', Fanon explains, 'take turns at dif- ferent levels in order literally to make of the native an object in the hands of the occupying nation.' Fanon is adamant that '[t]his object [person], without means of existing, without a raison d'être, [was] broken in the very depth of [their] substance'.[75] Fanon argues that torture was inherent to the colonial system, compelling French soldiers in Algeria to become its instruments. He asserts that the Algerian struggle transcended opposition to widespread violence – torture, rape and murder – and fundamentally rejected the colonial structure itself. For Fanon, the Algerian demand was unequivocal: total liber- ation from the system that necessitated and justified such atrocities.

In torture, the whole history of colonial conquest and violence crystal- lised; it became a key aspect of the war. Torture was the sum of this violence, the bottom line of colonial politics. It was a defining feature of colonial conquest, a by-product of nineteenth-century repression and pacification, and part of a long history of state violence against uprisings and resistance. The 'smoking out' of Dahra caves in 1845, led by Pélissier and de Saint-Ar- naud; the repression of the El-Mokrani uprising (1870–71) following the famine of 1866–68; and the suppression of the uprisings of 8 May 1945 in Sétif and 20 August 1955 in Philippeville, led by Aussaresses,[76] were all man- ifestations of the French colonial regime and its blind violence.

Torture reproduced the power relations underpinning the Manichaean economy of colonial society, pitting one category of people against another, coloniser against colonised, those who possessed human rights against those to whom such rights were deemed inapplicable. While torture was physi- cally inflicted upon individual suspects, its impact rippled out across entire populations. This disciplinary practice was inherently gendered, incorporating sexuality as both a productive and reproductive process.

In *Travail sur l'Algérie*, Alexis de Tocqueville asserts that the French surpassed the barbarity of the populations they sought to civilise, citing the execution of innocent civilians and massacre of entire communities during the Algerian conquest. This brutal campaign spanned four decades, evolving into a warfare strategy designed to exterminate the native population. However, the conquest faced an unexpected challenge: population growth. The French army deployed various methods to decimate the native population, but these yielded a different outcome and gave rise to Malthusian pressures. In response, colonial settlements were developed, and pacification efforts – both then and during the Algerian war – sought to dislocate Algerian society and pulverise its population.

Torture and violence during the Algerian war were by-products of this history. Initially framed as an 'operation of public order and policing', the Algerian conflict quickly escalated into a war of conquest. The violence unleashed was, in many ways, a returning violence – a *choc de retour*. Sartre, Fanon and Césaire characterised it as a manifestation of the 'boomerang effect'.[77] Sartre coined the term to describe how colonial violence, ultimately rebounding onto the colonisers, eroded their democratic principles and human rights. Dehumanising colonial practices and racist ideologies cultivated by empires boomerang back, oppressing marginalised groups and undermining the colonisers' claims to 'equality' and 'human rights'.

Sartre saw the violence in Algeria as a backlash resulting from colonialism's brutal history, striking back at the foundations of the colonising nation. Colonialism had sown the seeds of turmoil; the violence of decolonisation was the resulting whirlwind.[78] This violence not only mirrored the devastation of nineteenth-century colonial conquest but also turned back against mainland France. The perpetrators of this brutality undermined France's political institutions and democratic laws, exposing the contradictions at the core of the French Republic's civilising mission.[79] What was presented as a policing action devolved into a quagmire of repression, revealing the true nature of French domination.

7

Fanon, the French Liberal Left and the Colonial Consensus

The Algerian Revolution, as Macey astutely remarks, marked the high tide of third-worldism, with Fanon emerging as the pre-eminent spokesperson for a generation of French intellectuals disillusioned with the orthodox left as epitomised by the Parti communiste français (PCF).[1] The 'liberal left',[2] however, criticised his brand of third-worldism for promoting a humanism of violence.[3] Fanon risked his life to uphold the ideals of the Free World and French republicanism. How should one interpret his commitment to these ideals in light of his decision to join the French Resistance during the Second World War? Should one, as journalist Gilbert Comte's scathing review of *The Wretched of the Earth* suggests, view it as a 'pitiless hostility that screams in the mad darkness', reminiscent of Hitler's *Mein Kampf*?[4] How does one reconcile his interpretation of Marxism with the PCF's colonial policies that facilitated the use of raison d'état to justify human rights abuses during the Algerian war? Is it contradictory to present Fanon as an intellectual following in the footsteps of Zola and the Dreyfusards, who stood firmly against this very raison d'état?

This chapter has a twofold aim: first, to nuance the critique of Fanon by reinserting the issue of race into the Marxist debate on the colonial question; second, to shed light on a murky period in French history by showing that Fanon consistently defended the Republican tradition during a time when nationalism forged a consensus between the left and right, leading to colonial fascism. Initially, the chapter discusses the prevalent Marxist interpretation of Fanon and situates it in relation to the PCF's 'assimilationist' politics, which shaped this consensus and ultimately provided fertile ground for the emergence of colonial fascism in the 1950s. It then examines Fanon's journalistic writings to demonstrate that he upheld the Republican – and more specifically Dreyfusard – tradition, which the left abandoned at the height of the Algerian crisis. Finally, the chapter engages with Jean-François Lyotard's contention in *La Guerre des Algériens* that nationalism came to underpin racial antagonism. Fanon's reworking of Marxist theory helps us understand how the colonial issue was overshadowed by the internationalist rhetoric of the Comintern and the nationalist discourse of the PCF's anti-fascist front. This chapter seeks to demonstrate that *The Wretched of the Earth* is, in effect, an anthem that derives its significance from the 'Internationale', yet rethinks the Marxist-Leninist doctrine that colluded with colonialism.

THE MARXIST INTERPRETATION OF FANON

If colonialism brought white and black people into a partnership of uneven reciprocity,[5] it was a relationship that proved to be doubly alienating for Fanon. In *Black Skin, White Masks*, he subscribes to a cultural materialist approach which conceives of the issue of racism as a construct determined by economic conditions. He is adamant that the inferiority complex is engendered by a double process: the economic inferiority of the colonised people is coupled with the internalisation – or what he calls the 'epidermalisation' – of such inferiority.[6] In *The Wretched of the Earth*, he comes to recognise the limits of Marxist analysis in accounting for racism and colonialism: 'Everything up to and including the very nature of precapitalist society, so well explained by Marx, must here be thought out again.'[7] He cautions against orthodox Marxist theory, which considers the bourgeois phase as a necessary step towards the advent of the classless society. By reversing the roles Marx assigned to the proletariat and the lumpenproletariat, Fanon radically subverts Marxist theory. In his conception of the revolution, the proletariat is not revolutionary but rather constitutes 'the nucleus of the colonised population which has been most pampered by the colonial regime';[8] the lumpenproletariat is not a reactionary class, but rather the most revolutionary. The bourgeois phase in the post-independence state, Fanon argues, is a useless phase.

Focusing on the pitfalls of national culture, the Vietnamese historian and writer Nguyen Nghe identifies in Fanon's revolutionary politics vestiges of subjectivism drawn from the Sartrean existential phenomenology that was fashionable at the time, and he chides him for promoting the mythology of the peasantry's 'redemptive' violence as a panacea against the ills of colonialism.[9] Unlike Fanon, Nghe argues that the national bourgeoisie does not represent a useless phase in the process of decolonisation.[10] Fanon's revolutionary politics, he claims, misleads his readers into believing that the peasantry alone expresses the spontaneity of the masses, whereas the mobilisation of the peasantry would not have been possible without the

political organisation provided by the national bourgeoisie.[11] He criticises
Fanon for overlooking the significance of class alliance in the revolution,
an alliance which was crucial in marshalling Algerian nationalism; he also
criticises him for confusing the proletariat with the petty bourgeoisie.[12]
In Nghe's view, Fanon, while highlighting the privileges of the working
class in comparison to the impoverished peasantry, fails to comprehend
that the former was better positioned in relation to the mechanisms of
power: its privileges enabled it to grasp the extent of colonial exploitation and to instigate resistance.[13] Put simply, according to Nghe, Fanon
seems oblivious to the historical totality of the Algerian Revolution, which
had its bases in the city, and to the fact that the peasants who engaged in
armed struggle received their political education from bourgeois intellectuals who lived in the city.[14] In other words, the interaction between the city
and the countryside was crucial in determining the history of the revolutionary movement. For Nghe, then, the working class in Algeria's colonial
cities and the Algerian immigrants in mainland France were not disinter-
ested bystanders but played a crucial role.[15] He therefore criticises Fanon
for waxing lyrical about the peasantry and idealising its armed resistance.
Nghe effectively turns Fanon's argument on its head: without the nationalist leaders, the peasants who were influenced by the maraboutic religious
leaders in the pay of the colonial administration would have been incapable
of harnessing the revolution.[16]

Nghe also calls into question Fanon's international politics, dismissing his
call to the ex-colonised nations to abandon the chimera of following the path
taken by Europe.[17] More specifically, he criticises Fanon for his conception
of a new humanism to be founded in the Third World and for his politics of
non-alignment. Nghe contends that the Third World, in complete contrast
to the rhetoric of Fanon, was vacuous and could not provide the foundations
for political or historical development. He pours scorn on Fanon for sitting
on the ideological fence of Third World neutrality: for Nghe, it was not a
question of choosing between East and West, or, more precisely, between
the Third World and Europe, but between two differing conceptions of the
world, namely capitalism and communism. As persuasive and memorable as
this kind of critique might be, it nevertheless glosses over the specificities of
the context out of which Fanon intervened. To have a better understanding
of his third-worldism and his ideological neutrality, I want now to consider
Nghe's critique in the light of the PCF's problematic political stance vis-à-vis
the colonial question.

'ASSIMILATIONIST' POLITICS AND COLONIAL FASCISM

In the early 1930s, the Comintern altered its strategy on the colonial question by abandoning the class-against-class policy in favour of an anti-fascist front. After the Franco-Soviet Pact, the PCF underwent a process of nationalisation, renouncing its internationalist stance all the better to focus on French domestic affairs. In order to thwart the rise of fascism, Maurice Thorez, leader of the PCF, joined the Front populaire and sought subsequently to extend the alliance with the right in 1939, well after Blum's centre-left coalition government collapsed.[18] There was, however, a perceptible shift in the colonial policies of the PCF: the anti-fascist front ostensibly eclipsed the colonial question and Thorez jettisoned the anticolonial policies which the party previously advocated in the Riff war. This change of strategy exacerbated the close relationship that the Étoile Nord-Africaine (ENA) had established with the PCF in the 1920s. In June 1936, Blum banned the ENA from attending the Congrès musulman algérien. Following its dissolution in 1937, the ENA re-emerged as the Parti du peuple algérien (PPA), advocating for decolonisation. The PPA opposed not only the PCF but also the élus and oulemas for supporting the Blum–Viollette Bill and its assimilationist proposal in 1937. The bill failed to pass due to opposition from Algerian mayors on similar grounds. This failure raised concerns that Algerian nationalism might be co-opted by fascism. As discussed in Chapter 3, Radio Bari's anticolonialist propaganda exacerbated colonial tensions in Algeria and neighbouring North African countries.

In February 1939, just a few months before the outbreak of the Second World War, Thorez visited Algeria. On 11 February, he delivered a speech in Algiers defining the party's position with regard to the colonial question and the issue of fascism.[19] Thorez's representation of Algeria as a 'nation-in-formation' chimed with Gabriel Audisio's and Albert Camus's assimilationist rhetoric that refused the dichotomous language of colonialism and ran counter to the celebration of the *Greco-Latin genius* in Louis Bertrand's novel *Le Sang des races* (1899).[20] If, in the symbiosis of cultures, Bertrand maintained the supremacy of the Latin conquerors, in *Le Sel de la mer*, by contrast, Audisio denounces Bertrand's 'Afrique latine' as an instrument of coloniality, proposing instead a 'Mediterranean humanism' transcending racial and nationalistic chauvinism, contrasting the fascistic ideology of totalitarianism with the 'living sense of community'.[21] Under the auspices of the PCF – and two days after Thorez addressed the party – Camus made a presentation to the Maison de la culture in Algiers. Taking his cue from Thorez and Audisio, he differentiated his Mediterranean from Bertrand's 'abstract and conventional Mediterranean', the Mediterranean of 'human plagiarism', characterised by its 'military genius' and its 'academic image'.[22] Bertrand was one of the intellectuals who supported Mussolini's colonial endeavour in Ethiopia, and Camus denounced the proponents of Latinity for their pro-fascistic tendencies.[23] The Mediterranean was an important strategic site in the fight against fascism.

Thorez's intervention in Algeria – his pronouncements hailing Algeria as a nation-in-formation, as a melting pot in which twenty races merged to form one nationhood – was a rebuttal of Bertrand's racist discourse. In his speech, supplanting the notion of race with that of nationality, Thorez affirms:

> We, communists, do not recognise races. We only want to recognise peoples. [...] *There is the Algerian nation that is constituting itself historically and whose evolution can be facilitated, aided by the effort of the French Republic.* [...] there is an Algerian nation that is constituting itself, also, in the mixture of twenty races.[24]

At the PCF's ninth congress, held in Arles on 29 December 1937, Thorez had reiterated Lenin's idea that 'the right to divorce does not imply the obligation to divorce'.[25] He had warned that the anticolonialist agenda could only help fascism promote its movement in the colonies:

> If the decisive question of the moment is the victorious struggle against fascism, the interest of the colonial peoples lies *in their union* with the people of France and not in an attitude that could favour the enterprises of fascism and place, for example, Algeria, Tunisia and Morocco under the yoke of Mussolini or Hitler, or make Indochina a base of operations for militaristic Japan.[26]

On 11 February 1939, he cautioned the nationalists that 'the victory of fascism would by no means bring about their liberation and would not solve the problem of their emancipation'.[27] He stressed the urgent need to rally behind the anti-fascist front and defend the Republic. In light of the Blum–Viollette Bill's failure, Thorez's stance appeared outdated. He advocated for measures that had already been rejected, stating: 'This still very modest minimum [...] must be voted on, and the free exercise of their religion guaranteed to Muslims.'[28] His speech could be interpreted as an attempt to re-engage the disillusioned Algerian nationalist movement. However, the brand of 'Algerian nationalism' he reaffirmed to maintain the '*élus*' and *oulemas* within the coalition was anachronistically assimilationist, especially following the bill's rejection.

After the Second World War, France sought to reassert sovereignty over its overseas territories. At the Brazzaville conference in 1944, General de Gaulle presided over the reorganisation of the French Empire by initiating political reforms to ensure that the independence of the colonies would develop within the framework of the French Union. Significantly, de Gaulle was not the only political figure to believe that the grandeur of France depended on the maintenance of the empire. Various socialist leaders shared this belief: Blum in 1946, with the outbreak of the hostilities in Indochina, followed by Mollet and Lacoste in 1956-7, at the height of the Algerian war. There was a consensus in the post-war period which curtailed parliamentary division on the colonial issue and created a community of shared interests which worked to maintain France's hold over its empire.[29] As Tony Smith argues, 'there is ample evidence that the major concerns of the SFIO [Séction française de l'Internationale ouvrière] bound them to rather than divided them from the parties to their right.'[30] Blum's stance against the anticolonial policies of the PCF at the Congrès de Tours in 1920, and his policies as well as those of his successors – Ramadier in 1947 and Mollet in 1956 – are a case in point.[31] The issue of decolonisation in Indochina and Algeria did not exacerbate the political instability of the French political system; on the contrary, it created a consensus. The Algerian war consolidated such consensus – and Molletism came to epitomise it. Commenting on Blum's and Ramadier's policies in the Indochinese war in 1946–47 and on Mollet's Algerian policies in 1956–57, Smith contends that 'it was unity, resolution and action which at certain critical points were the hallmarks of the regime', adding: 'What marked these crucial periods of socialist leadership was not so much the fatal logic of a political system as the fatal logic of a colonialist perspective.'[32]

If we dwell on the Mollet government, it is because its policies shaped Fanon's views vis-à-vis the colonial question and the liberal left. The socialist Mollet campaigned in the legislative elections of January 1956 to form a coalition government on the basis of a political platform to negotiate with the FLN and restore peace. However, on 6 February 1956, shortly after his election, Guy Mollet faced a hostile reception in Algiers. An angry mob pelted him with rotten tomatoes in an incident known as '*la journée des tomates*'. This event symbolised the fierce opposition from French settlers to any perceived weakening of France's control over Algeria during the

War of Independence. Consequently, Mollet pursued a policy of pacification by deploying scores of conscripted soldiers to quell the FLN rebellion. He replaced General Catroux with Lacoste as governor-general. Lacoste's attempt to bring about social and political change was thwarted by French settlers. Frightened by the ultras who were calling for his resignation, the socialist Lacoste, in an attempt to show that France still maintained its control over Algeria, implemented repressive measures which triggered the Battle of Algiers. On 12 March 1956, Mollet (with the help of the communists) passed the Special Powers Act, implementing a programme of actions which bypassed the National Assembly and ultimately ceded power to the military – a course of action that was of dubious legality under French law and that went against the grain of the Republican tradition. Moreover, to stifle the support of Nasser's Egypt for the FLN, he opened another front by waging the Suez War in October 1956. The 10th Parachute Division, led by Massu, was deployed first to Egypt and then, at the end of the Suez hostilities, to Algiers. On 7 January 1957, the civilian authorities relinquished power to the military and Massu was given special powers to crush the FLN organisation. In sum, Molletism was a resolute stance to keep Algeria French, hypostatising the colonial consensus. It was in protest against the Mollet government that Fanon resigned his post in Blida. In his letter of resignation, written to Resident Minister Lacoste in late 1956, Fanon bemoans the systematic dehumanisation of the colonised Algerians.[33] It is no coincidence that Aimé Césaire resigned from the PCF at about the same time as Fanon because of Mollet's retrograde colonial policies.

JOURNALISM AND THE REPUBLICAN TRADITION

Fanon's critique of the liberal left in his journalistic writings targets the cosy relationship that French communists had with the ultras who worked to maintain the colonial status quo. His article 'La Minorité européenne d'Algérie', published in *Les Temps modernes* in May–June 1959 and reissued in *Studies in a Dying Colonialism*, should be considered alongside the series of three articles he published in December 1957 in *El Moudjahid* titled 'Les Intellectuels et les démocrates français devant la révolution algérienne' (translated as 'French Intellectuals and Democrats and the Algerian Revolution' in *Toward the African Revolution*). There are certainly inconsistencies in Fanon's assessment of the political position of the French liberal left, but these were not the outcome of his brand of nationalism; rather, they were determined by the political context out of which he intervened. To understand the significance of 'Algeria's European Minority', it is worth comparing the Algerian liberal left, which helped recruit him to the Algerian cause, with the French liberal left, led by the socialist Mollet or the liberal Bourgès-Maunoury, who worked to maintain French colonial presence in Algeria.

Whereas, in 'French Intellectuals and Democrats and the Algerian Revolution', Fanon tars the liberal left with the same brush because of their lack of commitment to the Algerian cause, in 'Algeria's European Minority' he is careful not to lump all the Europeans together. The European minority in Algeria, he contends, never constituted a monolithic colonialist block.[34] The leaders of the Mouvement pour le triomphe des libertés démocratiques (MTLD) and the Union démocratique du manifeste algérien (UDMA) established contact with the European minority precisely because they grasped this political fact and understood the important role that liberal Europeans could play in Algeria's decolonisation. Fanon describes the relationship these liberal Europeans had with their Muslim counterparts – men and women alike – as an association of joint endeavour for the establishment of a democratic Algeria.[35] He makes clear that this relationship was different from the so-called Franco-Muslim fraternisation which the colonial administration promoted as part of the psychological warfare to break the revolutionary movement.

Unlike their French counterparts, the French Algerians could not openly advocate for the principles of democracy. They could not militate outside the Communist Party which held an assimilationist stance and which acted in complicity with the colonial administration.[36] In 'French Intellectuals and Democrats and the Algerian Revolution', Fanon contrasts the French liberal left with its Algerian counterpart: in cahoots with the colonial administration, the French liberal left lent their support to the Mollet government and its colonialist policies, whereas the Algerian liberal left – albeit muzzled, persecuted and tortured by the administration – were unequivocal in their support for the Algerian people. Fanon notes that the French government was consistent in its policy of pacification. He remarks ironically:

From 1956 onward the Algerian war was accepted by the nation. France wants the war, as Mr. Guy Mollet and Mr. Bourgès-Maunoury have explicitly stated; and the people of Paris, on July 14th, 1957, conveyed to Massu's parachutist torturers the country's deep gratitude. The liberals abandoned the struggle at this stage. The accusation of treason to which the adversaries of the Algerian war exposed themselves became a formidable weapon in the hands of the French government. Thus in early 1957 many democrats ceased their protests or were overwhelmed by the clamor for vengeance, and a clumsily structured elementary patriotism manifested itself, steeped in racism – violent, totalitarian, in short, fascist.[37]

The Mollet government fell on 21 May 1957; the liberal Bourgès-Maunoury replaced Mollet on 25 June, but the change of leadership did not mean a change of direction in French politics. Instead, the newly appointed prime minister continued in the footsteps of Mollet, extending the special powers given to the army in Algeria. The triumphalist and bellicose policies undertaken by Bourgès-Maunoury enjoyed popular support in France. Fanon refers explicitly to the jingoistic parade of the paratroopers in the Champs-Élysées on 14 July 1957, the day before the trial of the Algerian revolutionary Djamila Bouhired, who was accused of planting a bomb in a café in Algiers, concluded with the death penalty.

In November 1957, in response to a book written by Georges Arnaud and Jacques Vergès entitled *Pour Djamila Bouhired*, Fanon published 'Concerning a Plea' in *El Moudjahid*. Echoing Sartre's 'Le Colonialisme est un système', published in *Les Temps modernes* in March–April 1956,[38] Fanon had already underscored in 'Algeria Face to Face with the French Torturers', published in *El Moudjahid* in September 1957, that colonial practice is premised on violence: 'The Algerian people are not unaware of the fact that the colonialist structure rests on the necessity of torturing, raping, and committing massacres.'[39] Two months later, in 'Concerning a Plea', Fanon cautions against political expedience in the name of a narrow nationalism that sought to sacrifice the rights of the individual. He berates the French intellectuals and liberal left for their failure to uphold and safeguard the universality of the Republican tradition which was undermined by French colonialism. Djamila Bouhired, the Algerian militant and nationalist, emerges as an emblematic figure – much like Dreyfus – a victim whose individual rights were sacrificed to uphold the raison d'état. For Fanon, Bouhired epitomises the violated Algerian: 'there have since been a multitude of Djamila Bouhireds, tortured, violated, and massacred on Algerian territory'.[40] He considers her trial as French colonialism's attempt to shatter the national will by sentencing her to execution. In this light, Bouhired is to be seen not as a convicted terrorist that French justice tried and sentenced to death, but as the subjugated colonised Algerian whose rights were denied by an oppressive colonialism. Fanon bemoans the failure of the Republican tradition: 'We can measure herein the historic belatedness of the French conscience. After the fruitful struggle that it waged two centuries ago for the respect of individual liberties and the rights of man, it finds itself today unable to wage a similar battle for the rights of peoples.'[41]

Fanon pours scorn on the French liberal left for their political apathy and for their misplaced patriotism. History, he contends, was being made without them: they could neither prevent Mollet pandering to the ultras nor stop the deployment of troops to Algeria. He excoriates the French liberal left for instituting the emergency laws that gave the ultras special powers, for being able to do nothing in the face of the putsch of 13 May, for toeing the official line and for believing that France was fighting terrorism.[42] In 'French Intellectuals and Democrats and the Algerian Revolution', he condemns the French justification for its actions in Algeria as totalitarian, racist, and fascist.[43] In 'A Victory', published in *L'Express* in March 1958 in response to Henri Alleg's *La Question*, Sartre echoes Fanon: 'in 1958, in Algiers, people are being tortured regularly, systematically, everybody knows, from Monsieur Lacoste to the farmer of the Aveyron, but nobody talks about it.'[44] Under the premiership of the socialist Mollet and the liberal Bourgès-Maunoury, Sartre contends, the army was given full powers and the 'torturer-in-chief' replaced the police.[45] Sartre and Fanon are as one in contending that France acted in complicity with a murderous colonialism in Algeria and that the liberal left colluded with fascism.

Under the aegis of Mollet, Fanon argues, the colonial administration instituted practices which sapped the universality of human rights and the principles upon which the constitution of government was founded in France: democracy was banished in colonial Algeria; it '[was] tantamount to treason'.[46] The colonial administration gagged, tortured and murdered those who advocated these principles; Alleg was incarcerated and tortured, while Maurice Audin paid the ultimate price for defending France's democratic principles. The French liberal left either collaborated with the colonial administration or sought refuge in silence. It is possible to establish a connection, as Fanon does in his comment about the violation of the human rights of the colonised people, between Bouhired, Alleg and Dreyfus. As a naturalised Frenchman, Alleg, like Dreyfus, was a victim whose rights as an individual were violated to maintain the raison d'état. Nonetheless, this figure was at the forefront of a neo-Dreyfusard movement represented by Jewish intellectuals. It seems that Fanon in 'Algeria's European Minority' attempted to galvanise the voice of the neo-Dreyfusards in their fight against the colonial system and the raison d'état which was put in place by Mollet, Lacoste and Massu.

Unlike their French counterparts, Fanon maintains, the liberal left in Algeria stood resolutely against colonial fascism: Audin and Alleg emerged as proponents of a Dreyfusard tradition that very few intellectuals on the left in mainland France were willing to champion. Fanon presents their resistance against colonial fascism as a decolonisation of France.[47] Fanon also stresses the contribution of the European minority to the Algerian cause, contending that they provided not only ideological and organisational but also strategic and military support to the FLN. His intervention in 'Algeria's European Minority' counteracted the psychological warfare conducted by the Fifth Bureau, which was attempting to fracture the movement of resistance. Referring to the Alleg case, Fanon writes:

> The European men and women who have been arrested and tortured by the police services and the French parachutists, by their attitude under torture, have shown the rightness of this position taken by the FLN. Not a single Frenchman has revealed to the colonialist police information vital to the Revolution. On the contrary, the arrested Europeans have resisted long enough to enable the other members of the network to disappear. The tortured European has behaved like an authentic militant in the national fight for independence.[48]

The European minority was ethnically diverse; religion complicated still further the issue of ethnicity and nationality. A sizeable proportion of the non-Muslim population was Jewish, who were granted political citizenship by the Crémieux laws.[49] Colonial Algeria was essentially a racist state; Fanon maintains that 'in it, one finds the various mechanisms of racist psychology'.[50] Some Jews identified with those who discriminated against them in the past, a paradoxical situation that Memmi describes in *The Colonizer and the Colonized*. Memmi presents the social structure of colonial Algeria in the form of a pyramid, with the coloniser at its apex and the colonised Algerians at its base.[51] It is true that the acculturated Jews enjoyed privileges, but these came at a price. In *Le Monolinguisme de l'autre*, Derrida bemoans the assimilationist policies which alienated Algerian Jews and led to the 'ossification' and 'necrotisation' of their culture.[52] Echoing Fanon's characterisation of colonial Algeria as a compartmentalised society, he decries the impassable '*frontières de nuit*' that consign the native Algerians to life in a state of apartheid.[53] Like Fanon, he argues that assimilation was a sham: the privileges afforded to the Jews were taken from them when Vichy France abolished the Crémieux laws in October 1940. For Dreyfusards like Alleg and Pierre Vidal-Naquet, Vichy collaboration and antisemitism undermined France's Republican principles, as did the Algerian war. Like Fanon, they considered their commitment to the Algerian cause to be a continuation of their resistance to fascism.

Fanon is adamant that the attitude of the Jews vis-à-vis the FLN and the Revolution was not homogeneous: those who sought shelter in the shadow of the colonial regime were in a minority; the majority of the Jews identified with the Algerians.[54] Jewish tradesmen contributed financially and Jewish intellectuals demonstrated their support for the Algerian Revolution. Alleg exemplifies the Dreyfusard spirit, demonstrating a readiness to make the ultimate sacrifice in support of the Algerian cause. 'Even today', Fanon emphasises, 'the Jewish lawyers and doctors who in the camps or in prison share the fate of millions of Algerians attest to the multiracial reality of the Algerian Nation.'[55] At the height of the Algerian war, these Jews realised that their '[a]ttachment to an artificial French nationality is a snare and a delusion at a moment when the young and powerful modern Algerian nation is rapidly taking shape'.[56]

While he criticised the liberal left in the articles he wrote in 1957, two years later Fanon clearly solicits their political support. In 'Algeria's European Minority', he cites two accounts: one by Yvon Bresson, a police officer who worked as an FLN agent; and another by Fanon's colleague Charles Geronimi. In line with Abane Ramdane's political project to inaugurate a multicultural Algeria, Fanon seeks to establish the foundation for a rapprochement between the Algerians and the Europeans, as he suggests that the issue of nationality is up for grabs in post-independence Algeria, where Europeans, Jews, Berbers and Arabs will play a key role in an Algerian nation governed by democratic political institutions. In stark contrast to the opening chapter of The Wretched of the Earth, the tone of Fanon's 'Algeria's European Minority' and his introduction to Studies in a Dying Colonialism is conciliatory. His project is clear: 'We want an Algeria open to all, in which every kind of genius may grow.'[57] Fanon's critique of the liberal left and his Marxist interpretation are tethered to the historical and political contexts of Algeria's decolonisation and the PCF's position on the colonial question. It is therefore important to disentangle his critique of the liberal left in Studies in a Dying Colonialism from his Marxist exegesis in The Wretched of the Earth, which centres on the role played by the peasantry in the revolution.

REDEFINING CLASS IN COLONIAL ALGERIA

In 'Colonialism Is a System', Sartre analyses the logic of colonialism as a manifestation of industrial capitalism that sought new markets for its products.[58] Jean-François Lyotard expands on Sartre's critique; according to the figures he provides in *La Guerre des Algériens*, the markets in North Africa – and principally in Algeria – remained very weak, catering for a very small, predominantly European class. Private investment was directed towards financial services, not industry, thus keeping the economy in a pre-industrial state. The colonial administration was against the modernisation of the agricultural sector for fear that the *fellahs* would be promoted to the ranks of the European proletariat, thus undermining social stability. The maintenance of such stability, Lyotard argues, involved the expropriation of 18 million Muslims in North Africa.[59] Fanon unearths this history of expropriation, asserting that colonialism created an immiserated lumpenproletariat.[60]

Lyotard concurs with Fanon's assessment of the Algerian war as a peasant revolution: 70 per cent of Algerian agriculture was not economically viable. The insurgents were peasants; predominantly 20 years of age, they entered the armed struggle because they had nothing to lose: they were born in 1938, a year after the failure of the Blum–Viollette Bill; they were brought up in the dire conditions of the Second World War that saw the majority of the indigenous population in the grip of famine; and at the age of 7 they experienced the Sétif massacre.[61] Lyotard underscores that these insurgents' intransigence was determined by colonial violence, by their expropriation, by their immiseration and marginalisation; the opening chapter of *The Wretched of the Earth* sets out the implications of this violence.

The colonial question rendered the left's conceptual language obsolete, revealing it to be out of touch with political reality.[62] Lyotard rejects an abstract Marxist approach which conceived of the Algerian conflict as a 'class manifestation'; he refuses to consider the Mouvement national algérien (MNA) – a trade-unionist party which was set up by Messali Hadj as a rival to the FLN and which represented immigrant workers in France and peasants in Algeria – as a brand of Algerian Bolshevism. He is quick to point out that Messalism never represented 'the revolutionary vanguard of the Algerian proletariat'.[63] The 400,000 Algerian workers in France were not an integral part of the French working class. Trotsky's notion of the permanent revolution was meaningless as far as they were concerned because these workers were kept segregated from their French counterparts by a whole culture in France – and by 350 kilometres of land and sea.[64] There was a cultural gap between the two peoples, a gap created by a history of brutal colonialism and exacerbated by a nationalistic conflict.

To fathom the politics that opened up such a gap, it is worth reconsidering Thorez's view of colonial Algeria as a nation-in-formation from Fanon's perspective. While Thorez replaces the notion of race with that of nationality, thus suppressing the colonial issue, Fanon considers 'race' as a superstructure, constitutive of colonialism's Manichaean politics. In *The Wretched of the Earth*, elaborating further on this notion of 'race' as a superstructure, he writes:

> This world divided into compartments, this world cut in two is inhabited by two different species. The originality of the colonial context is that economic reality, inequality, and the immense difference of ways of life never come to mask the human realities. When you examine at close quarters the colonial context, it is evident that what parcels out the world is to begin with the fact of belonging to or not belonging to a given race, a given species. In the colonies the economic substructure is also a superstructure. The cause is the consequence; you are rich because you are white, you are white because you are rich. This is why Marxist analysis should always be slightly stretched every time we have to do with the colonial problem.[65]

Class frontiers were consolidated by ethnic barriers to the extent that class attitudes were completely obfuscated or expressed in racial terms.[66] Thus, between those who exploited the means of agricultural production and those who were exploited – the European settlers and the dispossessed *fellahs* – there was a massive gap that was defined in racial terms. The same gap existed between the European workers and their Algerian counterparts. The Manichaean divide, as described by Fanon in *Les Damnés de la terre*, highlights the compartmentalised existence in colonial Algeria: a police cordon separated the European workers living in Bad-el-Oued from the Algerian workers in the Casbah. These groups never formed a community of shared political interests.[67] Even when they were exploited in the same way as the Algerian proletariat, the European workers never identified with the latter as a class. Identification was expressed in cultural and ethnic terms. The French proletariat never considered that its class interests converged with the class interests of the oppressed/colonised peoples.

According to Fanon and Lyotard, the Algerian conflict was intensified by two opposing nationalisms: colonialist and anticolonial, the latter mobilis-

188 • FRANTZ FANON

ing the dispossessed Algerian peasantry. While Nghe highlights the urban working class and bourgeois elite's role in the nationalist movement, historical and political factors complicated the Marxist notion of class struggle in colonial Algeria. Lyotard demonstrates how nationalism, whether anticolonial or fascistic, overshadowed this concept. The MTLD, founded in 1946 after the PPA's dissolution, attempted to present itself as a 'parti de masse',[68] despite its working-class immigrant origins. Its leaders, the national bourgeoisie, denied social/class distinctions and antagonisms in Algeria. This class-blind approach resulted in a monolithic organisation lacking a doctrine capable of addressing the problems of the dispossessed masses, particularly the peasantry. In contrast, the FLN promoted an ideology that permeated all aspects of Algerian society, recognising diverse social and class interests. It worked to incorporate the concerns of various groups – from the petty bourgeoisie and proletariat to the lumpenproletariat and peasantry – into the national struggle, bridging urban and rural divides. The FLN uniquely mobilised militants from the MTLD, UDMA, and *oulemas* to join the armed struggle. Its centralism emerged from the conflict itself. As a unified, centralised party, the FLN established itself in both rural and urban areas, gaining comprehensive control over the Algerian population. Fanon, while supporting the FLN's revolutionary movement as representative of the masses, critiqued its centralist and bourgeois inclinations in his analysis of nationalism's pitfalls. He maintained that the expropriated peasantry remained the only truly revolutionary class.

The FLN could not be 'the incarnation of the Algerian proletariat' but was rather a kind of sacred union of workers, peasants, and petty bourgeoisie.[69] The 'proletariat', 'middle class', 'bourgeoisie' and the 'peasantry' are not abstract entities but are determined by the specificities of colonial history and politics. The peasantry was specifically Algerian, a class that constituted the social basis of the nationalist movement: the revolution was nothing but the expression of the expropriated and uprooted Algerian peasantry. It was not an abstract definition of the peasantry that brought about 'class suture' in Algeria; it was the history of colonial exploitation that shaped this class solidarity and gave rise to national consciousness. In his critique of Fanon, Nghe, eliding the racialised terms of the colonial problematic and the nationalistic discourse which obscured class antagonism, overlooks that this history was defined not in terms of class – that is, the proletariat or peasantry – but in terms of ethnicity and nationality.

Chiming with Fanon's critique of the liberal left, Lyotard's criticisms of Marxism-Leninism are worth reviewing from the historical perspective of the colonial consensus. In *La Guerre des Algériens*, he raises three inter-linked issues: first, class and nationalist antagonisms; second, the power vacuum created by the Algerian war; and third, the French communists' stance on class solidarity and decolonisation. The Battle of Algiers changed the internal dynamics of French politics; it brought about an unholy alliance between left and extreme right, obscuring class differences. How did the left come to support the ultras and how did the FLN come to yoke together different, even contradictory, class positions in its anticolonial struggle? Marxist rhetoric was anachronistic as it could not conceive of the hidden contradictions inherent within the colonial society. The army, bent on restoring its pride in Algeria after its humiliating defeat in Indochina and the Suez crisis, instituted a raison d'état undercutting the Republican tradition and sacrificing individual freedom. It was not Lacoste but the ultras that held power in Algiers. By the same token, it was not Paris but Algiers which determined the political agenda of mainland France. Lyotard observes that while the FLN maintained an organisation in the country-side and the ultras controlled the colonial administration in the cities, Paris experienced a political vacuum. After pelting Mollet with tomatoes, the ultras dominated French politics: they imposed their fascistic slogans on France and oppressed its political atmosphere. Like Sartre and Fanon, Lyotard denounces the collusion of the French left (namely the PCF and the SFIO) with colonial fascism that undermined France's Republican prin-ciples and political institutions.

It is important to bear in mind that Fanon wrote 'Algeria Face to Face with the French Torturers', 'Concerning a Plea', 'French Intellectuals and Demo-crats and the Algerian Revolution' and 'Algeria's European Minority' in order to seek the support of the liberal left and to denounce the raison d'état which denied the rights of Bouhired and Alleg. Fanon clearly links the theme of violence with the raison d'état; the reference to Mollet in *The Wretched of the Earth* is significant in this respect.

The starving peasant, outside the class system, is the first among the exploited to discover that only violence pays. For him there is no compro-mise, no possible coming to terms; colonization and decolonization are simply a question of relative strength. The exploited man sees that his lib-eration implies the use of all means, and that of force first and foremost. When in 1956, after the capitulation of Monsieur Guy Mollet to the settlers in Algeria, the Front de Liberation Nationale, in a famous leaflet, stated that colonialism only loosens its hold when the knife is at its throat, no

190 • FRANTZ FANON

Algerian really found these terms too violent. The leaflet only expressed what every Algerian felt at heart: colonialism is not a thinking machine, nor a body endowed with reasoning faculties. It is violence in its natural state, and it will only yield when confronted with greater violence.[70]

The Manichaean economy which gave rise to such violence is not a confrontation of rational points of view; it is purely the expression of raison d'état maintained with the help of the army and the police. This violence was blind and unthinking, but emerged from the 'mad darkness' of colonialism: it operated within a consensus which, in order to uphold France's colonial interests, renounced one of the cornerstones of the Republican tradition. Just like the Dreyfus Affair, the Algerian war polarised French society – and the divisions were not along class or partisan lines. It did not set the liberal left against the clergy and the ultra-nationalists, those who defended the inalienable rights of the individual (the proponents of the Human Rights League) and those who put the interests of the state above these rights. The Algerian war confused these demarcation lines: it is one of the ironies of history that Mollet, a socialist and member of the Human Rights League, with the help of the communists, presided over (and covered up for) the systematic practice of torture; the liberals of *Témoignage chrétien* – those who recruited Fanon to the Algerian cause – emerged as neo-Dreyfusards resisting the raison d'état instituted by the left.[71]

As we have seen, the political direction taken by Thorez in the 1930s impinged on the history of the PCF as the party moved away from its former internationalist agenda and espoused a narrow nationalism in the defence of the Republic against the threat of fascism. The class-against-class strategy in Marxism-Leninism was effectively held in check by nationalism, which came to obfuscate racial and colonial antagonism. The PCF's colonial policies in the 1930s, Irwin Wall rightly argues, 'came back to haunt it in the 1950s when the party could not formulate an adequate response to the Algerian War'.[72] Thorez's anti-fascist front paradoxically determined the colonial consensus which, at the height of the Algerian crisis, brought together left and right, communists and ultras in a baneful coalition, giving rise to fascism in Algeria. This fascism brought down the Fourth Republic in the putsch of 13 May 1958. Lyotard denounces the PCF for being notoriously weak and spineless – as '*mol*' as Mollet[73] – and for colluding with the ultras. He is quick to point out that the liberal left turned a blind eye to the heavy-handed pacification led by the army and that the SFIO and the PCF participated indirectly and directly in this repression. In this respect, Césaire's correlation between colonialism and fascism in his *Discours sur le colonialisme* is particularly relevant. In his famous *Lettre à Maurice Thorez*, Césaire tenders his resignation after the PCF supported the Mollet government's Special Powers Act in 1956, exploding the contradictions in its stance on the colonial question. If the PCF resisted the rise of fascism in the 1930s, paradoxically it found itself in cahoots with the fascist ultras in the Algerian conflict. In *Studies in a Dying Colonialism* and his journalistic writings, Fanon decries such complicity; in *The Wretched of the Earth* he revises the conceptual language of the left which was anachronistically at odds with colonial reality.

In sum, the vestiges of subjectivism in *The Wretched of the Earth* are inherited from existential phenomenology and expressed in Marxist terms in *Black Skin, White Masks*. Fanon broaches the subject of Marxism explicitly in his rebuttal of Sartre's dialectical schema for objectifying the subjectivity of the black, and implicitly in his critique of the dichotomous language of racism that seals the black in their blackness and the white in their whiteness. In *The Wretched of the Earth*, he expands on this subject, contending that the specificities of race and ethnicity must be taken into account in the dialectics governing the Manichaean economy of colonial society. Lyotard adds to the debate initiated by Fanon, excoriating Marxism-Leninism for overlooking the significance of nationalism. However, Marxist theory should not be conflated with Marxism-Leninism or the politics of the PCF, just as Marx should not be confused with Thorez. I have chosen to read Fanon and Lyotard in tandem to show that whereas Marx, according to Fanon, suppresses the notion of 'race' and the colonial question in a grand narrative on class struggle, Thorez supplants the notion of 'race' with 'nation' and suppresses the colonial issue by deploying nationalism as a political device in his rhetoric of nation-in-formation.

It is worth reiterating that Fanon's take on Marxism is determined by the context of decolonisation and by the PCF's politics on the colonial issue, and that his Marxist analysis is intertwined with his critique of the liberal left. The insurgent Fanon is the product of the historical and political circumstances that gave rise to the raison d'état which forced him to join the FLN's '*délégation extérieure*', exiled in Tunis. His radicalism stems, then, from the specificities of anticolonial struggle.

As noted, the original French tile of Fanon's *Studies in a Dying Colonialism* (*L'An V*) references the French Revolutionary calendar to underscore the transformative potential of the War of Independence, not only on Algerian society but on anticolonial and liberation movements worldwide. His *The Wretched of the Earth* alludes to the famous left-wing anthem 'The Internationale', whose opening lyrics in French, 'Debout, les damnés de la terre', translate to 'Stand up, the damned of the earth' or 'Arise, wretched of the earth'. The title of Fanon's book draws a connection between the revolutionary spirit of the song and his analysis of colonialism and the struggle for decolonisation. Through these references, Fanon emphasises the global nature of the anticolonial struggle and aligns it with broader movements for social and economic justice. In his *El Moudjahid* critique of the colonial consensus, he obviously targets the French liberal left who colluded with the ultras; in *The Wretched of the Earth*, he cautions against the pitfalls of nationalism. The brand of nationalism he advocates is internationalist: it is at a variance with Thorez's nationalism; it follows in the footsteps of the 'Internationale', but the dubious history implicating the PCF in maintaining the colonial consensus led him to question Marxism-Leninism as a viable alternative to the colonial status quo.

Conclusion

Colonial biopolitics, with all its contradictions, cemented a consensus between left and right, serving state interests at the expense of individual rights. The history of French republicanism, built on colonial ambition, was inextricably tied to Algeria's colonial subjugation and subsequent decolonisation. Fanon, underscoring the pervasive colonial ideology in French political thought, illuminates these contradictions: both the left and right supported military efforts to maintain colonial interests. In *Studies in a Dying Colonialism*, Fanon examines the impact of French colonialism on Algerian society and its institutions, as well as the radical transformations brought about by the War of Independence. In *The Wretched of the Earth*, he describes its violence as a direct consequence of French military tactics intended to destroy Algerian social and cultural structures in order to reconstruct a neocolonial French Algeria. This violence cannot be attributed to Fanon himself; in fact, he spoke out against it in his resignation letter to Lacoste. Unlike some of his colleagues – who were arrested, tortured or executed – Fanon survived to document the realities of colonial violence. He asserts that the violence stemmed from the colonial encounter itself and was elevated to a guiding principle of colonial governmentality. Furthermore, he argues that decolonization was not a rational debate but rather 'the untidy affirmation of an original idea propounded as an absolute.'[1]

Critics like Comte, Arendt and Nghe misinterpret Fanon's treatment of violence by failing to acknowledge the historical context of French colonial oppression. Comte's review of *The Wretched of the Earth* controversially compares Fanon's work to Hitler's *Mein Kampf*, accusing Fanon of exuding a terrorising aggression akin to Nazism.[2] This comparison risks conflating anticolonial struggle with genocidal intentions. Comte's critique obscures the brutal war waged by the French army against Algeria's civilian population, including children and women. It overlooks crucial historical, political and moral contexts, failing to grasp the depth of Fanon's decolonial critique. Similarly, Hannah Arendt labels Fanon an 'apostle of violence' and a 'preacher of hate', comparing him to figures like Hitler, Sorel, and Pareto.[3] Her claim that Fanon 'glorified violence for violence's sake' and harboured 'a much deeper hatred of bourgeois society than the conventional Left'[4] overlooks a crucial point: it was the French left in its coalition with the ultra right that empowered the French army to impose special measures and devastate Algeria's civilian population. Arendt reduces Fanon's complex ideas to a cautionary tale about revolutionary excess. Her analysis of violence as a concept lacks consideration of its historical specificities and fails to fully integrate it into her broader understanding of totalitarianism as a 'novel form of government'[5] that uses terror to subjugate entire populations. Nghe also criticises Fanon from a Maoist perspective, accusing him of romanticising peasant violence and misapplying Marxist analysis. However, Nghe neglects the historical context that shaped this violence, which was a direct response to the French army's counter-revolutionary tactics during the Algerian War. Fanon's chapter 'Concerning Violence'[6] addresses the French counter-insurgency strategy, which involved expropriation and the forced resettlement of rural populations.

Fanon challenges colonial biopolitics – a health politics that colluded with the military apparatus. During the colonial conquest, this politics decimated civilian populations, encouraged expropriation and dispossession, dismantled family structures, and engendered poverty, disease and famine. During the Algerian war, it created forbidden zones of life. The 'pitiless hostility' Comte attributes to Fanon's work was not just present in the Blida-Ville hospital where Fanon worked and cared for the subjects of colonial alienation, but also in detention and regroupment camps. This hostility originated from the colonial system itself. To understand the violence Fanon discusses, it must be seen in light of French hostility and psychological warfare, which disrupted rural life and impacted both the French political and military landscape. Eric Wolf notes that the Algerian conflict inspired two influential theories of warfare: one by French officers, and one by Fanon regarding decolonial revolutions.[7]

Fanon's concept of peasant revolution must be interpreted in conjunction with colonial history, which systematically dispossessed and proletarianised the peasantry. Interestingly, if Mao had any influence on Algeria's decolonisation, it was indirect, through the French army's appropriation of his theories in psychological warfare. The French military relied on socio-psychological manipulation to divide colonised people from FLN insurgents, using mass control tactics. Trinquier, a key figure in French pacification theory, defined modern revolutionary warfare as a system of political, economic, psychological and military actions aimed at overthrowing established authority. He argued that unconditional support from the population was crucial for victory, citing Mao's analogy that fighters are like fish in water. Since peasants were central to the ALN, the conflict could only end by 'evacuating the water' and neutralising the peasantry through terrorism when support was lacking.[8]

Fanon's peasant revolution was a direct response to France's counter-revolutionary war against the civilian rural population, a brutal conflict that dislocated Algerian society. As Mahfoud Bennoune affirms: by 1962, approximately 3.5 million peasants – about 50 per cent of rural inhabitants – were either displaced or in regroupment camps.[9] The army declared rural areas 'forbidden zones', rebranded as 'permanent fire zones', effectively labelling anyone within them as a rebel. This 'scorched earth' approach involved large-scale sweeps, forced relocations, and the destruction of villages and livestock. Under President Charles de Gaulle from 1958 onward, operations intensified, often treating all rural inhabitants as suspects, resulting in widespread torture and killings. This strategy, later presented as 'the thousand villages policy',[10] was framed as a humanitarian effort but was ultimately designed for population control and counter-insurgency.

In conclusion, regroupment camps were not a novel concept; they had been used since the nineteenth century as a strategy for population control. Captain Charles Richard, head of the Arab Bureau in Orléansville (now Chlef), articulated their purpose: 'The essential thing is to group these people who are everywhere and nowhere. The essential thing is to make them graspable to us. When we hold them, we can then do many things that are impossible for us today, which will perhaps allow us to seize their spirit after we have seized their body.'[11] A century later, Soustelle adopted the same strategy, and General Parlange implemented it with perverse rigour. In his 22 July 1955 report, citing historian Stéphane Gsell, General Parlange declared: 'Material conquest must be accompanied by the conquest of minds.' 'To win hearts and minds,' he added, 'it is necessary to increase contact with the population; to speak simply and plainly, and to speak the same language.'[12] General Parlange's establishment of the first regroupment camps in the Aurès region stemmed from his belief that winning the war required conquering souls. This 'simple' and 'plain' language masked untold violence. From its inception, the regroupment system was cynically presented in biopolitical terms as an improvement in living conditions, while concealing its true aim: population control and cultural domination. Colonial biopolitics, purporting to be a politics of health, seized both the body and spirit, subjecting them to unspeakable genocidal violence.

Notes

ABBREVIATIONS

ACICR – Archives du Comité International de la Croix-Rouge
AN – Archives nationales (Pierrefitte-sur-Seine, Paris)
ANOM – Archives nationales d'outre-mer (Aix-en-Provence)
ECPAD – Établissement de communication et de production audiovisuelle de la défense (Fort-Ivry, Paris)
SHD – Service historique de la Défense

INTRODUCTION

1. Frantz Fanon, *Black Skin, White Masks* (London: Pluto Press, 1986) and Frantz Fanon, *The Wretched of the Earth* (New York: Grove Press, 1963).
2. English translation: Frantz Fanon, *Studies in a Dying Colonialism* (New York: Grove Press, 1965).
3. David Macey, *Frantz Fanon: A Life* (London: Granta, 2000), pp. 397–400.
4. Ibid.
5. Peter Geismar, *Fanon* (New York: The Dial Press, 1971), p. 113.
6. Alice Cherki, *Frantz Fanon, Portrait* (Paris: Seuil, 2000), p. 199.
7. Neelam Srivastava, 'Anti-colonial Violence and the "Dictatorship of Truth" in the Films of Gillo Pontecorvo: An Interview', *Interventions* 7(1) (2005), pp. 102–4.
8. The *régime de l'Indigénat*, also known as the *Code de l'Indigénat* or simply *l'Indigénat*, was a discriminatory penal-administrative system used in French colonial territories during the nineteenth and twentieth centuries, primarily targeting indigenous populations. Introduced in Algeria in 1834 and extended to the broader French colonial empire from 1887, the *régime* allowed for arbitrary administrative justice applied solely to 'indigenous' people, bypassing general French legal principles. Key features of the *régime* included: (i) sequestration of property, (ii) collective fines, (iii) internment (house arrest or detention), (iv) disciplinary powers enabling officials to impose fines or imprisonment for specific offences, such as refusing to assist authorities or not carrying a travel permit. The *régime* also imposed a colonial tax – the '*impôt arabe*', particularly in Algeria – to fund infrastructure such as roads, schools and hospitals, primarily benefiting the colonists. It affected all aspects of indigenous life: penal, civil and political. Modified in 1928, the *régime* remained in force until 1946, when it was abolished following condemnation by reformist movements like the Young Algerians (*Jeunes Algériens*) and the League of Human Rights. The 1944 Brazzaville Conference recommended its abolition,

and it was formally ended in Algeria by the March 1944 ordinance, though some practices persisted until independence. Some historians have compared the system to apartheid in South Africa.

1 COLONISATION MEDICINE AND COLONIAL BIOPOLITICS

1. Paul Picard, 'L'Assistance médicale des Européens en Algérie', in *Hygiène et pathologie nord-africaines: Assistance médicale*, vol. 2 (Paris: Masson et Cie, 1932), pp. 18–19. Please note that *Hygiène et pathologie nord-africaines* comprises two volumes edited by Lucien Raynaud, Henri Soulié and Paul Picard. Raynaud conceived of the project but died before its publication, as did Soulié. The work was part of the Collection du Centenaire de l'Algérie 1830–1930, a series commemorating a century of French presence in Algeria. The publication aimed to present the state of knowledge about Algeria after 100 years of occupation, focusing on hygiene, pathology and medical assistance in North Africa. The first volume was authored by Lucien Raynaud. The second volume consists of two large sections authored by Paul Picard and Henri Soulié.

2. Ibid., pp. 25–6.

3. Ibid., p. 131.

4. Ibid., pp. 63–4.

5. A '*douar*', derived from the Arabic دَوَّار (*dawwār*), denotes a small rural settlement in North Africa, typically comprising tents inhabited by one or two extended families. These encampments usually house populations ranging from 30 to 100 individuals, representing a traditional form of communal living in the region. The '*mechta*' means a hamlet or small village consisting of several traditional dwellings known as *gourbis* made of mud.

6. Picard, 'L'Assistance médicale des Européens en Algérie', p. 65.

7. Henri Soulié, 'L'Assistance médicale des indigènes en Algérie', in *Hygiène et pathologie nord-africaines*, vol. 2, p. 493. ANOM B 10264 Pierre Darmon, 'Criquets, famine et choléra 1867, l'année de la mort', in *Les Collections de l'histoire*, No. 95 (April–June 2022), pp. 35–7.

8. Soulié, 'L'Assistance médicale des indigènes en Algérie', p. 494. On 9 June 1874, Governor-General Chanzy approved the plans to build Saint-Cyprien des Attafs in the plain of Chélif; the hospital opened its wards for the sick in February 1876.

9. Ibid., pp. 495–7.

10. Ibid., p. 496.

11. Ibid., p. 520.

12. Yvonne Turin, *Affrontements culturels dans l'Algérie coloniale: Écoles, médecines, religion, 1830–1880* (Paris: François Maspero, 1971).

13. Jules Cambon, *Le Gouvernement Général de l'Algérie (1891–1897)* (Paris: Champion, 1918), p. 435.

14. Ibid., p. 437. 'As a result [of the Warnier Law], speculators deliberately bought up shares of property in order to pursue the acquisition of the entire estate, whole families were thus expropriated and, from one day to the next, reduced to poverty' (ibid., p. 107). Cambon was unapologetic that the 1873 law on the

constitution of indigenous property had disastrous consequences: unscrupulous speculators used its provisions to expropriate and ruin many families (ibid., p. xviii). He was adamant that the law on civil status was 'the necessary corollary of the constitution of individual property and the very condition of the progress of the indigenous race' (ibid., p. 30). According to Cambon, the native population's progress was ostensibly predicated on the ruinous dismantling of their economic and social structures.

15. Ibid., pp. 28–9.
16. Ibid., pp. 92–3.
17. Ibid., p. xiii.
18. Ibid., p. xviii.
19. Ibid., p. 438.
20. Etymologically, 'goum' originates from the Arabic word 'qaum' (قوم), meaning 'nation' or a community sharing common cultural traits. In the context of French colonisation in North Africa, it refers to a unit of native soldiers commanded by French officers. 'Goumi' denotes a collaborator or informer, often used interchangeably with 'harki'.
21. (Général) Ferdinand-Auguste Lapasset, *La Guerre en Algérie: Instructions sommaires pour la conduite d'une colonne* (Paris: Ch. Tanera, 1873), pp. 27–8.
22. Olivier Le Cour Grandmaison, *Coloniser. Exterminer: Sur la guerre et l'état colonial* (Paris: Fayard, 2005), pp. 145–52.
23. Cambon, *Le Gouvernement Général de l'Algérie*, pp. 38–9.
24. Ibid., pp. 153–4.
25. Ibid., p. 160.
26. As we will see later, Captain Vaissière uses a similar expression to reference the technique of the *razzia* and the laws that expropriated the native population. This technique was formalised into a potent military weapon by General Bugeaud during the colonial conquest, targeting civilian populations and their means of subsistence. Louis Vignon later adopted this expression, stating: 'it is important to always be ready to strike and repress. This is why we must have at our disposal two weapons: a weapon of war and a weapon of peace, if it is possible to use these expressions. On the one hand, it is sequestration and collective responsibility; on the other, it is the punishments outlined in the *Code de l'Indigénat*.' Louis Vignon, *La France en Algérie* (Paris: Librairie Hachette, 1898), p. 498.
27. Cambon, *Le Gouvernement Général de l'Algérie*, pp. 216–18.
28. Ibid., p. 46.
29. Ibid., p. 218.
30. Ibid., p. 46.
31. Ibid., p. 158–9.
32. Ibid., pp. 36–7.
33. Ibid., p. 169.
34. Ibid., p. 426.
35. Soulié, 'L'Assistance médicale des indigènes en Algérie', p. 499.
36. Ibid., pp. 499 and 560.

37. Michel Foucault, 'The Politics of Health in the Eighteenth Century', in Michel Foucault, *Power/Knowledge: Selected Interviews and Other Writings*, ed. Colin Gordon (New York and London: Harvester Wheatsheaf, 1980), p. 171. Drawing from Foucault's insights, it is crucial to emphasise that nosopolitics, or the 'medicalisation' of the family in colonial Algeria, specifically targeted native women (ibid., pp. 172–5). As I will demonstrate, this medicalisation was an instance of coloniality.
38. Dorothée Chellier, *Voyage dans l'Aurès: Note d'un médecin envoyé en mission chez les femmes arabes* (Tizi-Ouzou: Imp. Nouvelle J. Chellier, 1895), p. 6.
39. Ibid., p. 7.
40. Ibid., pp. 7 and 25.
41. Ibid., p. 7.
42. Ibid., p. 23.
43. Ibid.
44. Ibid.
45. Ibid.
46. Ibid., p. 25.
47. Ibid.
48. Cambon, *Le Gouvernement Général de l'Algérie* (1891–1897), p. 438.
49. Soulié, 'L'Assistance médicale des indigènes en Algérie', p. 508.
50. Ibid., p. 582.
51. Ibid., pp. 565–6.
52. Ibid., p. 534.
53. Ibid., pp. 535–6.
54. Ibid., p. 539.
55. Ibid.
56. Ibid., p. 519.
57. Issued by the Ministry of War, the decree of 5 November 1846 and 5 March 1847 regulated the organisation of the civilian hospital in Algiers. Subsequently, the decree of 13 July and 29 August 1849 declared Algerian hospitals public establishments, granting them all the rights and prerogatives enjoyed by civil institutions. The decree issued by M. de Saint-Arnaud on 3 September and 15 October 1852 regulated the admission of patients and treatment in hospitals. The decree of 9 and 12 June regulated the asylum for the elderly, incurable and indigent. Earlier, the decree of 21–28 August 1837 had defined the framework of the administrative commission of the Hospice of Algiers. Finally, the decree of 13 January and 4 February 1848 outlined the functions of the commission overseeing care for orphans and abandoned children. See Picard, 'L'Assistance médicales des Européens en Algérie', pp. 55–8.
58. Ibid., p. 180.
59. Ibid., pp. 131–2.
60. The *bureaux arabes* were special administrative units within the French military in Algeria, established in 1833 and officially sanctioned in 1844. Staffed by French Orientalists, ethnographers, and intelligence officers focused on indigenous affairs, their main functions were to assist in governing the colony, gather intelligence, and inform French colonial policy. They played a key role in the

military pacification of Algeria and the administration of the indigenous population until their dismantling after 1870.

61. Previously, several decrees regulated the medical professions in Algeria. The decree of 31 December 1830 established the legal framework for medical practice, while the subsequent decree of 12 September 1832 focused on the pharmaceutical profession. Furthermore, the decrees of 15 and 19 January 1835 introduced additional regulations for both doctors and pharmacists. See *Hygiène et pathologie nord-africaines*, vol. 1, p. 251.

62. Ibid. See also Picard, 'L'Assistance médicales des Européens en Algérie', p. 173.

63. Picard, 'L'Assistance médicales des Européens en Algérie', p. 174.

64. Ibid., pp. 175–6.

65. Ibid., pp. 94–5.

66. Ibid., p. 105. The European charity office in Algiers, created by decree of 13 July 1849, comprised two sections: the first dealt with European assistance, the second with Jewish assistance.

67. Ibid., p. 447.

68. Ibid., p. 448.

69. Ibid., pp. 108–9.

70. Ibid., p. 110.

71. *Les Délégations financières algériennes, session ordinaire de 1927* (Alger: Victor Heintz, 1927), p. 652. See also Picard, 'L'Assistance médicales des Européens en Algérie', p. 111.

72. Picard, 'L'Assistance médicales des Européens en Algérie', pp. 91–2.

73. Ibid., pp. 178–9.

74. Ibid., pp. 369–70, and *Hygiène et pathologie nord-africaines*, vol. 1, p. 284.

75. Picard, 'L'Assistance médicales des Européens en Algérie', p. 472.

76. Ibid., p. 106.

77. Ibid., p. 464.

78. Ibid., pp.458–64.

79. Foucault, 'The Politics of Health in the Eighteenth Century', pp. 176–7.

80. ANOM GGA 25 H 30. Malinas and Tostivint go on to add: 'This necessity imposes itself from the beginning of any occupation in colonial countries, but it is especially among the Arabs that, since the beginning of the last century, we have more particularly used the medical sciences to increase our prestige and ensure our authority.' M. Malinas and M. Tostivint, *Mutualité coopérative et projet général d'assistance médicale indigène en Tunisie* (Tunis: Impr. Rapide, 1905), pp. 1–2.

81. *Hygiène et pathologie nord-africaines*, vol. 1, p. 255.

82. Ibid., p. 256.

83. Ibid., p. 257.

84. Ibid., p. 273.

85. Ibid., p. 284.

86. The decree of 4 December 1924 created the Office national d'hygiène sociale in Paris. The office worked with the Ministry of Hygiene and the Ministry of Labour to coordinate propaganda work necessary for individual prophylaxis

and general hygiene. The decree defines the aims of the Office national d'hygiène sociale as follows:

1. To collect and keep up-to-date documentation on the health situation in France.
2. To centralise and make available to the public, national and local services of the medical profession, hygienists and the public, all French and foreign documents and all information relating to hygiene, social diseases and their prophylaxis.
3. To carry out in France and in the colonies a continuous and methodical propaganda to the public, with a view to informing them of the measures of hygiene and prophylaxis necessary for the preservation of health, the fight against social diseases and the preservation of the race.
4. To liaise between the public authorities and private works, in order to coordinate all efforts made to protect public health.

See *Bulletin de l'Association des Dames françaises*, 1 (January 1925): 12; and *Hygiène et pathologie nord-africaines*, vol. 1, pp. 283–4.

87. Fanon, *The Wretched of the Earth*, pp. 38–9.
88. For a detailed discussion of endogamy in Algeria, see Germaine Tillion's *Le Harem et les cousins* (Paris: Editions du Seuil, 1966). The English translation *My Cousin, My Husband* first appeared under the title *The Republic of Cousins* (London: Saqi Books, 1983). For a broader understanding of this concept, see Olivier Le Cour Grandmaison's *L'Empire des hygiénistes: Vivre aux colonies* (Paris: Fayard, 2014).
89. Le Cour Grandmaison, *L'Empire des hygiénistes*, p. 140.
90. Ibid., p. 143.
91. Soulié, 'L'Assistance médicale des indigènes en Algérie', pp. 505–7.
92. Le Cour Grandmaison, *L'Empire des hygiénistes*, p. 167.
93. Pierre Dumas, *L'Algérie* (Grenoble: B. Arthaud, 1931), pp. 25–6.
94. René Worms, *Congrès colonial français de 1905* (Paris: Bibliothèque des congrès coloniaux français, 1905), p. 304. See also Le Cour Grandmaison, *L'Empire des hygiénistes*, p. 172.
95. Edmond Sergent and Étienne Sergent, 'Hygiène de l'Afrique septentrionale', in *Hygiène coloniale*, vol. XI, ed. A. Chantemesse and E. Mosny (Paris: Baillière & Fils, 1907), pp. 147–8.
96. In *Nos grands problèmes coloniaux* (Paris: A. Colin, 1929), Georges Hardy addressed French colonial management challenges, favouring association over assimilation and criticising mainland France's 'negative formalism'. While emphasising respect for indigenous traditions, his approach remained paternalistic, aiming to guide development within a colonial framework. Hardy's views reflected a shift towards acknowledging local contexts while still supporting colonial control and the civilising mission.
97. Lucien Deslinières, *La France Nord-Africaine* (Paris: Éditions du Progres Civique, 1920), p. 9.
98. Ibid., p. 631.
99. Ibid., p. 656.

100. *Hygiène et pathologie nord-africaines*, vol. 1, p. 491.

101. Marshal Lyautey, 'Préface', in Jean Royer (ed.) *L'Urbanisme aux colonies et dans les pays tropicaux*, vol. 2 (La Charité-sur-Loire: Delayance; Paris: Editions d'urbanisme , 1932), p. 8.

102. Ibid., p.7

103. Edmond du Vivier de Streel, 'Introduction', in Royer (ed.) *L'Urbanisme aux colonies et dans les pays tropicaux*, vol. 2, p. 12.

104. Ibid., pp. 11–13.

105. In 1845, according to René Lespès, General Lamoricière created a 'regroupment centre' in Oran as a site of confinement for indigenous people who were expropriated and lost their land to colonial settlements; the centre was dubbed '*village nègre*'. René Lespès, *Oran, étude de géographie et d'histoire urbaines, 1830–1930* (Paris: F. Alcan, 1938), p. 158. See also Ammara Bekkouche, 'Un quartier nommé Ville Nouvelle: Du village nègre colonial à la Medina J'dida des Oranais', *Les Annales de la recherche urbaine* 98 (2005), pp. 114–21.

106. Fanon, *The Wretched of the Earth*, p. 39.

107. Said Faci, *L'Algérie sous l'égide de la France* (Toulouse : Imp. Régionale, 1936), pp. 24–6.

108. Frantz Fanon, *Les Damnés de la terre* (Paris: Gallimard, 1991), pp. 69–70. '*Bicot*' is an extremely offensive, racist French slang term that derogatorily refers to people of North African or Middle Eastern origin, especially from the Maghreb. Derived from '*arbicot*' a diminutive of '*arbi*' (Arab), its pejorative nature exceeds the English translation 'dirty Arabs' in *The Wretched of the Earth*, which fails to capture the term's full offensive impact.

2 TORTURE UNVEILED: REREADING FANON AND BOURDIEU IN THE CONTEXT OF MAY 1958

1. Nigel Gibson, *Fanon: The Postcolonial Imagination* (Cambridge: Polity, 2003), p. 139.

2. Germain Tillion, *The Republic of Cousins* (London: Saqi Books, 1983), p. 172 (first published in French, *Le Harem et les cousins* [Paris: Editions du Seuil, 1966]).

3. Christine Achour, *Frantz Fanon: L'Importun* (Montpellier: Chèvre-Feuille Etoilée, 2004), p. 38.

4. Ibid., pp. 39–40.

5. T. Denean Sharpley-Whiting, *Frantz Fanon: Conflicts and Feminisms* (Lanham, MD: Rowman and Littlefield, 1997).

6. M.-A. Helie-Lucas, 'Women, Nationalism, and Religion in the Algerian Liberation Struggle', in N. Gibson (ed.) *Rethinking Fanon* (New York: Humanity Books, 1999), p. 275.

7. Fanon, *The Wretched of the Earth*, p. 202.

8. Achour, *Frantz Fanon: L'Importun*, p. 45.

9. Ibid., pp. 38–9.

10. Ibid., p. 36. According to Achour, Fanon insists on the revolutionary impetus of this dynamic restructuring of Algerian society, Bourdieu on the 'destructuring' of rural life and the attendant uprooting of the population. She situates Fanon's discussion in this interpretive context, arguing that the veil is the signifier par excellence of this dynamism.

11. Anne McClintock, *Imperial Leather: Race, Gender, and Sexuality in the Colonial Conquest* (New York: Routledge, 1995), p. 364.

12. Ibid., p. 367.

13. Ibid., p. 364.

14. Ibid., p. 366.

15. Fanon, *Studies in a Dying Colonialism*, p. 65.

16. Ato Sekyi-Otu, *Fanon's Dialectic of Experience* (Cambridge, MA: Harvard University Press, 1996), p. 225.

17. Ibid., p. 224.

18. Ibid., p. 218.

19. Ibid., pp. 228–9.

20. Ibid., p. 224.

21. Pierre Nora, *Les Français d'Algérie* (Paris: Christian Bourgeois, 2012), pp. 194–195. As Nora affirms, the Algerian woman safeguarded tradition and stood as the last rampart against French colonial advances. She preserved family unity through the upheavals of conquest and settlement. Domestic and religious life constituted the two secret doors that the French never unlocked.

22. Albert Memmi, *Decolonization and the Decolonized* (Minneapolis and London: University of Minnesota Press, 2006), p. 88.

23. Fanon, *Studies in a Dying Colonialism*, p. 39.

24. Ibid., p. 48.

25. Ibid., p. 51.

26. Macey, *Frantz Fanon: A Life*, p. 404.

27. Fanon, *Studies in a Dying Colonialism*, p. 36.

28. Macey, *Frantz Fanon: A Life*, p. 407.

29. Ibid., p. 407.

30. Ibid.

31. Neil MacMaster, *Burning the Veil* (Manchester and New York: Manchester University Press, 2009), p. 139.

32. Fanon, *Studies in a Dying Colonialism*, p. 60.

33. Ibid., p. 61.

34. Fanon, *Black Skin, White Masks*, p. 10.

35. Gibson, *Fanon: The Postcolonial Imagination*, p. 140.

36. Fanon, *Studies in a Dying Colonialism*, p. 59.

37. Ibid., p. 45.

38. Gibson, *Fanon: The Postcolonial Imagination*, p. 141.

39. Ibid., p. 142.

40. Ibid., p. 143.

41. Ibid., p. 142.

42. Ibid., p. 143.

43. Albert Memmi, *The Colonizer and the Colonized* (London: Souvenir Press, 1974), pp. 142-6.
44. Pierre Bourdieu, *The Algerians* (Boston, MA: Beacon Press, 1962), pp. 156, 158.
45. Pierre Bourdieu, 'Guerre et mutation sociale en Algérie', *Études méditerranéennes*, 7 (1960), pp. 25-6.
46. Ibid., p. 26.
47. Bourdieu, *The Algerians*, p. 157.
48. Bourdieu, 'Guerre et mutation sociale en Algérie', p. 26.
49. Jacques Berque, *French North Africa: The Maghrib Between Two World Wars* (London: Faber and Faber, 1967), p. 341.
50. Bourdieu, *The Algerians*, p. 157.
51. Joan Scott, *The Politics of the Veil* (Princeton, NJ: Princeton University Press, 2007), p. 62.
52. Berque, *French North Africa*, pp. 340-1.
53. Bourdieu, *The Algerians*, p. 157.
54. Ibid., p. 158.
55. Ibid., p. 158.
56. Bourdieu, 'Guerre et mutation sociale en Algérie', and 'Révolution dans la revolution', *Esprit* 291(1) (Janvier 1961), pp. 27-40.
57. Ibid., p. 27.
58. Yves Courrière, *Les Fils de la Toussaint* (Paris: Fayard, 1968), p. 413.
59. MacMaster, *Burning the Veil*, p. 122.
60. Courrière, *Les Fils de la Toussaint*, pp. 413, 416-23.
61. MacMaster, *Burning the Veil*, p. 136.
62. Scott, *The Politics of the Veil*, p. 63.
63. MacMaster, *Burning the Veil*, p. 122.
64. ANOM GGA 14 CAB 162 Petition to the Director of Radio Casbah, 8 April 1958. ANOM 81 F 74. Also, in early October 1958, the SAS and the Mouvement de Solidarité Féminine organised similar petitions urging Algerian women to appeal to de Gaulle for reforms and the banning of the veil. Hundreds of women, many illiterate, were rounded up by military personnel to sign using their fingerprints. On 13 October 1958, Madame Lucienne Salan, President of the Committee for Social Aid, Action, and Women's Solidarity, wrote to de Gaulle, highlighting Muslim women's demand for reforms on issues such as minimum marriage age, forced marriages, polygamy, and repudiation. She forwarded several petitions from Beni-Saf, Ain-Temouchent, Laferrière, and Er-Rahel, believing they reflected the women's urgent desire for France to improve their situation and their hope that de Gaulle would be their saviour.
65. ANOM GGA 14 CAB 162 General Allard's letter to the Army General commanding the 10th Military Region, Joint Forces, and Fifth Bureau, 6 May 1958.
66. ANOM GGA 14 CAB 162 General Salan, 'Port du Voile', 12 May 1958.
67. ANOM GGA 14 CAB 162 Letter from General Massu Commander of the 10th Parachute Division to the Prefect of Algiers, 26 April 1958.
68. Marnia Lazreg, *Torture and the Twilight of Empire* (Princeton, NJ: Princeton University Press, 2008), pp. 146-9.

69. Ibid., p.148. See also SHD GR 1 H 2461/D1, Le Général de division Paul Vanuxem, 10e Région militaire, 2e D.I.M. & Z.E.C. État-major – 5e Bureau, Action psychologique, 'Action psychologique féminine, Travail de préparation', 20 June 1958.

70. Lazreg, *Torture and the Twilight of Empire*, p. 149.

71. Ibid., p. 150.

72. MacMaster, *Burning the Veil*, p. 130.

73. Ibid., pp. 131–2.

74. Ibid., p. 133.

75. Ibid., p. 132.

76. Helie-Lucas, 'Women, Nationalism, and Religion in the Algerian Liberation Struggle', p. 275.

77. Jean-Luc Einaudi, *La Ferme Améziane* (Paris: L'Harmattan, 1991), p. 105.

78. Ibid., p. 106.

79. Ibid., pp. 111–12.

80. Ibid., p. 112.

81. Ibid., p. 113.

82. Lazreg, *Torture and the Twilight of Empire*, p. 147.

83. Ibid., pp. 150–1.

84. Alastair Horne, *A Savage War of Peace* (London: Macmillan, 1977), p. 291.

85. Fanon, *Studies in a Dying Colonialism*, p. 62.

86. Ibid., p. 59.

87. Ibid., pp. 42–3.

88. Ibid., p. 45.

89. Malek Alloula, *The Colonial Harem* (Manchester: Manchester University, 1987), pp. 14 and 26.

90. Fanon, *Studies in a Dying Colonialism*, pp. 44–5.

91. MacMaster, *Burning the Veil*, pp. 139–40.

92. Fanon, *Studies in a Dying Colonialism*, p. 38.

93. Ibid., p. 46.

94. Ibid., p. 60.

95. For example: married to an FLN militant, Djemila was arrested and tortured, her veil was removed, her clothes torn, she was exposed naked to the gaze of French soldiers. Electrodes were then placed on her ears, on her nipples and on her sex. Djemila witnessed the rape of a 13-year-old child who was detained with her mother. Said was also detained in the Améziane Farm. He was undressed and his head was forced into a tub full of urine and excrement. Larbi had his testicles crushed. Hachemi Zitouni had electrodes put on his penis. Mouloud, the owner of the farm and Monique's half-brother, was made to sit on a bottle with a broken neck. Unveiling was one of the main instruments used in questioning; torture in Einaudi's account was sexed.

96. Helie-Lucas, 'Women, Nationalism, and Religion in the Algerian Liberation Struggle', p. 275.

97. Raphaëlle Branche, *La Torture et l'armée* (Paris: Gallimard, 2001), p. 298.

98. Ibid., p. 299.

99. Ibid., pp. 303–4.

100. Hélène Cixous and Eric Prenowitz, 'Letter to Zohra Drif', *College Literature* 30(1) (Winter 2003), pp. 82–90. Cixous uses two figures of speech to describe the Casbah where this battle took place. She deploys personification to attribute human, specifically feminine, characteristics to 'the oldest of Algiers's cities, the most folded up, the convoluted one, the cascade of alleyways with the odours of urine and spices'. She also employs synecdoche, using a part of the female body to refer to the whole, calling it by its 'hidden name', 'the savage genitals'. Cixous affirms that 'the Casbah with its folds and its powerful and poor people, its hunger, its desires, its vaginality … was always the clandestine and venerated genitals of the City of Algiers'.

101. Assia Djebar, *Women of Algiers in their Apartments* (Charlottesville: University of Virginia Press, 1999; first published in French, 1980), p. 6.

102. Ibid., p. 150.

103. Ibid., p. 44.

104. Ibid., p. 150.

105. Branche, *La Torture et l'armée*, p. 304.

106. According to Branche, electrodes were placed in her genitalia and finally a bottle and a toothbrush were rammed into her vagina (ibid., p. 305).

107. Fanon, *Studies in a Dying Colonialism*, p. 46.

108. Scott, *The Politics of the Veil*, p. 65.

109. Ibid., p. 61.

110. Ibid., p. 66.

111. Fanon, *Studies in a Dying Colonialism*, p. 44.

112. Scott, *Politics of the Veil*, p. 67.

113. Ibid., p. 67.

114. Diana Fuss, *Identification Papers: Readings on Psychoanalysis, Sexuality, and Culture* (New York: Routledge, 1995), p. 150.

3 THE BATTLE OF THE VEIL AND OF THE WAVES: COLONIAL AND ANTICOLONIAL RADIO TRANSMISSION

1. T.A.M. Craven, 'Radio Frontiers', *Annals of the American Academy of Political and Social Science* 213, (*New Horizons in Radio* special issue) (January 1941), p. 126.

2. Aurélie Luneau, *Radio Londres 1940–1944* (Paris: Perrin, 2005), pp. 21–45.

3. ANOM 9 H 50 'Note à Monsieur le Secrétaire Général du Gouvernement', 21 February 1938, pp. 1–7. The Directeur Général des Affaires Indigènes in Algeria, Louis Milliot, called for the deployment of a new radio station, Le Poste colonial, to counter the propaganda of transnational radio stations broadcast on different wavelengths reaching North African shores. Milliot drew attention to Radio Bari's anti-British and anti-French stance. Supporting Milliot's views, M. Delahaye noted that Radio Bari's programmes were marked by '[an] offensive directed first against English policy in Islamic countries and, since autumn 1937, against France's Muslim policy and, more generally, against France itself' (ANOM 15 H 32 'Note sur la Radiodiffusion et les populations

indigènes d'Algérie', 25 February 1938, p. 4). Radio Bari criticised 'the harmful policy that France was pursuing in Islamic countries' (ibid., p. 5). Fascist propaganda intensified following the decision taken in December 1937 by the Ente Italiano Audizioni Radiofoniche (Italy's state-run radio broadcaster from 1928 to 1944) to extend Radio Bari's Arabic programme from 30 to 40 minutes three times a week. This change in its broadcasting strategy was also accompanied by the publication of a review entitled *Radio Arabi di Bari* (see ANOM 15 H 32 'Propagande Italienne par radiodiffusion dans les milieu musulmans', Direction Générale des Affaires Indigènes, Centre d'Informations et d'Etudes, 19 December 1937). In response, the BBC Daventry station began broadcasting in Arabic on 3 January 1938, with Le Poste colonial following suit on 16 January of the same year.

4. Frédéric Brunnquell, *Fréquence monde – du Poste colonial à RFI* (Paris: Pluriel, 1982), p. 28.

5. Ibid., p. 31.

6. Ibid., p. 32. A propaganda campaign was undertaken largely by Germany and Italy, as well as by Spain, to promote pan-Islamism and Arabism. This propaganda was disseminated via wireless (namely Radio Berlin, Radio Bari and Radio Seville), and was also mediated through the printing press, leaflets, sound recordings, films, and public performances ranging from scripted and unscripted plays to public speaking, songs and poetry. French radio intervened locally to counter fascist and Nazi propaganda; the aim was to thwart pan-Islamism and Arabism and prevent Algeria's rapprochement and ideological alignment with Islamic and Arab countries in the Middle East. French colonial propaganda was clear: 'There is no interest in systematically linking Algeria to the Muslim Orient, because it is no longer and should not become again a specifically Arab country. On the contrary, we can posit that our discreet yet tenacious efforts should contribute to diverting our Colony from the Arab world and steering it towards Western forms of civilisation, without giving them the character of a religious struggle' (ANOM 9 H 50 'Organisation de la contre-propagande en Algérie', p. 16). The significance of radio as an instrument of propaganda and the necessity to keep it under surveillance was underscored by the Directeur Général des Affaires Indigènes, Jean Mirante (ANOM 15 H 32 'Note pour Monsieur le Secrétaire Général du Gouvernement', 21 February 1933). Mirante proposed a range of programmes covering topics such as France and Islam, hygiene and education, Antiquity, Arabic language and literature. These programmes would be presented by experts vetted by the colonial administration.

7. Rebecca P. Scales, 'Subversive Sound: Transnational Radio, Arabic Recordings, and the Dangers of Listening in French Colonial Algeria, 1934–1939', *Comparative Studies in Society and History* 52(2) (April 2010).

8. Ibid., p. 387.

9. Ibid., p. 391. In 1933–35, as Scales documents, Omar Guendouz, a teacher of Arabic and contributor to the pro-assimilationist newspaper *La Voix des Humbles*, presented a limited number of programmes in classical Arabic.

However, these programmes were largely inaccessible to the masses, who primarily spoke Algerian and Berber dialects.

10. Ibid., p. 410.
11. Ibid., p. 416.
12. Ibid. The number of radio receivers in Algeria grew steadily: from 50,000 in May 1936 to 54,600 in November, reaching 66,531 in April 1937 and 74,445 by December 1937. While approximate, these figures indicate a consistent upward trend in radio set acquisition. Determining the exact number owned by Algerians is challenging, but estimates suggest they possessed 4–5 per cent of the total – approximately 3,000 sets in April 1936, increasing to 4,000 by December 1937. Notably, many of these were not privately owned but found in shopkeepers' stores, Moorish cafés and small greasy-spoon restaurants. This information is based on Delahaye's 'Note sur la radio diffusion et les populations indigènes', prepared on 29 June 1937 for the October 1937 session of the Haut Comité Méditerranéen (ANOM 15 H 32).
13. Scales, 'Subversive Sound', pp. 388–9.
14. Ibid., p. 399.
15. In 1936, Marcel Pellenc, reporting to the Blum Cabinet, warned against the dangers of anticolonial propaganda. However, he also contended that France possessed in radio technology a potent weapon to counter such propaganda, maintain its colonial hegemony, and win the hearts and minds of indigenous people (in ibid., pp. 410–11).
16. ANOM 15 H 32 Talk given by Mr. Bachagha Smati, 'Le Disque de langue arabe'.
17. Ibid., pp. 1–2.
18. Ibid., p. 2.
19. Ibid., p. 4.
20. The Jonnart Law (1919) granted voting rights to the *évolués*, but not to the largely uneducated majority of the colonised people. It was a democratic gesture framed in segregationist terms; the newly enfranchised elite were grouped into a separate electoral college.
21. From the outset, the settlers rejected this programme of reforms: assimilation endangered the stability of the colonial system and jeopardised their interests. Jean Pomier and Louis Lecoq, ardent supporters of these interests, opposed the Jonnart Law, lamenting the religious and racial tensions arising from assimilationist policies and criticising France's failure in its mission for allowing the colonised to evolve apart in the confines of their culture. In 'L'Algérie en France', Lecoq denounced 'Jonnart the academician, a solemn statesman of the failed kind, inspirer of the absurd regulations of 1919 that amplified the system of the Arab evolving in "his society"' (Louis Lecoq, 'L'Algérie en France', *Afrique*, 32 [1927], p. 4). The Jonnart Law never intended to allow the natives to evolve in their culture; the necrotisation of the latter was one of the consequences of French colonialism and the colonised's exclusion from the political process which was played out in the public sphere. Lecoq and Pomier's criticism of Jonnart was disingenuous. They argued his policies went too far in assimilating indigenous people, while simultaneously reacting against the backlash of Algerian nationalism that denounced the law's shortcomings. Their critique

highlighted the bifurcation of colonial Algeria along ethnic, religious and gender lines. The literary movement *Algérianisme*, founded by Pomier and Lecoq in 1920, emerged as a reaction against both the Jonnart Law and the political demands of a burgeoning Algerian nationalism. In 'La propagande et les Ecrivains', Pomier traces the etymology of 'propaganda' to the missionary work of the Congregation for the Propagation of the Faith, insisting that literature must fulfil the task of 'assimilating' and 'proselytising' the colonised natives. Ultimately, radio – much like writing in Pomier's conception of colonial literature – was employed as a propaganda stratagem to 'pose, ex-pose and pro-pose Algeria' (Jean Pomier, 'La Propagande et les écrivains', *Afrique*, 251 [1953], p. 7).

22. The Blum–Viollette Bill of 1936 proposed granting French citizenship to about 35,000 Algerians. However, despite its limited scope, the bill faced fierce opposition from French settlers, who threatened rebellion and mass resignations of French mayors. Ultimately, the Blum government capitulated to this pressure, and the bill was abandoned without debate, foreshadowing a similar capitulation by the Mollet government two decades later. See Herbert Luethy, 'Algeria in Revolt', *The Atlantic*, November (1956), p. 76.

23. ANOM 15 H 31 *En Nadjah* (8 and 12 August 1939) drew attention to Radio Bari radio programmes, through which Mussolini exacerbated tensions by criticising France's policies towards Muslims in Algeria and calling for *jihad*.

24. In 'L'Algérie en France' (1927), Lecoq bemoans that the settlers were camping in a hostile society. In 'Prélude à l'exposition coloniale de Paris', *Afrique*, 68 (1931), pp. 4–5, Pomier asserts that Algeria was neither France nor an extension of France, and that religion remained in a state of medieval fanaticism, keeping races and ethnicities apart. A year before the publication of Maurice Viollette's 'L'Algérie vivra-t-elle?', Pomier insisted that harmony in Algeria could be achieved only when all religions were confined to the private sphere and ceased to interfere in the public space.

25. Jean Pomier, 'Attitude devant l'Islam', *Afrique*, 56 (1930), p. 5 (bold in original).

26. In 'La Radiodiffusion', Gustave Mercier writes:
   In this country where space remains the major obstacle, any means of communication acquires unparalleled value. Is there a more subtle messenger than these barely captured waves, which already transport thought, through speech or musical harmonies, at the speed of light, across indefinite distances? What a dream to connect all the pioneers of the countryside, all the isolated towns or farms in the interior, all the lost outposts, to Sudan, to the Equator, to the heart and brain of the Algerian capital, and through them to France and Europe! What an incomparable privilege to have a propaganda and information tool that can make Algeria's voice heard, every day and everywhere! This dream, this privilege, have become reality, thanks to the Centennial credits, and we can say that success has even exceeded expectations. (ANOM B 4844 Gustave Mercier, Commissaire Général du Centenaire, *Centenaire de l'Algérie, Voyage de M. le Président de la République 4–12 mai 1930*, pp. 18–19).

As we will see, these high hopes were dashed by political reality. The obstacles French colonialism encountered were not physical and spatial but political and cultural. See also 'Postes, télégraphes et téléphone en Algérie', another report written for the centenary, affirms that radiophony had a bright future in consolidating France's colonial enterprise. It was expected to develop business, increase agricultural production, build communication networks, improve education, and bring French progress to the smallest hamlets (ANOM B 4844 'Postes, Télégraphes et Téléphone en Algérie', p. 17). This celebratory rhetoric of the centenary served as a device that masked the colonial malaise and latent political tensions.

27. ANOM 15 H 31 'Lettre de la part de 72 Sanfilistes de Paris E.S.E.', sent to M. le Rédacteur en Chef de Radio P.T.T. Alger, 26 October 1937. The term 'sans-filiste' stems from 'sans-fils', associated with the Compagnie Générale de Télégraphie Sans Fil (CSF), a French company founded in 1918 that developed wireless technology. 'Sans-fils', meaning 'without wires' in French, relates to wireless communication technology. CSF pioneered broadcasting equipment, electroacoustics, shortwave radio, radar systems and television. The term sans-filiste refers to radio operators and specialists or involved in wireless communications.

28. The élus, or 'elected natives', were a group of French-educated Algerian Muslims who engaged with the colonial political system. Members of the Fédération des Élus Indigènes, formed in 1927, they advocated for the assimilation and integration of Algerians into French society. This group sought equal rights and citizenship for Muslims within the French system, aiming for reform through existing colonial structures. Prominent figures such as Ferhat Abbas initiated and led these efforts, pushing for gradual political and social changes whilst working within the confines of the colonial framework.

29. See Delahaye's note on radio broadcasting and the indigenous populations, prepared on 29 June 1937 for the October 1937 session of the Haut Comité Méditerranéen. ANOM 15 H 32 'Note sur la Radiodiffusion et les populations indigènes d'Algérie', p. 1.

30. Jacques Derrida, Le Monolinguisme de l'autre (Paris: Éditions Galilée, 2006).

31. Memmi, The Colonizer and the Colonized, p. 140.

32. Fanon captures a structure of feelings prevalent in traditional society, as reflected in En Nadjah newspaper by Algerian listeners who cautioned against purchasing a radio receiver: 'Traditions of respectability are so important for [Algerians] ... that it is practically impossible for [them] to listen to radio programs in the family. The sexual allusions, or even the clownish situations meant to make people laugh, which are broadcast over the radio, cause an unendurable strain in a family listening to these programs.' Fanon, Studies in a Dying Colonialism, p. 70.

33. ANOM 15 H 31 En Nadjah, 9 and 14 October 1936, and 25 June 1937.

34. Fanon, Studies in a Dying Colonialism , pp. 37–8.

35. Ibid., pp. 38–9.

36. Ibid., p. 65.

37. Ibid.

38. Ibid., pp. 71–2.

39. Ibid., p. 72.

40. Ibid.

41. Ibid., p. 69.

42. Ibid.

43. Frantz Fanon, *The Wreched of the Earth* (New York: Grove Press, 1963), p. 39.

44. As she puts it:

> In the evening, the men always gathered. *Saout El Djezaïr* (*The Voice of Algeria*) reached them again from Cairo. People wrestled with their hunger, denying their already hungry stomachs a few mouthfuls of bread to buy a radio. The advent of the transistor was a revolution in itself, spreading information to the most remote villages without electricity. Transistors exploded in the solitude of mountains and desert plains like so many bombs … [the] impact was considerable. Those who lived in total isolation, forgotten by the rest of the world, suddenly became aware, thanks to it, that they belonged to a country, an entity in motion, driven by noble and exhilarating aspirations. (Malika Mokeddem, *Les Hommes qui marchent* [Paris: Editions Ramsay, 1990], pp. 87–8).

45. Fanon, *Studies in a Dying Colonialism*, p. 81.

46. Ibid., pp. 82–3.

47. Ibid., p. 83.

48. Ibid., p. 84.

49. AN R19860074/6 'Voeu relative à la radiodiffusion', Tunis, 16 March 1954. See also letter from E. Hugues, Secretary of State, to the President of the Council, 22 April 1954; and 'Brouillage des émissions radiophoniques étrangères en langue arabe', letter from Contre-Amiral M. Conge, President of the Telecommunications Coordination Committee of the French Union, to the President of the Council, Permanent General Secretariat of National Defense, Paris, 29 November 1954.

50. AN R19860074/6 'Note pour Monsieur Cabannes, Cabinet de Monsieur le Ministre de l'Industrie et du Commerce', Radiodiffusion-Télévision Française, Direction des Services Techniques, 21 December 1954, p. 1.

51. AN R19860074/6 Robert Lacoste, 'Letter à Monsieur le Secrétaire d'Etat à la Présidence du Conseil chargé de l'Information (Cabinet)', 18 September 1956.

52. AN R19860074/6 Presidence du Conseil, 'Procès-verbal de la réunion du 20 septembre 1956', pp. 1–3. Technically, this jamming was only possible using powerful and well-placed transmitters. Two or three days were needed to set up jamming frequencies on one or two RTF transmitters. However, jamming would require the interruption of some RTF programmes. A sum of 120 million francs was pledged for the jamming operation.

53. AN R19860074/6 See the directive of 13 October 1956 from the Presidency of the Council's Central Bureau of Documentation and Information directed to the Major General Director of RTF Technical Services and the Colonel Director of the Radio Control Group at Fort Mont-Valérien, instructing them to implement the jamming of Radio Tunis and Radio Maroc.

54. AN R19860074/6 'Brouillage de Radio Tunis et de Radio Maroc', Letter from Bourgès-Maunoury, Minister of Defence and the Armed Forces, to the Prime Minister (Military Cabinet), 5 October 1956.

55. AN R19860074/6 GCR Fiche no. 12, 'Emissions en langue arabe. Efficacité des brouillages pendant le mois de juillet. Modifications intervenues entre le 16 juillet et le 20 août 1957', p. 1. See also AN R19860074/6 Le Directeur du Bureau Central de Documentation et d'Information, 'Note' to Undersecretary to the Prime Minister's Office, 25 June 1957. The 'Note' ordered that the RACL be jammed; it had begun a new bi-weekly programme targeting Algerian workers in France. The broadcast aired from 23:30 Sunday to 00:30 Monday and 23:30 Wednesday to 00:30 Thursday on 6.666 kHz.

56. See AN R19860074/6 GCR Fiche no. 12, p. 1.

57. AN R19860074/6 GCR Fiche no. 14, 'Emissions en langue arabe. Mise à jour des caractéristiques des émetteurs et des brouilleurs', 16 November 1957, p. 1.

58. Ibid., pp. 1–2.

59. Fanon, *Studies in a Dying Colonialism*, p. 96.

60. GCR Fiche no. 12, p. 10.

61. Ibid., p. 8. It broadcast on 12.025 kc/s rather than its customary 17.915 kc/s.

62. Ibid., pp. 8 and 17. Hostile in its denunciation of France's murderous colonialism, Radio Damascus's 'La Voix du Maghreb arabe' was comfortably received and followed by many listeners (ibid., p. 13). Additionally, Radio Baghdad started airing a programme discussing the struggle of the Algerian people (ibid., p. 14). Radio Cairo denounced the 'human butchery' committed by France in Algeria, a butchery which would only restore a 'sinister example of barbarism and the safeguard[ing] of imperialism' (ibid., p. 17). Radio Karachi criticised French colonialism, just as Radio Sana called on Arab countries colonised by the British to follow in the footsteps of their brothers in Algeria (ibid., p. 19).

63. Ibid., p. 18.

64. AN R19860074/6 Présidence du Conseil, Ministre de la Défense Nationale et des Forces Armées, 24 January 1958, p. 4.

65. Ibid., p. 5.

66. Ibid., p. 6.

67. AN R19860074/6 Pierre Maisonneuve, 'Mise en oeuvre du Centre de brouillage des Eucalyptus', 24 December 1957, pp. 1–2.

68. AN R19860074/6 Présidence du Conseil, Ministre de la Défense Nationale et des Forces Armées, 24 January 1958, p. 7.

69. AN R19860074/6 GCR Fiche no. 19, 'Emissions subversives en langues arabe et française. Evolution. Brouillage', 16 September 1958, p. 13.

70. Ibid., p. 15.

71. Ibid., p. 18.

72. Ibid., p. 21.

73. In August 1959, the RALC's programme from 21:00 to 23:00 was extended until 00:18 and transmitted on four frequencies: 6.250, 6.400, 6.500 and 8.100 kc/s, with shifts of ±50 kc/s. The RALC also broadcast on three frequencies: 6.300, 6.400, and 7.100 kc/s, with what appeared to be a fixed frequency of

6.428 kc/s and a progressive shift reaching 6.285 or 6.290 kc/s at the end of transmission. The third frequency operated on the 8 Mc/s band and eventually stabilised at 5900 kc/s with variations of ±10 kc/s. A similar strategy was used by Radio Tunis: transmission in Arabic shifted from 962 to 629 kc/s on 31 August 1959 and subsequently to 635 kc/s (AN R19860074/6 GCR Fiche no. 24, 'Emissions subversives en langues arabe et française. Evolution. Brouillage', 28 September 1959, pp. 5–7). From 8 October 1961, broadcasts on 5.930 and 11.810 khz were discontinued, and by 19 October, transmissions on 5.760 khz ceased. The stable frequency of 8.698 khz and the variable frequency of 8.735 khz were alternated during the same transmission. Each broadcast used two synchronous frequencies: a stable one at 6.429 khz and a variable one, which could be either 8.698 khz (stable) or 8.735/8.740 khz (variable). Frequency hopping occurred up to three times per broadcast. It is likely that two transmitters were used in tandem to boost transmission power (AN R19860074/6 GCR Fiche no. 33, 'Emissions subversives des pays de langue arabe. Evolution. Brouillage. Renseignements divers', 23 November 1961, pp. 6–8).

74. 'La Voix des Arabes' was aired as 'La Voix du peuple' on 24 January 1959, a programme in colloquial Algerian that proved very popular. Additionally, Radio Cairo began broadcasting 'La Voix de la République Algérienne' at 19:15 instead of 19:00. This programme remained as virulent as ever and developed themes similar to those presented by La Voix des Arabes (AN R19860074/6 GCR Fiche no. 21, 'Emissions subversives en langues arabe et française. Evolution. Brouillage', 29 January 1959, pp. 2–5. Radio Baghdad also aired 'La Voix de la République Algérienne' daily, a programme as acerbic as 'La Voix des Arabes' (ibid., p. 11).

The RALC maintained its hostile stance in the anticolonial campaign, while programmes such as 'La Voix de la Mauritanie combattante', 'La Voix de l'Algérie combattante', 'Tel est notre Sahara' and 'La Voix de l'Algérie', transmitted by Moroccan Radio, moderated their criticism (AN R19860074/6 GCR Lettre and Fiche no. 23, 'Emissions subversives en langues arabe et brouillage', 28 September 1959, p. 1). Radio Tunis, on the other hand, increased the impact of its broadcasts by choosing to air 'La Voix de l'Algérie arabe soeur' in colloquial Arabic, a modification that made the programme more accessible to Algerian and Tunisian listeners (GCR Fiche no. 21, p. 12).

Working in tandem with the RALC and 'La Voix de l'Algérie arabe soeur', 'Vive l'Algérie' – transmitted weekly by Libyan Radio – added further complexity to La Croix's task of silencing the voice of 'Free Algeria'. In October 1959, Radio Amman began broadcasting pro-FLN programmes as virulent as those of Radio Cairo. The powerful transmitters in Jordan were clearly audible in Algeria. On 12 November 1960, Radio nationale marocaine launched a weekly programme, 'La Voix de l'Algérie', which must not be confused with 'La Voix de l'Algérie combattante'. This new programme, broadcast in Arabic every Saturday at 20:25, just after the news bulletin, was highly audible in Paris on three frequencies (AN R19860074/6 GCR Fiche no. 29, 'Emissions subversives en langues arabe et française. Evolution. Brouillages. Renseignements divers', 28 November 1960, p. 4). Moreover, Radio nationale marocaine also introduced another programme, 'La Voix de la Mauritanie combattante', broadcast on the same frequency (11.737 kHz) as the FLN's 'La Voix de l'Algérie combattante' (GCR Fiche no. 29, pp. 4–5, 23). The strategy of Radio nationale marocaine was to merge the two programmes, confusing the GCR and bypassing its scrambling devices.

75. AN R19860074/6 GCR Fiche no. 23, p. 1, and Fiche no. 24, pp. 1–2.
76. AN R19860074/6 GCR Fiche no. 19, pp. 1 and 3, and Fiche no. 21, p. 12.
77. AN R19860074/6 GCR Fiche no. 29, p. 2.
78. Ibid., p. 3.
79. Ibid.
80. Ibid., pp. 3–4. Faced with an increasing number of broadcasts from Morocco, Tunisia and Egypt – not to mention those from other Arab countries and from the communist bloc – the GCR, concedes La Croix, could not manage and had to allow the transmission of some nationalist propaganda from the Middle East.
81. The RAU – the newly formed United Arab Republic – announced the installation of three powerful new transmitters, supplied by Telefunken, for 'La Voix des Arabes'. Two transmitters had already been installed in Tunisia by the same German firm. Jordan also reported the installation of a 100 kW transmitter, intended to broadcast to North Africa, parts of Europe, and Asia, including Iran, Pakistan, and Indonesia. Radio Omdurman in Sudan began broadcasting on 11,855, 9,505, and 5.039 kHz with a 20 kW transmitter. Other countries supporting the FLN bolstered their broadcasting infrastructure: Iran launched Radio Tehran on 19 July 1960 with a 100 kW transmitter; the German Democratic Republic built a radio station in Guinea; and Radio Mali installed a new 100 kW transmitter on 18 June. AN R19860074/6 GCR Fiche no. 28, 'Emissions subversives en langues arabe et française. Evolution. Brouillages. Renseignements divers', 12 September 1960, pp. 19–21.
82. AN R19860074/6 GCR Fiche no. 12, p. 19.
83. AN R19860074/6 GCR Fiche no. 14, p. 2.
84. The most hostile broadcasts against French colonialism came from the Soviet bloc, particularly Radio Moscow, Radio Sofia and Radio Tirana. In May 1961, the German Democratic Republic launched a new programme, 'Afrique du Nord', which aired twice a week in Algerian vernacular. The programme featured Algerian war songs, the FLN anthem and provided news of the revolution to support the Algerians in their struggle for independence. (AN R19860074/6 GCR Fiche no. 32, 'Emissions subversives en langues arabe et française. Evolution. Brouillages. Renseignements divers', 22 July 1961, p. 36; see also Fiche no. 21, p. 13).
85. AN R19860074/6 GCR Fiche no. 29, p. 27. Radio Amman aired a programme sympathetic to the FLN, 'The Voice of Arab Algeria', similar to Algerian broadcasts on other Arab stations. It depicted Algerian suffering and condemned French forces for their alleged genocide and extermination in the name of freedom (ibid., p. 26.)
86. Ibid., p. 27.
87. AN R19860074/6 GCR Fiche no. 24, p. 5.

88. AN R19860074/6 GCR Fiche no. 30, 'Emissions subversives en langues arabe et française. Evolution. Brouillages. Renseignements divers', 31 January 1961, p. 27.
89. Ibid., p. 27.
90. AN R19860074/6 GCR Fiche no. 28, p. 25.
91. AN R19860074/6 GCR Lettre et Fiche no. 28, 'Emissions subversives en langue arabe et brouilleurs', 28 November 1960, pp. 1–2 ; GCR Fiche no. 29, pp. 1–4.
92. AN R19860074/6 'Note concernant les possibilités de brouillage de RTF', 14 November 1961, p. 2.
93. AN R19860074/6 GCR Lettre et Fiche no. 32, 'Emissions subversives des pays de langue arabe et brouillages', 23 November 1961, p. 2.
94. AN R19860074/6 GCR Fiche no. 33, p. 2.
95. Fanon, Studies in a Dying Colonialism, p. 85.
96. Ibid.
97. Ibid. pp. 86–7.
98. Ibid. p. 88.
99. Ibid. p. 87.
100. Ibid.
101. Ibid.
102. Ibid., p. 73.
103. Ibid., p. 74.
104. Ibid., p. 93.
105. Ibid., p. 91.
106. Ibid., pp. 89–90.
107. Ibid., p. 91.
108. Ibid.
109. Ibid., p. 92.
110. Ibid., pp. 90–92.
111. Ibid., p. 89.
112. Ibid., p. 92.
113. Ibid., p. 83.
114. Ibid., p. 84.
115. Ibid., p. 86.
116. Ibid., p. 87.
117. Ibid., p. 73.
118. Ibid., p. 89.
119. Ibid.
120. Richard Boyd, Broadcasting in the Arab World: A Survey of the Electronic Media in the Middle East (Ames: Iowa State University Press, 1993), p. 205.
121. Ibid., p. 206.
122. Ibid.
123. Antoine Sabbagh, 'La propagande à Radio-Alger', in Michèle de Bussierre, Cécile Méadel and Caroline Ulmann-Mauriat (eds) Radios et télévision au temps des 'événements d'Algérie (Paris: Harmattan, 1999), p. 30.
124. Ibid., p. 29.
125. Brunnquell, Fréquence monde, pp. 90–92.

126. Cherki, *Frantz Fanon, Portrait*, p. 194.
127. Fanon, *Studies in a Dying Colonialism*, pp. 92–3.
128. Ibid., p. 70.
129. Ibid.
130. Ibid., p. 93.
131. Ibid., p. 92.
132. As Marc Martin affirms, on 13 May 1958, Radio-Alger was taken over by the Comité du Salut Public, and the journalists appointed by mainland France were replaced (Marc Martin, 'La radio dans les crises françaises liées à la guerre d'Algérie', in de Bussierre et al. (eds) *Radios et télévision au temps des 'événements d'Algérie*, p. 19.
133. Ibid.
134. As Martin succinctly puts it:

> Overall, during this crisis, Radio Alger played a significant role in shaping public opinion in France in two distinct ways. By surprising the public (through the theme of fraternisation), it rendered opinion more uncertain and fluid. By alarming it (with the martial and threatening tone observed by *Le Monde*), it steered public opinion toward the political solution that could bridge the divide between Paris and Algiers: the return of General de Gaulle to power. (Ibid., p. 22).

135. Sabbagh, 'La propagande à Radio Alger', p. 29.
136. Ibid., pp. 31 and 33.
137. Ibid., p. 32.
138. MacMaster, *Burning the Veil*, p. 172.
139. Ibid.
140. Mokeddem, *Les Hommes qui marchent*, pp. 87–8.
141. MacMaster, *Burning the Veil*, p. 172.
142. ANOM 20250 'Courrier des auditrices', in *Ici Alger: Revue mensuelle des émissions en langues arabes et Kabyle de Radio-Algérie* 71 (December 1958), p. 23.
143. Ibid.
144. ANOM 14 CAB 162 Petition 8 April 1958.
145. MacMaster disputes *El Moudjahid*'s claim that the army, aided by Mouvement de solidarité feminine, coerced poor domestic servants and prostitutes into participating (*Burning the Veil*, p. 137).
146. AN R19860074/6 *Bulletin d'écoutes du monde islamique*, 'La Voix des Arabes'. After the failure of the Melun talks in June 1960, 'La Voix des Arabes' made new accusations that torture and sexual violence had been used against Algerian women. It condemned these crimes and de Gaulle's 'senseless policy', which it argued was driving the country towards economic and moral bankruptcy.
147. Fanon, *Studies in a Dying Colonialism*, p. 62.
148. AN 65AJ/1266 Radio Algérie, 18 and 19 May 1958, Nos 4.082 and 4.083, AFN/43. Radio-Alger announced the venue for the meeting at 15:30 – Birmandreis Town Hall Square – where twenty trucks would be available to transport participants to the Tagarins. A similar appeal was also made to the inhabitants of El-Biar.

149. AN 65AJ/1266 Radio Algérie, 20 May 1958, No 4.904, AFN/23.
150. AN 65AJ/1266 Radio Algérie, 18 and 19 May 1958, Nos 4.902 and 4.903, AFN/21.
151. AN 65AJ/1266 Radio Algérie, 18 and 19 May 1958, Nos 4.902 and 4.903, AFN/52.
152. AN 65AJ/1266 Radio Algérie, 18 May 1958, Nos 4.902 and 4.903, AFN/53. A similar statement, scripted by the agents of the Fifth Bureau, was made in another unveiling ceremony. 'We are aware of how far our traditional dress, our reclusive existence, are factors that separate us from our French sisters of different religion to ours. We wish to engage fully in the route to modernity and to profit from the exciting epoch which Algeria is currently traversing to accelerate our progress' (MacMaster, *Burning the Veil*, pp. 131–2).
153. AN 65AJ/1266 Radio Algérie, 20 May 1958, No. 4.904, AFN/2.
154. AN 65AJ/1266 Radio Algérie, 22 May 1958, No. 4.906, AFN/11.
155. AN 65AJ/1266 Radio Algérie, 28 May 1958, No. 4.912, AFN/5.
156. 'My brothers, you have just heard the speech delivered by one of the most authoritative voices in Islam. I stand before you with the veil. Through the renewal we must bring to our emancipation (applause), my sisters, let us not squander the only opportunity offered to us for complete and absolute emancipation (cries, ovations).' AN 65AJ/1266 Radio Algérie, 28 May 1958, No. 4.912, AFN/6.

4 REPUBLIC OF COUSINS OR CITIZENS?

1. Karl Marx, 'Le Système foncier ancestral en Algérie au moment de la conquête française', trans. A. Gisselbrecht and A. Tabouret-Keller, *La Nouvelle Critique*, 109 (Sept.–Oct. 1959), pp. 69–88.
2. Bourdieu, *The Algerians*, pp. 120–1.
3. Captain Vaissière (*Les Ouled Rechaich* [Algiers, 1863], p. 90) cited in ibid., p. 121.
4. Ibid., p. 122.
5. Ibid., p. 117.
6. Ibid., pp. 2–4.
7. Ibid., p. 4.
8. Ronald Matthews's translation of *L'Algérie en 1957*, published by Knopf in 1958.
9. Tillion, *The Republic of Cousins*, p. 161.
10. Ibid., p. 160.
11. Ibid., p. 164.
12. Ibid., p. 150.
13. Ibid., p. 162.
14. Ibid., p. 163.
15. Ibid., p. 164.
16. Ibid., p. 158.
17. Ibid., pp. 36–37 and pp. 61–63.
18. Bourdieu, *The Algerians*, p. 145.
19. Ibid., p. 146.

20. Ibid.
21. Tillion, *The Republic of Cousins*, p. 161.
22. Ibid., p. 162.
23. Ibid., p. 27.
24. Ibid., p. 172.
25. Ibid.
26. Ibid., pp. 172–3.
27. Fanon, *Studies in a Dying Colonialism*, p. 114.
28. Ibid., p. 99.
29. Ibid., p. 100.
30. Ibid., p. 101.
31. Ibid., p. 103.
32. Ibid., p. 105.
33. Ibid., p. 106.
34. Ibid., p. 107.
35. Ibid.
36. Ibid., pp. 109–10.
37. Ibid., p. 110.
38. Ibid., p. 107.
39. Ibid., p. 120.
40. General Allard provided this estimated figure to the Conseil d'État in 1867; see Annie Rey-Goldzeiguer, *Le Royaume arabe: La politique algérienne de Napoleon III, 1861–1870* Alger: Office des Publications Universitaires, 2014, pp. 452–3.
41. ANOM B 10264 Pierre Darmon, 'Criquets, famine et choléra 1867, l'année de la mort', p. 36.
42. Ibid., pp. 35–7. It was dubbed the 'demographic disaster' by Djilali Sari in *Le Désastre démographique* (Alger: Société Nouvelle d'Édition et de Diffusion, 1982).
43. The overall toll defies precise quantification, with estimates ranging from 220,000 to 500,000 fatalities. Rey-Goldzeiguer proposes 800,000, while Darmon puts the figure at 1 million. However, any global assessment fails to capture the nuanced reality. Djilali Sari termed it the 'demographic disaster' in *Le Désastre démographique*. Bertrand Taithe examines the intricacies of this calamity and its media portrayal in the press ('La famine de 1866–1868: anatomie d'une catastrophe et construction médiatique d'un événement', *Revue d'histoire du XIXe siècle* 41 [2010]).
44. Rey-Goldzeiguer, *Le Royaume arabe*, pp. 275–336.
45. Grégor Mathias, *Les sections administratives spécialisées en Algérie* (Paris: L'Harmattan, 1998, p. 15.
46. Ibid., p. 16.
47. Ibid., p. 17.
48. Ibid., p. 68. On 30 April 1955, General Parlange was put in charge of civilian authorities and all troops stationed in the Aurès region. On 26 September, Soustelle issued a decree creating the SAS.
49. Keith Sutton, 'Army Administration Tensions over Algeria's Centres de Regroupement, 1954–1962', *British Journal of Middle Eastern Studies* (1999),

26(2), p. 261. See also Jean Nicot, 'Les S.A.S. et la pacification en Algérie', *Revue Historique des Armées*, 189 (1992), pp. 26–39.

50. Sutton, 'Army Administration Tensions', p. 250.

51. Michel Cornaton, *Les Regroupements de la decolonisation en Algérie* (Paris: Les Editions Ouvrières, 1967), p. 68. See also Sutton, 'Army Administration Tensions', p. 252.

52. Sutton, 'Army Administration Tensions', pp. 254–5.

53. Cornaton, *Les Regroupements de la decolonisation en Algérie*, pp. 70–77. Sutton, 'Army administration tensions', p. 257.

54. *Le Déracinement: La crise de l'agriculture traditionnelle en Algérie* (Paris: Minuit, 1964). English translation: *The Uprooting: The Crisis of Traditional Agriculture in Algeria* (Cambridge: Polity Press, 2020).

55. Mohammed Harbi, *Le FLN, mirage et réalité* (Paris: Editions Jeune Afrique, 1980), p. 280.

56. *El Moudjahid*, 'La "pacification" dans l'impasse: les camps de regroupement', 10 May 1959 (41), p. 10.

57. *El Moudjahid*, 'La barbarie colonialist: 1.000.000 d'Algériens parqués dans les camps de regroupement', 24 April 1959 (40), p. 12.

58. 'Les événements d'Afrique du Nord', *Le Monde*, 18 April 1959, p. 2. See also: '"Réfugés" et "regroupés" en Algérie, une interview de Mgr Rodhain à La Croix', *Le Monde*, 13 April 1959, p. 5; 'La situation des Algériens "regroupés"', *Le Monde*, 21 April 1959, p. 3; 'Autour d'un rapport', *Le Monde*, 18 May 1959, p. 2

59. *El Moudjahid*, 'La barbarie colonialist', p. 12.

60. *El Moudjahid* provides the following figures: out of 1,200 people 900 were children. Ibid.

61. Fanon, *Studies in a Dying Colonialism*, pp. 29–20. The report affirms that 'the general physiological state of the population is such that medicine is no longer effective. It is therefore the standard of living that must first be ensured'.

62. Michel Rocard, 'Rapport de Michel Rocard sur les camps de regroupement', in Pierre Vidal-Naquet (ed.) *Les crimes de l'armée française, Algérie 1954–1962* (Paris: La Découverte, 2001), p. 151.

63. Ibid.

64. *El Moudjahid*, 'La barbarie colonialist', p. 12.

65. 'Des sénateurs s'émeuvent de l'atroce misère des Algériens du camp de Bessombourg' (*Le Monde*, 24 July 1959, p. 6) reports on severe famine in regroupment camps, prompting senators' outrage. The article also confirms the findings of a *Le Monde* report from April 18, which highlighted the dire conditions in these camps. Inadequate food and poor living conditions exacerbated the suffering, prompting growing concerns. The situation in Bessombourg, near Collo, drew particular attention due to its devastating poverty and the impact of forced displacement on the local population. This situation is also referenced by Mathias in *Les sections administratives Spécialisées en Algérie*, p. 74.

66. Ibid., p. 75.

67. *El Moudjahid*, 'La "pacification" dans l'impasse', p. 10.

68. *El Moudjahid*, 'La barbarie colonialist', *El Moudjahid*, p. 12.

69. Ibid.
70. The SAS promoted the creation of *Groupes d'auto-défense* (GADs) as the population's endorsement for French Algeria. These administrative units organised the GADs and mobilised the rural population. Sutton estimates that alongside the *harka*, GAD numbers grew from 400 groups comprising 8,000 people in May 1958 to 1,840 groups with 56,000 members in July 1960, reaching 1,918 groups by July 1961. Sutton, 'Army administration tensions', p. 123.
71. The precise events in Catinat remain difficult to establish with certainty. However, according to Patrick Buisson, women were recruited into the *harka* in northern Constantine and Kabylia. Buisson describes this recruitment as a 'doubly symbolic revolution' (*La Guerre d'Algérie* [Paris: Albin Michel, 2009], pp. 124–125). As the following two chapters will demonstrate, this process was marked by brutal violence, including rape and murder.
72. Mathias, *Les sections administratives spécialisées en Algérie*, pp. 81–86.
73. Benjamin Claude Brower, 'Regroupment Camps and Shantytowns in Late-colonial Algeria', *L'Année du Maghreb* 20 (2019), p. 6.
74. Fanon, *Studies in a Dying Colonialism*, p. 65.
75. See Fanon's reference in ibid., p. 64: the appendix, published in *Resistance Algérienne* on 16 May 1957, reflects the FLN leaders' awareness of the significant role played by Algerian women in the Revolution. 'Algeria Unveiled' and its appendix draw on two FLN texts: 'L'Algérienne au Maquis' (1956), which emphasises the active role of Algerian women in the Revolution, and 'La Femme', which argues that the marginalisation of women leads to societal atrophy and eventual demise (Mohammed Harbi and Gilbert Meynier, *Le FLN, documents et histoire 1954–1962* [Paris: Fayard, 2004], p. 605).
76. Fanon, *Studies in a Dying Colonialism*, p. 64.
77. Ibid., p. 65.
78. Ibid.
79. Ibid., p. 66.

5 THE USES OF MEDICINE: COLONIAL AND REVOLUTIONARY

1. Jennifer Johnson, *The Battle for Algeria: Sovereignty, Health Care, and Humanitarianism*, (Philadelphia, PA: University of Pennsylvania Press, 2016), pp. 2–3.
2. Ibid., p. 3.
3. Ibid., p. 4.
4. Ibid.
5. Ibid.
6. ANOM SAS DOC/3 'Sections Administratives Spécialisées, Goums et Harkas', Instructions comptables, Algiers, 1955, pp. 3–4.
7. Ibid.
8. Mathias, *Les sections administratives spécialisées en Algérie*, p.107
9. Johnson, *The Battle for Algeria*, p. 49.
10. Lazreg, *Torture and the Twilight of Empire*, p. 147.
11. Ibid., p. 96.

12. SHD 1 H 2524 'Sociologies musulmane. Causerie no 9. Les caractères essentials de F.M., 1. See also Nora, *Les Français d'Algérie*, pp. 194–195.
13. SHD GR 1 H 2461/D1 Le Général de division Paul Vanuxem, 10e Région militaire, 2e D.I.M. & Z.E.C. État-major – 5e Bureau, Action psychologique, 'Action psychologique féminine, Travail de préparation', 20 June 1958.
14. SHD GR 1 H 2461/D1 *Action sur les milieux féminins en Algérie*, État Major Interarmées, 3e Bureau, 27 March 1960, pp. 13–19. See also Lazreg, p. 147.
15. SHD GR 1 H 2461/D1 Fiches No. 2 and 3. Traditional garments such as *burnouses, djellabas* and veils were framed as potential sources of uncleanliness, subtly delegitimising indigenous clothing practices while promoting Western hygiene standards. By linking unclean clothing to the transmission of diseases, such as fleas and lice spreading plague and typhus, the Fifth Bureau's propaganda biopoliticised hygiene practices. This strategy gave scientific authority to the cultural imposition of Western cleanliness standards. The propaganda exemplified how hygiene discourse could be weaponised to reinforce power structures, stigmatise poverty and undermine traditional cultural practices under the guise of public health concerns.
16. SHD GR 1 H 2461/D1 Jacques Carret, 'La Femme musulmane', *Bulletin de Liaison et de Documentation du Service de l'Action Administrative et Economique, de la Délégation Générale du Gouvernement en Algérie*, 30 May 1958, pp. 52–3.
17. Johnson, *The Battle for Algeria*, pp. 10–12.
18. Mustapha Makaci, *Le Croissant-rouge algérien* (Alger: Alpha, 2007), pp. 1–59, documents the systematic persecution of medical professionals during the War of Independence. This persecution took various forms, including assassination, torture, imprisonment and house arrest. The victims can be categorised as follows:

   1. Assassinated doctors:
      Dr Benzedjeb, Dr Issad Hassani, Dr Chérif Zahar, Dr Asselah Hocine, Professor Lacroix, Dr Nedir, Dr Smail Bouderba, Dr Damardji Youcef, and Dr Bendjeloul.

   2. Medical professionals placed under house arrest or imprisoned:
      • Doctors: Durand, Ouakli, Cherfa, Zemirli, Medjebeur, Djebari, Pastor, Benbahmed, Khene, Shatz, Kerbouche, Mokhtar Kharoubi, Laliam Mustapha, Maouche, Krouri Benaissa, Belabed, Nefissa Hamoud, Bouayad, Damardji Youcef, Tebbal, Benarbia, Balaska, Belouizdad, Belkhodja J., Sadek Hadjeres, Masseboeuf, Martini, Hadjadj, Salhi and Frantz Fanon.
      • Dr Jean-Pierre Schatz (Tlemcen) was specifically sentenced to two years in prison.

   3. Persecuted dentists:
      Hocine Mimoune, Oucharef, Hafiz Mahièdine, Farid Redjeb, Bouchouchi, and Abdelouahab.

   4. Other medical professionals:

- Mrs. Martini, a midwife and wife of the chief physician of Chlef hospital.
- Medical students Timsit and Smadja.

Makaci underscores the widespread nature of the persecution against medical professionals during this period.

19. SHD GR 1H1691/2 FLN Service de santé, organisation du service de santé, June 1957.

20. ACICR BAG 202 008-004 As Jean-Pierre Schoenholzer, Secretary to the Diplomatic Conference and member of the ICRC Legal Service, notes in his report 'Personnel sanitaire algérien' (16 March 1959), these cases were highly controversial and led to numerous appeals to the ICRC. See also the letters from Pierre Gaillard, Head of the ICRC Executive Division, to William Michel, ICRC Delegate in France, regarding: 'Condamnation de médecins en Algérie' (29 April 1958 and 9 May 1958), and the cases of Dr Pastor (2 July 1958) and Laliam (5 January 1959).

21. ACICR BAG 202 008-004 Henri Jean Langlais, 'Note' to Pierre Gaillard concerning the 'Condamnations de médecins en Algérie', 25 April 1958.

22. ACICR BAG 202 008-004 President of the French Red Cross, Letter to the President of the Syrian Red Crescent, 28 April 1958.

23. ACICR BAG 202 008-004 Letter from the Algerian Red Crescent conveyed by Dr Bentami to Mr Gaillard, 27 May 1959.

24. ACICR BAG 202 008-004 See Mostafa Benbahmed's telex addressed to Dr Bentami and P. Gaillard's file note, 'Plainte du Croissant-Rouge algérien', 24 Novembre 1958.

25. Letter from Hocène Boukli, president of the CRA, to Jean de Preux, ICRC delegate in Tunis, 16 March 1958.

26. 'White Paper, On the Application of the Geneva Conventions of 1949 to the French-Algerian Conflict', Algeria Office, May 1960, p. 23.

27. Cherki, Frantz Fanon, Portrait, p. 131. Like Cherki, Macey argues that Fanon's support for the FLN in Blida-Joinville extended beyond medical care: the open-door policy provided sanctuary and treatment for wounded FLN operatives (Macey, Frantz Fanon: A Life, p. 265).

28. Richard C. Keller, Colonial Madness: Psychiatry in French North Africa Chicago, IL: University of Chicago Press, 2007), p. 159.

29. Fanon, Studies in a Dying Colonialism, p. 139.

30. Ibid., pp. 121-2.

31. Ibid., p. 123.

32. Ibid., p. 128.

33. Ibid., p. 130.

34. Ibid., p. 134.

35. Ibid., p. 133.

36. Ibid., p. 134.

37. Ibid., p. 136.

38. Ibid.

39. Ibid., p. 138-9.

40. Branche, La Torture et l'armée, pp. 467-8.

41. Fanon, *Studies in a Dying Colonialism*, p. 139.
42. Ibid.
43. Ibid., p. 141.
44. Makaci, *Le Croissant-rouge algérien*, pp. 1–59.
45. Fanon, *Studies in a Dying Colonialism*, p. 141.
46. Ibid., p. 142.
47. Ibid.
48. Ibid., p. 145.

6 TORTURE AND GENDER: INTERROGATION, RESETTLEMENT AND PACIFICATION

1. *Lettres du Maréchal de Saint-Arnaud 1832–1854*, 3rd edn (Paris: Michel Lévy Frères, 1864), p. 139.
2. Ibid., pp. 141–2.
3. Ibid., p. 147.
4. Ibid., p. 147–8.
5. ACICR BAG 202 008-011 See the telegram to the Red Cross from Mr Ferhat Abbas, President of the Council of the Provisional Algerian Government, sent from Tunis on 14 May 1959. See also the letter from the CRA sent by Dr Bentami to Gaillard on 5 May 1959, and the communiqué regarding Douar Terchioui issued on 12 May and forwarded to the ICRC on 28 May.
6. ACICR BAG 202 008-011 Letter from Henri Langlais to William Michel, ICRC Delegate in Paris, 23 May 1959. 'Un démenti de l'État-Major d'Alger', dated 6 May and 'Le massacre de Mac-Mahon était en réalité une libération', dated 13 May, sent from the Ministry of Armed Forces to the ICRC.
7. SHAT 1 H 2423 'Un Émule de Bugeaud ou bréviaire de répression', an extract chosen by Harbi and Meynier from 'Rapport sur le moral des tirailleurs pour 1956', offers a chilling insight into the colonial military mindset during the Algerian war, especially through the lens of gendered violence. See Harbi and Meynier, *Le FLN: Documents et histoire 1954–1962*, pp. 59–60.
8. Ibid., p. 60.
9. Ibid., p. 59.
10. SHD GR 1 H 3088 Robert Lacoste, 'Directive particulière concernant la lutte contre l'organisation politico-administrative rebelle', 18 August 1956. General of Army Corps Lorillot, Commander of the 10th Military Region and Senior Joint Forces Commander, 'Note de service', 6 September 1956.
11. Vidal-Naquet, *Les Crimes de l'armée française*, p. 157. As Capitain Estroup puts it: to 'do intelligence' meant to 'press the question', or in simple French, to 'torture'.
12. Fanon, *Studies in a Dying Colonialism*, p. 119.
13. SHD GR 1 H 3088 'Instruction sur la conduite de la recherche et de l'exploitation dans le cadre des operations de renseignements', Commandement Supérieur Interarmées, 10ème Région Militaire, État-Major – 2ème Bureau, 30

September 1957, pp. 3–4. See also SHD GR 1 H 3453 General Huet's 'Rapport d'opération', pp. 1–20 and Fiche 71, p. 7.

14. Branche, *La Torture et l'armée*, p. 302.

15. Colonel de Montagnac, *Lettres d'un soldat* (Paris: Librairie Plon, 1885), p. 299.

16. Émile Larcher, *Traité élémentaire de législation algérienne*, vol. 2 (Paris: Arthur Rousseau; Alger: Adolphe Jourdan, 1903), p. 101.

17. The battalion doctor examined the detainees to facilitate questioning. The DOP operated 'at the margins of legality' by instituting unlawful and inhumane procedures. Within this framework, torture was routinely used to extract information. The Centre de renseignement et d'action was designed to streamline the flow and exploitation of information. Alongside the Équipes de renseignement et d'action (ERA), the Centre de renseignement worked to 'clean up the masses'. These teams had special powers to apprehend suspects without warrants. See Branche, *La Torture et l'armée*, p. 365–72.

18. Cornaton, *Les Regroupements de la décolonisation en Algérie*, pp. 23–4.

19. Charles-Robert Ageron, 'Une dimension de la guerre d'Algérie: les "regroupements" de populations' in *De l'Algérie française à l'Algérie algérienne et genèse de l'Algérie algérienne* (Paris: Éditions Bouchène, 2018).

20. ANOM DOC SAS 3 Robert Lacoste, Memorandum from the Resident Minister to the IGAMEs and Prefects of Algeria, 'Action civique par les S.A.S', 4 February 1958.

21. Mouloud Feraoun, *Journal, 1955–1962* (Paris: Seuil, 1962), p. 297.

22. Branche, *La Torture et l'armée*, pp. 226–7.

23. Ibid., p. 323.

24. De Gaulle appointed Delouvrier as Civilian Delegate General to prepare for civilian rule. Delouvrier aimed to win over the Muslim population through economic development, job creation, and stimulating French investment. While he collaborated with General Challe, Delouvrier emphasised economic reforms and development, in contrast with Challe's hardline military stance against the FLN.

25. Branche, *La Torture et l'armée*, p. 388.

26. Frantz Fanon, 'Algeria Face to Face with the French Torturers', *Toward the African Revolution* (New York: Grove Press, 1967), p. 66.

27. Jean-François Lyotard, *Le Différend* (Paris: Éditions de Minuit, 1983).

28. Fanon, *Studies in a Dying Colonialism*, p. 138.

29. Ibid., p. 57.

30. SHD GR 1 H 2579/2 Salan's Letter to army Corps Commanders, 27 April 1957.

31. Fanon, 'Algeria Face to Face with the French Torturers', p. 64.

32. Ibid., pp. 70–71.

33. AN 304 AP 701 Mr Garçon's report, 19 June 1957.

34. Branche, *La Torture et l'armée*, p. 252.

35. Ibid., pp. 246–7.

36. SHD GR 1 H 3088 The Fifth and Second Bureaus launched a large-scale psychological operations campaign targeting the Muslim population under the slogan 'INFORM US'. General Allard argued that its success depended on leaders at all levels supporting it and actively gathering intelligence. He vowed

to create a 'religion of intelligence', pledging to personally oversee its implementation within the Army Corps (Army Corps General Allard, Commander of the Algiers Army Corps Military Region and Second Bureau, 'Directive particulière sur le renseignement', 25 September 1957, p. 5). Following General Allard, Branche refers to the OR as 'missionnaire du renseignement' (*La Torture et l'armée*, p. 253).

37. Branche, *La Torture et l'armée*, p. 260.
38. Ibid., p. 397 and ACICR BAG 202 008-004 'Mise au point du ministère des Armées', a clarification from the Ministry of the Armed Forces appeared in *Le Figaro* on 28 May 1959, denying allegations that the bodies of summarily executed Algerians were displayed.
39. Germaine Tillion, *Les Ennemis complémentaires* (Paris: Éditions Tirésias, 2005), p. 347.
40. Branche, *La Torture et l'armée*, pp. 400–1.
41. Antoine Argoud, *La Décadence, l'imposture et la tragédie* (Paris: Fayard, 1974), pp. 157–8.
42. Branche, *La Torture et l'armée*, p. 395.
43. Fanon, *Studies in a Dying Colonialism*, p. 26.
44. Branche, *La Torture et l'armée*, pp. 272–3.
45. Ibid., p. 294–5.
46. SHD 1K 625 On 17 February 1959, the chaplaincy published *Étude d'un comportement moral en face d'une guerre subversive*, commonly known as the 'green document' due to its cover. The document urged French soldiers to reflect on the morality of their actions in light of military regulations, international conventions and Church teachings, emphasising that 'no vacuum of morality and law exists during wartime'. It condemned acts such as collective reprisals, executions and torture. Striking a balance between prohibitions and an appeal to personal moral responsibility, the chaplaincy emphasised that individuals were not absolved from the need for discernment, nor from seeking support from chaplains. Despite the army's chief of staff initially banning its distribution, the document soon gained wider attention, prompting the chaplaincy to release a revised and expanded edition by late 1959, which included new reflections on psychological warfare. See Xavier Boniface, 'L'Aumônerie militaire française en guerre d'Algérie', *Vingtième Siècle: Revue d'histoire* 77 (janvier–mars 2003), p. 54 and Branche, *La Torture et l'armée*, p. 355.
47. Feraoun, *Journal, 1955–1962*, p. 286.
48. Fanon, *Studies in a Dying Colonialism*, p. 66.
49. Harbi and Meynier, *Le FLN, Documents et histoire 1954–1962*, pp. 59–60. Branche, *La Torture et l'armée*, p. 403.
50. In *L'Amour, la fantasia*, referring to Le Comte de Castellane, Assia Djebar writes: 'These Algerian women smear their faces with mud and excrement when they are led in the conqueror's procession.… They are not only protecting themselves from the enemy, but from the Christian, who is at once conqueror, foreigner and taboo!' Assia Djebar, *L'Amour, la fantasia* (Paris: Albin Michel, 1995), p. 83.
51. Feraoun, *Journal, 1955–1962*, p. 290.

52. Benoît Rey, 'Scènes de l'activité d'un commando de chasse, 1959–1961', in *Les Crimes de l'armée française*, ed. Pierre Vidal-Naquet (Paris: La Découverte & Syros, 2001), p. 112. Benoît Rey, *Les Égorgeurs* (Paris: Éditions de Minuit, 1961), p. 19.

53. Horne, *A Savage War of Peace*, pp. 402, 416.

54. Fanon, *Studies in a Dying Colonialism*, p. 119–20.

55. ANOM 81 F 528 Croissant-Rouge algérien, *Les Réfugiés algériens* (June 1959). The booklet included newspaper reports detailing disturbing cases of violence and atrocities against civilians, depicting extreme brutality, rape, sexual assaults, grave human rights violations and war crimes. These cases were reported by *Petit Matin*, 2 March 1958.

    Case 1: An elderly man from Mrij was tied up while two soldiers reportedly raped his wife before his eyes. His daughter attempted to defend herself but was sexually assaulted and pushed into a burning *douar*.

    Case 2: T- B- M- was stabbed in the back with a bayonet. While this occurred, the report states that Senegalese troops raped his young wife in front of their five children.

    Case 3: S- A-, from the settlement known as 'Pierres jaunes', violently struggled against paratroopers who attempted to rape her. In retaliation, they allegedly threw her four-month-old baby under a tank.

    Case 4: An unnamed young man was thrown into a ditch and left for dead after trying to prevent a lieutenant and his men from raping his wife.

    These cases depict horrific acts of violence, sexual assault, and disregard for human life and dignity. The level of brutality described is deeply disturbing and constitutes grave violations of human rights and war crimes.

56. Feraoun, *Journal, 1955–1962*, p. 290.

57. Ibid., p. 292.

58. Fanon, *The Wretched of the Earth*, p. 257.

59. Branche, *La Torture et l'armée*, p. 415.

60. Feraoun, *Journal, 1955–1962*, p. 269.

61. As noted in Chapter 2, the female body, particularly the vagina, was transformed into a site of brutal violence and pain infliction. Branche, *La Torture et l'armée*, pp. 424–5.

62. The *gégène*, a portable electric generator, became a preferred torture device due to its efficiency, cleanliness, and immediate results. Torturers applied electric shocks to genitals and other sensitive areas, often facilitating sexual assaults during interrogations. This practice symbolically re-enacted the war's violence within torture chambers, without risks to the torturers. Torture evolved into a means of subjugating the Algerian population, a goal the French army struggled to achieve on the battlefield alone. For torturers, the exhaustion following a session was often likened to sexual satisfaction, representing a perverse possession of the Other and reassurance of their own virility. The disturbing description of electric torture as '*jouissance*' (sexual pleasure) underscored the depraved nature of these acts. Branche, *La Torture et l'armée*, pp. 466–7.

63. Fanon, *Black Skin, White Masks*, pp. 104–41.
64. ANOM 2 SAS 7 Captain L.P. Fauque, *Stades d'évolution de la cellule familiale musulmane d'Algérie* (Algiers: Official Printing Office, 1959), pp. 1–28.
65. Lazreg, *Torture and the Twilight of Empire*, pp. 145–52 and 167–8.
66. SHD GR 1 H 3088 Robert Lacoste, 'Directive particulière concernant la lutte contre l'organisation politico-administrative rebelle', 18 August 1956. General of Army Corps Lorillot, Commander of the 10th Military Region and Senior Joint Forces Commander, 'Note de service', 6 September 1956. See also Marie-Catherine Villatoux, *Guerre et action psychologiques en Algérie* (Vincennes: Service historique de la Défense, 2007), pp. 5–72.
67. ANOM GGA 13 CAB 7 Robert Lacoste, Memorandum from the Minister Resident in Algeria to the Prefects of Algiers and Oran and the IGAMEs of Constantine, Bône, Batna, and Tizi-Ouzou, 5 November 1956.
68. ANOM GGA 14 CAB 233 On the subject of integration, excerpt from Cadi Mohammed Benhoura's 'Un cri d'alarme', *Le Monde*, 13 June 1958.
69. Le Cour Grandmaison, *Coloniser. Exterminer: Sur la guerre et l'état colonial*, pp. 137–52.
70. In *De l'humanité*, Bodichon argues that clearing Algeria of its native populations and marshes would rid humanity of sources of contagion and pernicious and redundant populations that hinder progress. He views human history as a struggle between inferior and superior races, advocating for the destruction of the former to achieve 'anthropological progress' and racial unity. For Bodichon, colonisation is beneficial, as it eliminates inferior races, such as the North African Arabs, and helps Europe dispose of its surplus populations. Eugène Bodichon, *Considérations sur l'Algérie* (Paris: Comptoir Central de la Librairie, 1845) pp. 114–15 p.142; *De l'humanité*, vol. 1 (Bruxelles: A. Lacroix, Verboeckhoven et Cie, 1866), pp. 91–2, 119, 126–7, 181, 342.

In *La Démographie figurée de l'Algérie*, René Ricoux estimates the indigenous population at 3 million in 1830, which declined to 2,652,072 in 1866 and 2,125,051 in 1872. He calculates a deficit of 874,949 people over 42 years, averaging 20,000 deaths annually. During the period 1866–72, due to typhus, famine and insurrection, the death toll rose to 87,000 per year. Ricoux views the colonial issue as fundamentally demographic, attributing the decline of the native population to their racial constitution and ethnic background. He considers Arabs and Berbers inferior and degenerate compared to Europeans, predicting their inevitable extinction. Ricoux uses the term *déchet* (refuse, rubbish) to describe this demographic deficit, implying that the natives were disposable. He anticipates that confinement, disease and famine will further confirm his theory of their certain demise. René Ricoux, *La Démographie figurée de l'Algérie* (Paris: G. Masson, 1880), pp. 260–1.
71. Nora, *Les Français d'Algérie*, p. 194.
72. Hélène Cixous and Eric Prenowitz, 'Letter to Zohra Drif', pp. 82–90.
73. Feraoun, *Journal, 1955–1962*, p. 290.
74. Paul Aussaresses, *Services spéciaux - Algérie 1955-1957* (Paris: Perrin, 2001), pp. 143–150.
75. Fanon, *Toward the African Revolution*, p. 35.

76. Twelve thousand people were massacred by Aussaresses.
77. Jean-Paul Sartre, 'Preface' to *The Wretched of the Earth*, p. 20.
78. Ibid., p. 24.
79. Aimé Césaire posited that the brutal repression and violence employed in colonies ultimately rebounded on Europe itself. The dehumanising subjugation tactics developed in the colonies were later turned inward against European populations, contributing to the rise of Nazism and Fascism. Thus, the inherent violence of colonialism haunted the colonisers, shaping both decolonisation movements and the emergence of totalitarian regimes in Europe.

7 FANON, THE FRENCH LIBERAL LEFT
AND THE COLONIAL CONSENSUS

1. See David Macey, *Frantz Fanon: A Biography*, 2nd edn (London: Verso, 2012), pp. 21–2.
2. I am using the term 'liberal left' to refer to the broad coalition that represented the parliamentary left, namely the Section française de l'Internationale ouvrière (SFIO) and the Parti communiste français (PCF), as well as the non-parliamentary democratic elements that militated on 'the left'. The crux of my argument centres on the Algerian war, the legacy of the Dreyfus Affair and the split in French society which blurred the demarcation lines between left and right so that it was no longer possible to distinguish ideologically between the SFIO, the PCF and liberal Catholics like André Mandouze and Jean-Marie Domenach and Jews like Pierre Vidal-Naquet. Members of *Les Cahiers du témoignage chrétien* represented political views that were traditionally championed by the left, while socialists like François Mitterrand supported the retrograde pacification policy undertaken by Guy Mollet's government.
3. See Hannah Arendt, *On Violence* (London: Penguin Press, 1970), and Lewis Coser, 'Fanon and Debray: Theorists of the Third World', in *Beyond the New Left*, ed. by Irving Howe (New York: McCall Publishing Co., 1970), pp. 120–34.
4. Gilbert Comte, 'Un *Mein Kampf* de la décolonisation', *La Nation française*, 21 March 1962, cited in Macey, *Frantz Fanon*, p. 21.
5. See Dennis Forsythe, 'Fanon: The Marx of the Third World', *Phylon*, 34(2) (1973), p. 165.
6. Fanon, *Black Skin, White Masks*, p. 13.
7. Fanon, *The Wretched of the Earth*, p. 40.
8. Ibid., p. 108.
9. Nguyen Nghe, 'Frantz Fanon et les problèmes de l'indépendance', *La Pensée*, 107 (February 1963), p. 27.
10. Ibid., p. 28.
11. Ibid., p. 29.
12. Ibid., p. 30.
13. Ibid., p. 31.
14. Ibid., pp. 31–2.
15. Ibid., p. 32.

16. Ibid., p. 32. Like Nghe, Renata Zahar hails the proletarianisation of the colo-
    nised as a coming-into-consciousness and suggests that Fanon's generalisation
    'leaves open the question whether revolutionary processes cannot after all be
    initiated among the proletariat with its much higher degree of organisation'; see
    R. Zahar, *Frantz Fanon: Colonialism and Alienation* (New York and London:
    Monthly Review Press, 1974), p. 105. She also argues that what Fanon offers is
    'a phenomenological description of neocolonialism which is in general correct
    but which is restricted to the conditions in the former colonies'; moreover,
    this description is characterised by a lack of 'any analysis of international rela-
    tions of dependency nor of the background and motives of modern imperialist
    policies' (ibid., p. 101).
17. Nghe, 'Frantz Fanon et les problèmes de l'indépendance', p. 33.
18. See Irwin M. Wall, 'Front Populaire, Front National: The colonial example',
    International Labor and Working-Class History 30 (1986), pp. 32–43. As Wall
    notes: 'When it became apparent in August 1936 that the Blum government
    coalition's reformist impulse was spent and its anti-fascist resolve showed signs
    of flagging under the impact of the Spanish Civil War, the PCF proposed the
    Front français. The party proposed extending the electoral alliance to all those
    on the right willing to rally around an anti-German standard' (p. 33).
19. Maurice Thorez, 'La Nation algérienne en formation', in *Textes choisis sur l'Al-
    gérie* (Paris: Parti communiste français, 1962), pp. 16–24. Thorez's speech is
    cited in Jakob Moneta, 'Le Peuple algérien uni autour de la France', in *La Poli-
    tique du Parti communiste français dans la question coloniale, 1920–1963* (Paris:
    Maspero, 1971), pp. 134–8.
20. See Azzedine Haddour, *Colonial Myths: History and Narrative* (Manchester:
    Manchester University Press, 2000), pp. 24–9.
21. Gabriel Audisio, *Sel de la mer* (Paris: Gallimard, 1936), pp. 118–21.
22. Ibid., pp. 107, 113.
23. Albert Camus, 'La Culture indigène, la nouvelle culture méditerranénne', in
    Essais, ed. by Roger Quilliot and Louis Faucon (Paris: Gallimard, 1965), p. 1324.
24. Thorez, 'La Nation algérienne en formation', pp. 20–1 (emphasis in original).
25. Thorez, 'La France du Front populaire', in *Textes choisis sur l'Algérie*, p. 12.
26. Ibid., p. 12 (emphasis in original).
27. Thorez, 'La Nation algérienne en formation', p. 22.
28. Ibid., p. 19.
29. Tony Smith, 'The French Colonial Consensus and People's War, 1946–58',
    Journal of Contemporary History 9(4) (1974), 217–47.
30. Ibid., p. 229.
31. Ibid., p. 229.
32. Ibid., p. 220.
33. Fanon, 'Lettre au Ministre Résident', in *Toward the African Revolution*, pp. 52–4.
34. Fanon, *Studies in a Dying Colonialism*, p. 148.
35. Ibid., p. 148–9.
36. Ibid., p. 150.
37. Fanon, 'French Intellectuals and Democrats and the Algerian Revolution', in
    Toward the African Revolution, pp. 78–9.

38. See Jean-Paul Sartre, 'Le Colonialisme est un système', in *Situations V* (Paris: Gallimard, 1964), pp. 25–48.
39. Fanon, 'Algeria Face to Face with the French Torturers', in *Toward the African Revolution*, p. 72.
40. Fanon, 'Concerning a Plea', in *Toward the African Revolution*, p. 74.
41. Ibid., p. 74.
42. Fanon, 'Algeria's European Minority', p. 149 and 'French Intellectuals and Democrats and the Algerian Revolution', p. 79.
43. Fanon, 'French Intellectuals and Democrats and the Algerian Revolution', p. 79.
44. Jean-Paul Sartre, 'A Victory', in *Colonialism and Neocolonialism* (London and New York: Routledge, 2001), p. 65. Criticising the Mollet government for instituting torture, Sartre goes on to add: 'Alleg naked, shivering with cold, tied to a plank which is still black and sticky from old vomit, reduces all this posturing to its pitiful truth. It is an act played out by imbeciles. An act, the fascist violence of their comments, their promise to go and "fuck up the Republic"' (p. 69).
45. Ibid., p. 71.
46. Fanon, *Studies in a Dying Colonialism*, p. 150.
47. Ibid., p. 150.
48. Ibid., p. 151.
49. Ibid., p. 153.
50. Fanon, 'La Minorité européenne d'Algérie', in *L'An V de la révolution algérienne* (Paris: La Découverte, 2001), p. 144. My translation.
51. See Memmi, *The Colonizer and the Colonized*, p. 10.
52. Derrida, *Le Monolinguisme de l'autre*, p. 89.
53. Ibid., p. 66.
54. Fanon, *Studies in a Dying Colonialism*, pp. 154–5.
55. Ibid., p. 157, italicised in the original.
56. Ibid.
57. Fanon, *Studies in a Dying Colonialism*, p. 32.
58. Sartre, 'Colonialism Is a System', in *Colonialism and Neocolonialism*, pp. 33–5.
59. Jean-François Lyotard, *La Guerre des Algériens* (Paris: Galilée, 1989), p. 44.
60. Fanon, *The Wretched of the Earth*, pp. 129–31.
61. Lyotard, *La Guerre des Algériens*, p. 93.
62. Ibid., p. 90.
63. Ibid., pp. 102–3.
64. Ibid., p. 103.
65. Fanon, *The Wretched of the Earth*, pp. 39–40.
66. Like Fanon, Lyotard contends that it was because of their ethnicity, not because of their class position, that the Algerians were completely crushed:

> C'est donc la totalité des musulmans qui est saisie et broyée par la poigne des colons: la société maghrébine est une société totalitaire, où l'exploitation suppose la terreur. Et comme les frontières de classes sont à peu prés exactement recouvertes par les frontières 'ethniques', une conscience de classes est impossible: c'est autant comme Algérien ou Tunisien que comme

ouvrier ou paysan que l'homme est écrasé. Le flic qui matraque ou qui torture est européen, le patron ou le contremaître est européen, l'officier est européen, le professeur est européen, le mépris est européen et la misère 'arabe'. La lutte se situe d'emblée sur le plan national, elle cherche spontanément à supprimer l'appareil terroriste comme immédiate de l'oppression, et l'indépendance, c'est-à-dire cette suppression, apparaît à tous comme le contraire de l'exploitation.

It is therefore the entire Muslim population that is seized and crushed by the grip of the colonisers. Maghreb society is a totalitarian society, where exploitation is inseparable from terror. Since class boundaries almost exactly coincide with 'ethnic' boundaries, class consciousness becomes impossible: the individual is crushed as much by being Algerian or Tunisian as by being a worker or peasant. The cop who beats or tortures is European, the boss or foreman is European, the officer is European, the professor is European, the contempt is European, and the misery is 'Arab'. The struggle is immediately framed in national terms; it spontaneously seeks to eliminate the terror apparatus as the immediate form of oppression, and independence – that is, the elimination of this apparatus – appears to all as the opposite of exploitation (*La Guerre des Algériens*, pp. 45–6).

67. Ibid., p. 106.
68. Ibid., p. 70.
69. Ibid., p. 103.
70. Fanon, *The Wretched of the Earth*, p. 61.
71. As Michel Winock notes, 'pendant la guerre d'Algérie, au moment du grand débat sur la torture, un néo-dreyfusisme entraîna de nouveau nombre d'intellectuels contre la raison d'État' ('during the Algerian War, at the time of the great debate on torture, a neo-Dreyfusard movement once again led many intellectuals to oppose the reason of state'); see M. Winock, 'L'Affaire Dreyfus comme mythe fondateur', in *La France politique* (Paris: Seuil, 2003), pp. 151–65, at p. 164.
72. Wall, 'Front Populaire, Front National', p. 35.
73. Lyotard, *La Guerre des Algériens*, p. 100.

CONCLUSION

1. Fanon, *The Wretched of the Earth*, p. 41.
2. Gilbert Comte, 'Un *Mein Kampf* de la décolonisation', *La Nation française*, 21 March 1962.
3. Hannah Arendt, *On Violence* (San Diego, New York and London: A Harvest/ HBJ Book, 1970), p. 12, p. 14.
4. Ibid., pp. 30, 65.
5. Hannah Arendt, 'Ideology & Terror: A novel Form of Government', in *The Origins of Totalitarianism* (Cleveland and New York: The World Publishing Company, 1962), pp. 460–79.
6. Fanon, 'Concerning Violence', in *The Wretched of the Earth*, pp. 35–107.

7. Eric Wolf, *Peasant Wars of the Twentieth Century* (New York: Harper & Row, 1969), p. 242–3.

8. 'Now, we know', writes Trinquier, 'that the essential means to win in modern warfare is to secure the unconditional support of the population; it is as indispensable to the fighters as water is to fish (cf. Mao Zedong). This support may sometimes be spontaneous (which is very rare, and even in such cases, it may only be temporary); if it is not, it will be obtained through appropriate organisation, which will maintain it by any means, the most effective being terrorism.' Roger Trinquier, *La Guerre moderne* (Paris: La Table ronde, 1961), p. 18. Trinquier not only advocated for terrorism to neutralise the Algerian peasantry but also implemented it with disturbing proficiency. As Mahfoud Bennoune affirms, Trinquier adopted these very tactics in his counter-insurgency efforts to isolate and alienate the population from the ALN. See Bennoune, 'La Doctrine contre-révolutionnaire de la France et la paysannerie algérienne: les camps de regroupement (1954–1962)', *Sud/Nord*, 2001, no. 14, p. 54.

9. Bennoune, 'La Doctrine contre-révolutionnaire de la France et la paysannerie algérienne', p. 57.

10. Ibid., p. 58.

11. Charles Richard, *Étude sur l'insurrection du Dhara* (Alger: Bastide, Dubos & Marest Libraires, 1846) p. 191.

12. Lieutenant Lasconjarias and Sous-lieutenant Jouan, 'Les "Sections administratives spécialisées" en Algérie: Un outil pour la stabilisation', *Les cahiers de la recherche doctrinale*, Centre de Doctrine d'Emploi des Forces (CDEF), 21 October 2005, p. 17.

Index

The Pluto Press Newsletter

Hello friend of Pluto!

Want to stay on top of the best radical books
we publish?

Then sign up to be the first to hear about our
new books, as well as special events,
podcasts and videos.

You'll also get 50% off your first order with us
when you sign up.

Come and join us!

Go to bit.ly/PlutoNewsletter